DISCARDED

D1611666

DISCARDED

29.95

ENVY UP, SCORN DOWN

DISCARDED

ENVY UP, SCORN DOWN

HOW STATUS DIVIDES US

Susan T. Fiske

Russell Sage Foundation • New York

Shelton State Libraries
Shelton State Community College

The Russell Sage Foundation

The Russell Sage Foundation, one of the oldest of America's general purpose foundations, was established in 1907 by Mrs. Margaret Olivia Sage for "the improvement of
social and living conditions in the United States." The Foundation seeks to fulfill this
mandate by fostering the development and dissemination of knowledge about the
country's political, social, and economic problems. While the Foundation endeavors to
assure the accuracy and objectivity of each book it publishes, the conclusions and interpretations in Russell Sage Foundation publications are those of the authors and not of
the Foundation, its Trustees, or its staff. Publication by Russell Sage, therefore, does
not imply Foundation endorsement.

BOARD OF TRUSTEES
Mary C. Waters, Chair

Kenneth D. Brody	Kathleen Hall Jamieson	Shelley E. Taylor
W. Bowman Cutter III	Lawrence F. Katz	Richard H. Thaler
Robert E. Denham, Esq.	Sara S. McLanahan	Eric Wanner
John A. Ferejohn	Nancy L. Rosenblum	
Larry V. Hedges	Claude M. Steele	

Library of Congress Cataloging-in-Publication Data

Fiske, Susan T.
  Envy up, scorn down : how status divides us / Susan T. Fiske.
     p. cm.
  Includes bibliographical references and index.
  ISBN 978-0-87154-464-3 (alk. paper)
  1. Social classes—United States. 2. Class consciousness—United States.
  3. Comparison (Psychology) 4. Equality—United States. 5. Envy. I. Title.
  HN90.S6F57 2011
  305.5′120973—dc22

                                                                    2010050297

Copyright © 2011 by Russell Sage Foundation. All rights reserved. Printed in the
United States of America. No part of this publication may be reproduced, stored in a
retrieval system, or transmitted in any form or by any means, electronic, mechanical,
photocopying, recording, or otherwise, without the prior written permission of the
publisher.

Reproduction by the United States Government in whole or in part is permitted for
any purpose.

The paper used in this publication meets the minimum requirements of American
National Standard for Information Sciences—Permanence of Paper for Printed Library
Materials. ANSI Z39.48-1992.

Epigraph on p. 149 of this text is from *The Conquest of Happiness by Bertrand Russell*.
Copyright © 1930 by Horace Liveright, Inc., renewed © 1958 by Bertrand Russell. Used
by permission of Liveright Publishing Corporation.

Text design by Genna Patacsil.

RUSSELL SAGE FOUNDATION
112 East 64th Street, New York, New York 10065
10 9 8 7 6 5 4 3 2 1

Contents

About the Author

Susan T. Fiske is Eugene Higgins Professor of Psychology at Princeton University.

Preface

IN THE United States today we are divided by envy and scorn, brought on by the status concerns that pervade our society. Income inequality, now at historically high levels, aggravates these status divides. Many of us envy those above us in status and scorn those below us, but whether we are the object of these comparisons or the person making them, feelings of envy and scorn can be hazardous to our health. So why do we always compare ourselves with each other, what happens when we do, and how can we harness this obsession for good—in ourselves, our relationships, our work, and our society?

I got interested in these issues for reasons that were equal parts political, scientific, and personal. Every election season we pit Main Street against Wall Street—and implicitly, both against Skid Row. Who are the American heroes? Why do we distrust elites? Why do we not want educated people to run the country? Why do we neglect our poor more than do most other industrialized countries? This book explores the psychology behind these American political questions.

These are exciting times for psychological science, especially experimental social psychology and social neuroscience. We're learning a great deal about people's immediate reactions to each other, whether thinking or unthinking, both up and down the status hierarchy. This book draws deeply on work conducted by the Fiske Lab at Princeton University, a team of students and post-docs who constantly motivate me (see http://www.princeton.edu/~fiskelab/), and on the work of colleagues who are doing some experiments that would amaze even the most jaded kibitzers.

How did I come to write this book? It is not as obvious as it may seem. As a Princeton professor, I hold an enviable position, about which I feel both grateful and lucky—but my good fortune sometimes divides me from people I hold dear. So I am motivated to understand better how the potentially envied can defuse uncomfortable encounters with people who think they may be scorned. In addition, even though I try to avoid it, occasionally I have to cope with my own envy of others, and I worry about how my position may allow unthinking scorn to creep into my daily life.

This book, then, is a political-scientific-personal meditation on these themes. No book is written alone, and my first thanks go to the Guggenheim and Russell Sage Foundations, which supported my year in academic heaven, and Princeton, which granted me a leave from teaching. Thanks especially to RSF president Eric Wanner, publications director Suzanne Nichols, information services director Claire Gabriel, librarian Katie Winograd, administrative assistant Alexsa Rosa, and research assistant Sophia Leung, as well as other staff who perfected the paradise. Among our wonderful cohort of visiting scholars, I thank Diana Sanchez and Tim Salthouse for responding to partial drafts, as well as Julia Ott and Ann Swidler, who provided references. Thanks to Tom Pettigrew (still mentoring after all these years) for a rapid and constructive review. Commentators John Clayton, Annette Lareau, and Paul DiMaggio also responded to partial drafts. And Shelley Taylor gave me the courage to undertake the project at all. This book is dedicated to Doug, who inspires and supports me, and Lydia, who provided cultural leads, read drafty drafts, and continues to amaze me every day.

Chapter 1

Comparing Ourselves to Others: Envy and Scorn Divide Us

I try to be good. But sometimes I see something and say, "Oooh, I want that."
—Small-business owner

People tell us we are lucky, but we've worked really hard to make this happen.
—Same person

W E ARE constantly comparing ourselves with others, and comparison is only natural. Even dogs and chimps do it, as we will see. At the same time, comparisons divide and depress us by making us envy those above us and discount those below us. So why do we persist in making comparisons? Could we harness this tendency so that some good comes of it?

Chrissie and Steve own a coffeehouse in a small town in rural western New England. When they took over from the previous owners, the business needed paint, ran at unreliable hours, and carried unpredictable offerings. Fresh out of college and full of energy, the new owners turned the coffeehouse into a thriving business, now frequented by both locals who drink regular coffee and second-homers whose drink orders require more adjectives (for example, "a triple, skim, foamy, extra-hot cappuccino, in my travel mug"). Chrissie and Steve love all of their customers, but they live in a two-tier economy. Most of the locals work two jobs, and many of the local young people join the military for the pay and benefits. Second homes are common among the visiting flatlanders, and few of their children join the military. The locals are justifiably proud of their town, their history, and their dedication, and the visitors are justifiably proud as well, but their satisfaction runs more to individual accomplishment than to community ties. Although most encounters between the locals

1

and the second-homers are polite—with annoying exceptions of course—
they remain divided into these two tiers.

Americans both recognize and minimize class distinctions. We pit Main
Street against Wall Street, elites against the honest working people, lazy
freeloaders against the deserving poor. The tensions generated by these
distinctions have always occupied center stage during election years,
but increasingly they pervade our society as it becomes ever more class-
divided. The gaps between the top and bottom parts of the income distribution are wider than ever. We have become segregated by social class
almost as much as by race, and because social class prejudices are less taboo
than those based on race, religion, and gender, we often express social class
biases without a second thought. What is more, the latest research reveals
that status prejudices of all kinds—not just social class but any status
dimension that pits people against each other, one up and one down—are
prevalent and persistent in our society. All these observations underlie this
meditation on comparison and how it divides us.

What, Me Worry?

For years, my collaborators and I have been studying how people form
impressions up and down the status hierarchy. People's ordinary lives
require forming efficient and effective impressions of incredible numbers
of other individuals. Where is the pattern in this daily social challenge?
In examining how people make sense of each other, both individuals and
groups, my colleagues and I have discovered two apparently universal
dimensions that differentiate people.[1] For regular people, researchers, and
policymakers alike, these two fundamental dimensions organize the psychology of everyday social cognition: one is status (our focus here), and
the other is intent to cooperate or not (providing the backdrop for people
who do or do not trust each other, regardless of status differences).

Walking down a dark alley, you spot an approaching figure. What is
the first thing you want to know? If you are a sentry, you cry out, "Halt!
Who goes there? Friend or foe?" You need to know the stranger's intentions, for good or ill. If the person seems to be on your side—a friend—
you assume that the person is trustworthy, friendly, and sincere. If the
stranger seems like a foe, however, then you probably do not assume that
the person has those warm traits, and indeed you may wonder whether
the person has some bad ones besides. We decide who is on our side by
knowing who intends to cooperate or compete with us—that is, who has
goals compatible with ours and who has zero-sum goals.

After inferring the stranger's intentions, you will want to know whether
he or she can enact those intentions. After all, why does an angry bunny
matter (except in the Monty Python killer-rabbit episode)? If the stranger
can act effectively, his or her intentions will matter to you. Curiously—and
this is the key point—we decide who matters, that is, who can act effec-

Table 1.1   The BIAS Map: Stereotypes of Warmth (Friend-Foe) and Competence (Status)

	Low-Status– Incompetent	High-Status– Competent
Friend-warm (friendly, trustworthy)	Disabled people, older people	Middle-class people, Americans
Foe-cold (hostile, exploitative)	Poor people, addicts, homeless people	Rich people, professionals

Source: Author's compilation based on Fiske et al. (2002); Fiske, Cuddy, and Glick (2007).

tively, by knowing their status. Worldwide, people believe that high status confers competence (hard to believe sometimes when we consider some of the buffoons in charge.[2]) But in theory and usually in practice, we believe in meritocracy and think that other people generally deserve what they get. All over the world, high-status people, those who hold down prestigious jobs and have achieved economic success, are assumed to be more competent than low-status people. Amy Cuddy, Peter Glick, and I have developed these ideas into the BIAS Map shown in table 1.1.

The distinctions matter because they divide us from each other in our everyday encounters, whether in a New England village, Chicago's Gold Coast, the beaches of Waikiki, or anywhere in between. We have strong feelings about clusters of people in society. As shown in the top half of table 1.1, many of us feel pride about iconic middle-class Americans. On the other hand, we pity disabled people and older people. Although these reactions can disturb us, they mostly reflect benign intentions because these are all people who are on our side, whether they are allegedly competent (middle class, American) or allegedly not (older, disabled).

More bothersome is the bottom half of the BIAS Map. We all too often envy the rich and scorn the poor. Neither is an admirable reaction, but both are all too natural. These comparisons up and down the status system divide us from each other. What is most disturbing is that we persist in denying what ails us.

Americans Minimize Status Distinctions, So Aren't We All Equal?

Americans are famously egalitarian. Our founding documents confirm that we share equal starting points and equal rights to pursue happiness. Yet the reality is that we are less equal than we think we are. Americans are deeply divided by class and status.

After this chapter, the rest of the book focuses on more personal status divides, based in the everyday comparisons that bother us, from the hierarchies at work to the better bodies seen at the gym to the threatening comparisons we make in close relationships. To get a good look at status in the big picture, let's start with the taboo topic of social class.

Aren't We All Middle Class?

We boast that we live in a classless society. In the United States, "the overwhelming majority of people identify themselves as 'middle class,' " according to no less than Bill Keller, executive editor of the *New York Times*.[3] Informally, sociologists agree: many of us believe this received wisdom. That most Americans identify as middle class both reassures us that we are not a class-obsessed society and leads us to believe that we have escaped Europe's divisive class-conscious ideology. Two-thirds of us do not believe in strong class conflict.[4] We minimize social class by trusting the middle class; 75 percent of us say that "most [middle-class people] can be trusted," unlike our beliefs about other named groups (for example, health maintenance organizations net only 20 percent trust).[5] We trust familiar middle-class occupations (83 percent trust teachers, 76 percent small-business owners, 68 percent coaches, and 66 percent ministers) more than we trust people in general (only 41 percent). And we trust the middle class much more than CEOs (23 percent), lawyers (25 percent), and car dealers (16 percent). As the novelist Richard Russo put it in his study of small-town status systems, "The middle . . . was the real America, the America that mattered, the America that was worth fighting wars to defend."[6] We all believe that Middle Class–R–Us.

There is only one problem with this belief: the "we are all middle class" truism is not exactly true. "The myth of a classless society . . . is itself a myth," observes *Harper's* magazine editor Roger Hodge.[7] To make his point, Hodge lists about one hundred terms in common usage, A-to-Y if not A-to-Z, from "artsy" and "blue-collar" to "wrong side of the tracks" and "yuppie." For decades, Americans have identified themselves about equally as "working class" and "middle class" (45 to 49 percent each) when pollsters provide these options along with "upper class" and "lower class" (see figure 1.1).[8]

In surveys, "middle class" still fails to describe fully half of us, so we cannot easily agree with Bill Keller's claim that the "overwhelming majority" of Americans identify as middle class. None of the polls in standard survey databases show most of us identifying as middle class. Nevertheless, we cannot help but believe that this myth deserves to be true. How did we come to this belief?

Maybe the origins of the "we are all middle class" myth trace back to the early days of polling, before World War II, when Gallup once asked the question about social class with a nice symmetrical list of possible answers—lower, lower-middle, middle, upper-middle, and upper class—that produced a lovely bell curve: 6, 12, 63, 11, and 5 percent, respec-

Figure 1.1   Most Commonly Self-Reported Social Class, 2000 to 2004

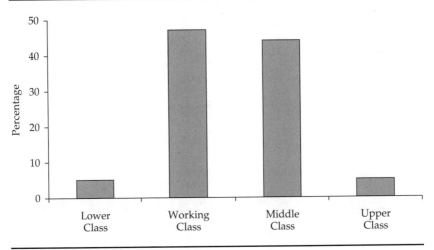

Source: Author's compilation based on Hout (2008) and data from General Social Survey (2000 to 2004).

tively.[9] "Middle class" won a sizable majority, and if we collapse lower-middle, middle, and upper-middle into a generic middle, we do indeed get Keller's "overwhelming majority" of 86 percent identifying as some version of middle class. Perhaps this is the result underlying the urban myth, but it has been holding on, evidence-free, for an average pollster's lifetime. After 1939, Gallup and every other survey started tinkering, and pollsters soon agreed that "working class" sounded better than "lower-middle class," so that term was never used again (see figure 1.2). One thing remains constant: Americans rarely call themselves "rich" or "poor" and are reluctant to place themselves at the unqualified *upper* or *lower* extremes.[10]

If in fact we have not been democratically middle class since early last century, how do we decide where we belong? In researching their essay collection, *Class Matters,* *New York Times* writers finally settled the class hand we're dealt as including four suits: income, wealth, education, and occupation.[11] As *Times* writers Janny Scott and David Leonhardt put it, face cards in three suits can land you in the upper-middle class, just as 2s and 3s in several suits can demote you, so no one suit is necessary and sufficient.[12] Family income is the most important factor in our sense of social class, with occupation close behind, according to Hout's data and going back to the earliest surveys.[13] Because we decide what class we are based on income and occupation, we are just as likely to identify as "working class" as "middle class" on surveys, contrary to received wisdom.

**Figure 1.2   The Last Middle-Class-Centered Bell Curve:
Self-Reported Social Class**

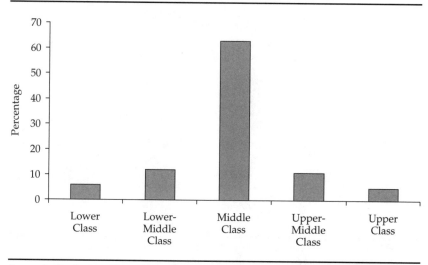

Source: Author's compilation based on data from Gallup Organization, poll 150 (1939).

Not only do we not feel predictably middle class, but Americans certainly lack the "passionate middle-class" consciousness of Europeans, according to Louis Hartz: "A triumphant middle class . . . can take itself for granted."[14] In Hartz's classic account, the American colonies had neither church canon nor feudal law to overthrow. The colonists had neither a uniform religion, having emigrated to protect the religious freedom of many small refugee sects, nor a hereditary nobility, having imported none. Alexis de Tocqueville observed that Americans were "born equal without having to become so."[15]

More recent research also suggests that Americans are not strongly invested in social class identities. In ethnographic interviews, blue-collar people rarely talk spontaneously about class in daily life, though they do discuss race, immigrants, religion, region, and extreme wealth or poverty.[16] In general, Americans do not overwhelmingly insist on a middle-class identity because they do need not to.

If We're Not All Middle Class, Whatever Happened to the American Dream?

If claiming middle-class status does not unite us, at least the American Dream does. Right? Yes. We are nearly unanimous (85 percent of us) about what the American Dream means: at a minimum, having high-quality health care and being able to feed yourself and your family. But most of us also think of loftier things as part of the American Dream, such as educational opportunities and freedom of speech.[17] Our shared American Dream embraces inspiring values such as having freedom and opportunity and prioritizing our children's future, but not necessarily materialistic values such as personally becoming rich or even middle class.[18]

It is a good thing that money does not embody the American Dream because wealth and income divide us more than ever. Americans are less equal now than at any point in the last fifty years, as noted by Isabel Sawhill and Sara McLanahan.[19] In our current "gilded era," CEO incomes average 185 times the average worker's income, compared with a mere 24-fold when many of those CEOs were in high school forty years ago. Over the last thirty years, the *after-tax* income of the super-rich (the top 1 percent) increased 129 percent, while the income of the lower class (the bottom fifth) increased only 4 percent. More concretely, in 2008 the bottom fifth received 3 percent of all household income, whereas the top fifth received a full 50 percent, according to the Census Bureau's current population report.[20]

To cut through all these numbers, economists have developed a single-number measure of income inequality that predicts a lot else about a country. The Gini index goes from 0, a utopia of perfectly equal sharing of income, to 100, a dystopia of perfect inequality where one person holds all the income. Over the last decade, the United States has hovered around 47; the median has been the more-equal Israel at 39, the most equal has been Sweden at 23, and the least equal has been Namibia at 71. Mozambique represents the twenty-fifth percentile (very unequal) and Canada the seventy-fifth (very equal). Most of the unequal countries are less developed, and most of the more equal countries are highly developed. But the United States, flanked by Uruguay and Cameroon—not our typical comparisons—ranks almost among the least-equal third of countries (see figure 1.3).[21] Around World War II, we were in the middle of the pack, but now our inequality outstrips all other developed countries.[22]

We are a land of inequality; the American rich are far richer than the rest of us. Are we a land of opportunity—or at least status mobility? Most of us are never going to rise from our current location, according to mobility statistics. Men's incomes substantially reflect the incomes of their fathers.[23] In a different route to the same outcome, women's incomes depend critically on their husbands, and they tend to marry men whose income resembles their father's, so women's incomes also are substantially stable over generations.[24]

The stability story is similar for jobs. Relative to their father's occupational prestige, only about one-third of sons rise above it, while one-third maintain it and one-third sink below it.[25] On the two common measures, income and occupation, American occupational mobility at best matches the world averages, and our actual earned-income mobility is much

Figure 1.3   Gini Inequality Ranks by Country

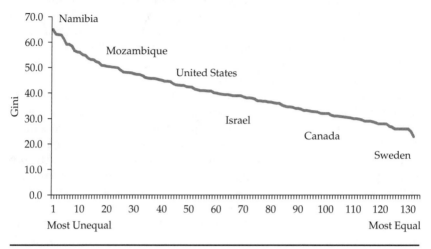

Source: Author's compilation based on data from Central Intelligence Agency (2010; see note 21, this volume).

lower. Contrary to our collective delusion, we are not leading the pack on opportunity.

So if the American Dream is not so devoted to material wealth as stereotype would have it, and if most of us cannot get rich anyway, we are clearly divided by our resources. What, if anything, unites us? Let's go back to the inspiring but elusive link of shared ideology: opportunity.

People Get the Class They Deserve

It is our national orthodoxy that America is the land of opportunity. According to a pivotal survey by James Kluegel and Eliot Smith, Americans' stable consensus endorses an opportunity syllogism:

(a)   Assuming equal opportunity, then

(b)   people get what they deserve, and

(c)   the system is fair.[26]

The first step, *equal opportunity as a shared assumption,* wins a full 70 to 88 percent agreement, whether in 1952, 1966, or 1980.[27] More recent Gallup data show certainty declining from the peak of 77 percent who were satisfied with the level of opportunity in the United States in 2002 to 57 percent in 2009, but that still represents a comfortable majority.[28] Despite war and recession, Americans continue to believe that opportunity is available to almost anyone who works hard. Collectively, ensuring opportunity itself matters to twice as many of us (66 percent) as reducing actual inequality

(28 percent).[29] Nearly everyone (87 percent) thinks "our society should do what is necessary to ensure that everyone has an equal opportunity."[30] Opportunity is our mantra.

The second step in our opportunity logic is that *people get what they deserve*. If opportunity arises only for those who work hard, then effort determines economic fate. We presumably control our own efforts, and when we have control we are not innocent victims of circumstances. Indeed, common explanations for poverty and wealth often blame the victim and credit the victor. About half of us (47 percent) blame people's poverty on their lack of effort, whereas the other half of us (48 percent) blame poverty on circumstances beyond poor people's control.[31] At the other end of the spectrum, about half of us (54 percent) say that people who make a lot of money deserve it, whereas the other half of us (45 percent) disagree. A later section discusses this in more detail, but for now assume that at least half of us subscribe to the syllogism's second step.

Consistent with the common idea that people get what they deserve, poor people around the world are viewed as intrinsically incompetent, whereas rich people are viewed as competent, according to data collected by Amy Cuddy, myself, and our international collaborators.[32] What is more, poor people are especially blamed. As Ann Marie Russell shows, observers judge poor people more than rich people on their work ethic.[33] This pattern typifies what social psychologists call a controllable stigma. People with HIV/AIDS are blamed more if they contracted the disease through casual sex than if it was transmitted through a blood transfusion. If you bring about your own misfortune, others are angry with you and do not want to help you. On the other hand, if the misfortune seems to be beyond your control (caused by circumstances), others feel pity for you and do help, according to Bernard Weiner's decades of research.[34] Indeed, the poor are pretty much universally seen as deserving their fates because they are lazy, immoral, and stupid.[35] We are particularly concerned about explaining bad outcomes, so it is poor people especially who provoke this kind of attributional gymnastics. But explanations for wealth also tend to credit the rich for their status. In short, meritocracy ensures that people seem to deserve their fates.

Undeniably, our belief in meritocracy is of two minds. How far we take it depends, first, on domain: we endorse meritocracy most highly in the economic sphere, where we tolerate inequality according to merit. In her interviews with both rich people and poor people, Jennifer Hochschild found that rich and poor both resist inequality in politics and social settings, where everyone should be equal. But they tolerate inequality in economic spheres because it merely expresses the value of effort.[36] Michèle Lamont's interviews with the upper-middle class also distinguish between the economic sphere, which values competence and ambition, and the social sphere, which values friendliness and teamwork.[37] So we are of two minds about meritocracy, depending on domain.

Admittedly, we may be ambivalent *within* the economic domain. At the same time that we expect poor people to take individual responsibility for themselves, at least half of us also understand bad luck. For example, fully 56 percent of polled Americans view homeless people as victims of circumstances beyond their control.[38] Still, a popular alternative view (38 percent) holds them responsible for their situation. Earlier, we saw that half of us blame poor people in general and half do not. On balance, we say *both* individual and circumstantial causes of poverty are "very important."[39] Most of us (85 percent) refuse to say explicitly that poor people somehow "deserve" to be poverty-stricken,[40] and 61 percent of us think that poor people work but cannot earn enough money.[41] On surveys, our consensus on individual responsibility coexists with our support for social responsibility.[42]

In our preferences, we compromise between an economic system that efficiently rewards individual effort (high incomes should serve as incentives) and one that provides income equality (incomes should be more equal).[43] Especially under the meritocracy that we all endorse, we not only show social responsibility toward the poorest but also reward individual effort. In answering the pollsters, we value opportunity and individual responsibility, although these values are tempered by social concern. All this supports our consensus that people mostly get what they deserve—the opportunity syllogism's second step.

Now we arrive at the syllogism's final step. Assuming equal opportunity and people getting what they deserve, *the current system is fair:* people succeed or fail according to their intrinsic merit. This assumption flies in the face of the evidence we have just seen that economic inequality is on the rise and upward mobility is at a standstill.[44] Nevertheless, by the syllogism's meritocratic logic, the system is fair and people get what they deserve by individual effort.[45] If so, then we should admire elites because they represent everything we value; they deserve their prestigious status. But do we admire them?

If Meritocracy Rules, Why Do We Hate Elites?

During the 2008 presidential election season, "elite" was everyone's favorite insult. Hillary Clinton hurled the term "elitist" at Barack Obama after he said that small-town Pennsylvanians, frustrated by economic inequality, "get bitter, they cling to their guns or religion or antipathy."[46] "Elitist" usually appears alongside "out of touch," as it did in Clinton's critique. Obama countered, "No, I'm in touch."[47]

When Politico.com asked John McCain how many homes he owned, he could not answer; later estimates ranged from four to eight.[48] McCain's campaign countered that Obama's "mansion" had four fireplaces and a wine cellar. Obama's campaign responded that his single mother had used food stamps when he was young. When McCain's campaign replied that Obama's income had cleared $4 million, Obama's defenders came back with Cindy McCain's net worth of over $100 million. Neither side wanted to be labeled "rich," though both were currently privileged—as was Hillary Clinton.

Clinton's campaign reminded delegates that previous Democratic nominees had been viewed as fatally out of touch. John Kerry allegedly lacked "the common touch."[49] Al Gore was just another of the "sons of privilege."[50] In a report that soon went viral, George H. W. Bush revealed his apparent ignorance about how grocery scanners work.[51] Altogether, most candidates in recent presidential campaigns attended Ivy League schools, which, for many high-level jobs, might seem like a pretty good credential. But in American elections this background counts as an insult. Elites make us nervous. David Brooks of the *New York Times* notes that we want our "toffs" to lower themselves by campaigning at diners; we want Republicans to endorse Bible-belt cultural populism and Democrats to endorse working-class economic populism. [52]

In polls, we do indeed sound like populist radicals: a stunning twice as many of us agree (versus disagree) that "inequality continues to exist because it benefits the rich and powerful."[53] A clear majority of us (71 percent) believe that the increasing wealth of the richest 1 percent is a "serious" or "very serious" problem.[54] Although we believe in equal opportunity, all the same, some of us seem more equal than others: most of us (63 percent) believe that upper-income people have had the greatest opportunity for financial gain.[55]

Americans all know how it feels to resent elites. But do we all know how it feels to be resented? Ivy League students, when asked, mumble that they go to college "somewhere near Boston," "in Connecticut," or "in the city," because they know their Ivy identity can be a conversation stopper. As a Princeton professor, I prefer in social settings that this elite identity not be the first thing that people know about me. Professors already spend a lot of time deflecting the perception that they never work for a living. Ivy identity just makes the stereotype even worse. Most elite professionals defend their hard work, and so do most Americans, period. Americans hold up their heads when they view themselves as reflecting the mainstream values of seeking opportunity and putting in the hard work that earns results. If those efforts pay off, as one friend put it, "I don't want to be envied, but I don't mind being enviable." Deep inside, most of us believe that we are as down to earth as the next person.

Don't Look Now, but the Enemy Is US

Much as Americans may resent their elites, Americans themselves are the elite of the world. To our collective dismay, even as supposedly class-free Americans, we all risk getting a reputation as being out of touch and privileged in the global neighborhood. With our cultural belief in being a classless society and protecting opportunity, Americans feel free of arrogance, but other countries often view us as clueless and opportunistic. Over the last decade, the Pew Global Attitudes Project has polled people in twenty-five countries on their views of the United States. We have not always fared well. In twelve countries, a majority view our economic influence as negative, and the median of the remaining countries hovers at a substantial 39 percent holding cynical views toward us.[56] In most countries (68 percent), a majority think that we do not consider their country's interests. Our influence is more often seen as negative than as positive. And these latest views are an improvement over the years of the George W. Bush administration, when the reputation of the United States was even more negative.

We run the world's most powerful economy and military.[57] This profile forces respect but does not win affection. Our power and competence are respected, but our intentions are distrusted, according to surveys of over five thousand respondents in eleven nations assembled by my collaborator, Peter Glick.[58] People in other countries view our government as competent but arrogant and cold. As a result, they report a mixture of admiration and contempt for us. This American experience of being resented as the global rich and powerful parallels the elite experience of being resented as the locally rich and powerful. While our country's high status has its advantages, it has reputational drawbacks as well.

Americans as citizens fare little better than our government; as a people, we are seen as dumber but nicer than our administration. David Brooks exaggerates this dynamic: calling us the "bimbos of the world" living *On Paradise Drive,* he notes that we are viewed as comfortable but empty.[59] Our materialism reflects our ambition, in his analysis, but we are saved from the stereotype of utter mindlessness by our utopian imagination, which keeps us focused on the future. We are driven, and our work ethic evokes both respect and resentment in global opinion. But why do other countries even care what we think, feel, and do? Why do we matter to them? Power is only part of the story.

Comparison Is Only Natural

> The rewards . . . in this life are *esteem* and *admiration* of others—the punishments are *neglect* and *contempt.* . . . The desire of the esteem of others is as real a want of nature as hunger—and the neglect and contempt of the world as severe a pain as the gout or stone.
> —John Adams, *Discourses on Davila* (1805), 341

People are obsessed by admiration and neglect, envy and scorn, the world over. We are divided from each other by the often correlated differences between power (resources) and status (prestige).[60] Elites within the United States and Americans in the world evoke envy and run the risk of scorning those who are less well off.

More generally, people in positions of power are vulnerable to neglecting those with less power. People without power, in contrast, focus closely on the powerful but may resent them. Just how do human beings understand the thoughts and feelings of other people who have more or less power? Does empathy allow us to understand and appreciate others despite the separations caused by individual, group, and national power differences? And when do power differences damage empathy and cause us to dehumanize each other? When do we scorn those below us and envy those above us? And what happens between us when we do?

In "The Housebreaker of Shady Hill," John Cheever describes Johnny Hake, a Westchester resident with a cash-flow problem. Just laid off and totally broke, he "had never yearned for anyone the way [he] yearned that night for money." He envies and resents his wealthy neighbor ("rich . . . the kind of man that you would not have liked at school. He has bad skin and a rasping voice and a fixed idea—lechery. The Warburtons are always spending money, and that's what you talk about with them"). After lifting Warburton's loaded wallet, Hake scorns a coffee-shop customer who pockets the previous customer's thirty-five-cent tip ("What a crook!").[61] While few of us are driven to burgle our neighbors, let alone the waitress, each of us is caught between those whose position we envy and those whose situation we scorn. We are comparison machines.

Even dogs know when another dog is getting something they themselves deserve. Friederike Range and his colleagues asked pairs of dogs to offer their paw for food rewards; the catch was that one dog received nothing after the other received a chunk of dark bread (this took place in Vienna).[62] In the company of a rewarded partner, the cheated dog soon refused to perform for no reward. When both dogs received rewards—even if the other dog received that doggie manna, sausage, while the subject dog received only bread, or when both received bread—they cooperated. The totally unrewarded, cheated dogs showed more signs of canine distress: scratching, yawning, lip-licking, and avoiding the other dog's gaze (see figure 1.4). Closer to humans, chimps and monkeys also monitor their peers' relative rewards and boycott inequity, according to Frans de Waal and his colleagues.[63] Comparison seems only natural.

What about comparison's side effect: envy toward those doing better than us and scorn toward those doing worse? Social psychologists have much to say about social comparison, but this book's focus is specifically comparison's by-products, envy and scorn. So let's get specific, the better to decide the whether, how, who, when, and why of comparison.

Envy: I Wish That I Had What You Have (And That You Did Not)

Psychologists agree, notes Richard Smith, that envy combines hurt and anger.[64] A long-standing expert on the subject, Smith explains that a person

Figure 1.4   When Do Dogs Give a Paw?

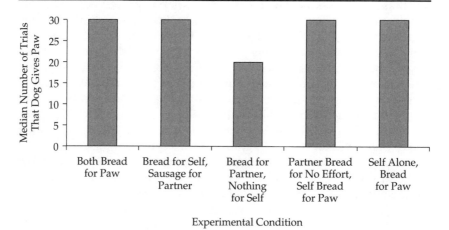

Source: Author's adaptation of data from Range et al. (2009).
Note: The maximum number of trials was thirty.

who feels envy is experiencing an illegitimate threat to a deserving self.[65] The experience of illegitimacy provokes anger, and the threat to self creates hurt. Envy homes in on disadvantage. As Gerrod Parrott notes, envy involves seeing that another person has something you want and wishing that person did not have it because their having it makes you feel inferior.[66] Envy can be malicious when it focuses on taking something away from another person, not just obtaining it for yourself. Wanting to damage the privileged other person is the essence of envy because the envied person causes your disadvantage. Consider that paragon of envy, Shakespeare's Iago. Bypassed for the coveted post of Othello's lieutenant, Iago develops a deadly envy that catalyzes his revenge on Othello, his wife Desdemona, and his aide Cassio.[67] In wreaking havoc, Iago does not even wish to have Desdemona for himself but instead wishes to deprive Othello of her. Envy thus has both a passive side (longing) and a potentially active side (aggression).

Unfair disadvantage is irksome. Envious people resent the overprivileged person but also the fate that bestows that advantage. In his analysis of everyday reports of envy, Parrott found that we resent not only the human agent of our disadvantage but also the unfair circumstances. We say that envy means longing and frustrated desire, as well as distress over feeling inferior and anxiety over losing status.[68]

Envious people sometimes are self-aware enough to feel guilty about it. Social norms frown on envy, so we are reluctant to admit to the feeling. In work on the emotions felt toward social out-groups, my colleagues and I found that people are least willing to report envy, perhaps because to admit envy is to reveal a sense of inferiority.[69] Ironically, envy is pervasive precisely because all social systems entail inequality. Envy endures because social systems endure. As Molière observed, the envious will die, but never envy.[70] Envy survives even in our own allegedly classless American society. All kinds of social systems, not just our equality-oriented one, must condemn envy to keep the peace. An overtly class-driven society maintains stability by advising people that "knowing your place" is a humble virtue. Even in our allegedly class-free, mobility-driven society, expressing envy is bad form.

To avoid confusion, let's agree on what envy is not. Envy is not jealousy. A jealous person fears losing a cherished personal relationship to a rival. Jealousy is more intense and more acute than envy because personal attachments change faster than the social system does. To be jealous is often to feel afraid, worried, threatened, rejected, suspicious, or betrayed, whereas the envious person more often feels inferior, ashamed, frustrated, bitter, or deprived, according to Parrott's informants.[71]

Envy is also not admiration, at least not as most English speakers use the term. The Dutch, Polish, and Thai languages have a term for benign envy ("benijden," "zazdrość," and "it-chαa") that connotes emulation, inspiration, and motivation to improve.[72] If malignant envy is "I wish you did not have what you have," then benign envy is "I wish I had what you have."[73] Sometimes people are inspired enough to admit someone else's superiority, to admire it, and to strive to achieve it themselves. Benign envy may turn out to be part of the solution, but malicious envy is always part of the problem, as we will see.

Scorn: You Are Not Worth My Attention (And I Wish You Would Go Away)

The flip side of envy is scorn. Otherwise known as disdain, contempt, or disrespect, scorn is rarely studied, probably for two reasons. When we envy someone else, we are usually aware of it and ruminate about it; our envy bothers us. We are often unaware, however, of scorning others; precisely because scorn is thoughtless, it often does not bother us. Psychologists most often study what bothers them, and being people, they are more bothered by envy than by scorn.

Another reason psychologists do not study scorn is that it is often a matter of neglecting and ignoring someone. "Silence is the most perfect expression of scorn," claimed George Bernard Shaw, who would know.[74] Scorn is the absence of respect, a lack of attention, a failure to consider. A failure to acknowledge another person provides evidence of scorn. In a famous story entitled "Silver Blaze," Sherlock Holmes solves a case that hinges on "the curious incident of the dog in the night-time": when a watchdog fails to bark at an intruder, Holmes deduces that the criminal must be the dog's owner. In a variant on this absence-as-evidence, not only would a scornful dog not bark in alarm, but a scornful dog also would not even wag its tail in recognition.[75] Scorn is known by what it fails to do.

Political systems can create scorn: "The centrality of hierarchy suggests a link between contempt and indifference. The underling is pathetically weak, so contempt can take the form of dismissing him," according to the political theorist Don Herzog.[76] John Adams, always acutely attuned to (dis)respect, describes the shame of the poor man, who

> is neglected and despised. He feels himself out of the sight of others, grop-
> ing in the dark. Mankind take [sic] no notice of him. He rambles and wan-
> ders unheeded. In the midst of a crowd . . . he is not disapproved, censured,
> or reproached; *he is only not seen.*[77]

To be sure, scorn does not stop with passive neglect. In its more active form, scorn is an aggressive wish to banish the scorned other. Thus, the scorned person does get a tiny bit of notice, but it is not good. Charles Darwin was the first scientist to describe the human facial expressions of scorn, disdain, contempt, and disgust: a sneer (uncovering the canine teeth on one side), a derisive, not-funny smile (all lips, no eye-crinkle), or a turning away ("puhleez!") all express disdain.[78] Disgust is conveyed when the muscles on the sides of the nose (the levator) are lifted; this expression wrinkles the nose, as if at a bad smell.

Paul Ekman, originator of the Facial Affect Coding System and consul-tant to the television program *Lie to Me,* claims that contempt is one of the very few facial expressions universally recognizable across all cultures. He describes the most common expression of contempt as a unilateral lip raise, also known as a half-smile. Contempt expressions appear reliably in certain situations, such as when we encounter "an acquaintance bragging about accomplishing something for which the acquaintance was not responsible." More generally, we express contempt when we are feeling "superior over another person, who has acted in a negative way."[79,80]

Although we recognize contempt when the situation suggests it, con-tempt is a neglected emotion, in that people report expressing and encoun-tering contempt the least of any emotions. Contempt is hardly polite. Its cousins—scorn, disdain, and disrespect—are even more rarely addressed in the social and behavioral sciences. Yet we know these emotions when we see them. And just as envy—though rarely admitted—clearly matters, so does scorn, because comparisons, both up and down, can be corrosive.

Comparison Corrupts

Keeping up is exhausting, and keeping others down has its own costs. Keeping up entails either emulating the trendsetters (benign envy) or, our issue here, slowing them down (malignant envy). To keep others down, you must suppress them so that they know their (inferior) place. Neither process is good for your health, not to mention the health of your target. A closer look shows why.

Scorn Scars the Scornful

Powerful individuals frequently fail to be compassionate in dealing with others.[81] For example, power increases exploitation, teasing, stereotyping, and even sexual harassment. Power-holders treat others instrumentally. In a study by Deborah Gruenfeld and her colleagues, some adults recalled a time when they had had power, and other adults, in a control condition, recalled a time when they had gone to the grocery store (not at all an experience of power).[82] Writing an essay about a time when they had power reliably primed participants to act powerful: they were sensitized to self-interest, regardless of interpersonal concerns. Most people, for example, avoid a jerk (in this study, someone who had neglected to help a handicapped person); control participants avoided the jerk even when they would have made money from performing as a team. When they could make money off their monumentally unkind partner, in contrast, the power-primed participants were willing to tolerate the jerk who could benefit them. When there was no money in it for them, the power-primed participants rejected the jerk, as did the baseline control participants. The power-holders seemed perfectly willing to approach the jerk when it suited their own needs but rejected the person otherwise. Using someone this way is an expression of scorn.

Scores of studies show that power-holders act with self-serving scorn for the needs of others; in experimental games conducted by David De Cremer and Eric van Dijk, for instance, power-holders took more for themselves.[83] Whereas most players split profits about equally, people designated as "leaders" are more likely to appropriate the lion's share. Leaders do the power grab especially when they feel legitimately entitled to lead, such as when leadership has been determined by a selection test—even if their position as leader actually was randomly determined by the experimenter (see figure 1.5).

Scornful power-holders are not only selfish but willfully clueless. Priming a powerful person has silly but also scary effects. Try this: Draw an upper-case letter "e" on your forehead. (If you are in public, do it in your imagination.) Which way do the "tines" of the e-fork face? Drawing the "e" so that it reads correctly from inside your head—with the tines pointing to your own right—correlates with failing to take the perspective of other people; drawing the "e" so that the tines point to your own left correlates with taking the perspective of other people outside your head. This demonstration and others come from the social psychology laboratory of Adam

Figure 1.5   Amount Allocated to Self by Designated Leaders, Followers, and an Equality Rule

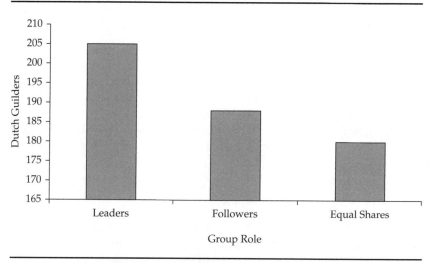

Source: Author's adaptation of data from De Cremer and van Dijk (2005).

Galinsky and his colleagues.[84] Their scarier study shows that priming power makes us worse at reading other people's facial expressions. This attitude of "I couldn't care less about you" shows scorn.

Other power researchers have replicated Galinsky's priming results with people given actual power over other people.[85] In our experiments, Stephanie Goodwin, our colleagues, and I recruited students who were expecting to work with other students from various majors.[86] In this scenario, supposedly based on a Harvard Management Aptitude Scale but actually by random assignment, some students got to be "the boss" and others had to be "the assistant" on a joint task that included significant prize money as an incentive. In a preliminary management exercise, they were to judge a series of other students described only by college major and personality traits. (On campus, majors serve as shared stereotypes; consider the common images of engineers versus artists.) In their ratings, "bosses," as predicted, used their personal stereotypes about college majors more than "assistants" did. That is, they made superficial judgments. Conversely, assistants used the individually revealing personality traits more than bosses did. As in the other studies, then, these power-holders were less sensitive to others as unique individuals—yet another form of scorn.

To be sure, power-holders sometimes can take responsibility for others, under the right circumstances. Power and status are always accompanied, however, by the risk of developing a scornful insensitivity to subordinates as power-holders control them, derogate them, fail to individuate them, and undermine their agency, all the while being self-serving and instrumental.[87] Recent studies show that people induced to feel powerful develop deficits specific to understanding others' emotions and thoughts. They fail to identify others' emotional expressions, to consider others' perspectives, and to appreciate others' knowledge. Such disregard for people raises the disturbing possibility that power inhibits our ability to see others as fully human entities possessing minds; that is, power may allow scorn.

Consistent with this suggestion, people often view social out-groups as less than human, a scorn-filled judgment if ever there was one. The emotional logic runs like this: we are more human than *they* are because we have a more complex inner life. As Jacques-Philippe Leyens and his collaborators have shown, we more readily see the in-group as experiencing subtle, complex, uniquely human emotions such as love, hope, grief, and resentment.[88] Out-group members—people unlike us—seem to experience only the same simple, primitive emotions that animals do (such as happiness, fear, anger, or sadness). Viewing "them" as feeling momentarily sad but not deeply grieving over the loss of family members, for example, makes it easier to avoid worrying about their misfortunes. This infrahumanization dynamic dampened empathy in the Hurricane Katrina debacle. Generally, white and black observers reported the other-race victims as experiencing less of the uniquely human emotions (anguish, mourning, remorse). To the extent that observers did perceive those emotions, however, they were more likely to offer help.[89]

Certain forms of social power reduce our ability to understand others' inner experiences (thoughts and feelings), thereby reducing our capacity for empathy and resulting in scorn directed downward. The social neuroscientist Lasana Harris and I took these ideas into the brain-scanning laboratory. Based on our lab's previous work, much of it with Amy Cuddy, we predicted that the least sympathetic, lowest-of-the-low out-groups would be homeless people and drug addicts. Look again at the BIAS Map (table 1.1). Homeless people are outliers, located the farthest from the center of society. In our survey data, they were so far away from all other social groups, along both negative dimensions, that, statistically speaking, they differed from all other humans in people's minds.[90]

Brain scans confirmed precisely this pattern. How might brain patterns display scorn? Human brains have adapted beautifully to social life. The brain's social cognition network reliably activates (comes on line) when we encounter other people, especially when we are thinking about their thoughts and feelings.[91] In particular, a swath of cortex curves vertically just behind the forehead (about where mystics locate the third eye, but I could be booted from social neuroscience for saying so). The medial prefrontal cortex (mPFC) lights up when we encounter people; this is our young field's most reliable finding. As a social psychologist, I love this result, which points to our neural attunement to other people.

Figure 1.6   The Medial Prefrontal Cortex (mPFC)

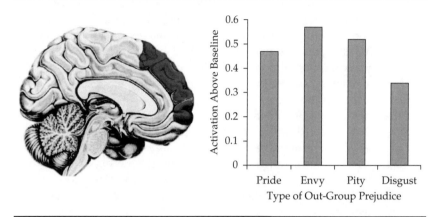

Source: Graph is author's compilation based on data from Harris and Fiske (2006).
Note: (Left) Shown in darker gray, the mPFC is typically the part of the brain involved in thinking about people. (Right) Levels of activation of the mPFC when exposed to people from different social groups. Alone among others, groups that elicit disgust (such as the homeless) do not activate the mPFC significantly above baseline.

However, some people do not light up our mPFC. Social groups that elicit contempt and disgust, alone among all other out-groups and in-groups, do not excite our mPFC in the way everyone else does. Harris and I built on the Fiske lab's finding that homeless people and drug addicts disgust other people—that is, people scorn them. After sliding into Princeton's scanner, our volunteers viewed dozens of photos of supposedly disgusting out-groups as well as other not-disgusting out-groups, such as older people or people with disabilities (who are pitied), rich people (who are envied), and in-groups, such as all-around Americans and college students (who inspire pride). The supposedly disgusting, most extreme out-groups failed to light up the mPFC (see figure 1.6).[92] (This neural dog definitely did not bark.) In regular questionnaires, participants reported these supposedly disgusting out-groups to be less warm or familiar, less competent, articulate, or intelligent, and less typically human. They also reported having a harder time attributing a mind to members of these out-groups—just as the quiet mPFC would suggest—and they did not expect to interact with them.

This disgust-contempt-scorn response fits a dehumanizing neglect of the minds of certain other people. Admittedly, we not only scorn but also pity homeless and drug-addicted people, yet our pity is not as great as it is for old or disabled people. And disgust uniquely targets these social outcasts. Sadly, this unfortunate reaction is only natural. We need to avoid disgusting people and things because they often are contaminated, as Steve Neuberg and Cathy Cottrell have shown.[93] It makes adaptive sense that we would avoid people who could endanger us. Cuddy's survey confirms this avoidance of disgusting out-groups: respondents reported that others will neglect and demean these lowest of the low, a kind of passive harm.[94] People also report that others will even attack them, a tragic kind of active harm that features all too often in incidents of unprovoked violence against the homeless. People in the lower left part of the BIAS Map space are allegedly "good for nothing."

When we dehumanize people, we deny them not only *typically* human attributes such as warmth and familiarity, but also *uniquely* human attributes, such as subtle emotions, articulate language, and complex minds. As in the earlier work on denying subtle emotions to out-groups, Nick Haslam describes this form of dehumanization as likening people to animals. People all over the world associate certain kinds of out-groups with animals automatically, not deliberately.[95] In a parallel reaction, people also withhold admiration and sympathy from some out-groups.[96] All these forms of dehumanization refuse to acknowledge the complex human experience of other people.

Not only are we clueless and unconscious when we scorn others, but we may also literally be making ourselves sick. According to an idea popularized in the 1970s, type A personalities, known for their driven styles, are at risk for heart disease; more recent work, however, identifies the hostility of this personality type as the main culprit. Health psychologists now blame a specific kind of hostility that is dominance-oriented.[97] This may be an extreme version of scorn. As Paul Ekman and his colleagues note, facial expressions of contempt (but not anger) relate to hostility in heart patients, a finding that supports a more focused hostility as the risk factor. If borne out, this would fit the idea that contempt or scorn is worse for your health than sheer anger itself.[98] Just as positive emotion promotes health, bitter emotions generally undermine it.[99] Although the current evidence for the link between scorn and health is admittedly tenuous, some enterprising researcher will soon demonstrate that contempt and scorn could be a major public health enemy.

A radical theory proposed by James Jackson fingers one type of scorn, namely racism, as a health risk to racists. Racial prejudice adds stress to a community as it reverberates between targets and racists, damaging the health of both.[100] All told, scorn can make high-status people exploitative, self-serving, insensitive, and unhealthy. Scorn scars the scornful.

Scorn Scars the Scorned

Being exploited, ignored, snubbed, and dehumanized obviously makes us unhappy—so obviously that a review of the evidence is hardly necessary. As later chapters will elaborate, ostracism and rejection are among the worst punishments that we can experience because we are such social beings. Beyond hurting and annoying, does scorn harm us in the long run?

Much circumstantial evidence does implicate racism as harming the health of its targets. The evidence often has to count as circumstantial because most of it shows a correlation at one moment in time. Most likely, being hassled about your race—in daily annoyances, in major life events, or in actual risks to life and limb—creates stress that undermines health. But we cannot conduct an experiment to establish causal direction, and to my knowledge the effects over time have not yet been documented, so we have to allow the possibility that stressed or irritable people more often evoke or perceive racism. Still, the racism-stress linkage seems likely.[101]

Being the target of any kind of stigma—marked for society's scorn—endangers health.[102] Involuntary physiological responses to stress can undermine heart health and immune function, whether in people or in primates.[103] Scorn can make its targets sick. Dehumanization damages all concerned, so scorn hardly seems adaptive.

Envy Harms the Envied

What about envy, which is directed upward? While being envious of high-status, allegedly exploitative people might not seem important, in fact our feelings toward higher-status groups and individuals can catalyze a volatile mix of reactions toward those we grudgingly respect but dislike.

In Haslam's system, a unique kind of dehumanization targets envied groups: they are denied the *typically* human attributes, such as warmth and sociality. These cold but effective out-groups are likened to robots. Perceived as threatening because they seem like automatons, out-groups dehumanized in this way are not so much disgusting as chilling. Think cyborgs. Businesspeople and their paraphernalia, from briefcases to suits, are associated in our minds with automatons, from androids to software.[104] On the downside, we link both businesspeople and robots to being cold, conservative, heartless, and shallow, though we acknowledge that they are also organized, polite, and thorough. What both CEOs and computers are *not* is typically human: curious, friendly, sociable, and fun-loving.

In our own work we have found that members of ethnic groups who succeed as entrepreneurs (Jews, Asians) and subordinate out-group members who succeed as professionals (middle-class blacks, career women) fall into this ambivalent space, eliciting envy and resentment. Society views them as sacrificing their humanity to get ahead, a finding that parallels the chilling cyborgs of Haslam's system. In surveys, people report that members of these groups—often seen as rich—are cold but competent.[105] These particular out-groups also provoke more envy than other groups do. People in the lower right part of the BIAS Map are allegedly not on our side, but their competence makes them threatening (see figure 1.7).

The volatility of our mixed reactions to envied groups is dangerous. Envied groups are especially targeted when we make the common assump-

Figure 1.7   Envied Groups and Scorned Groups

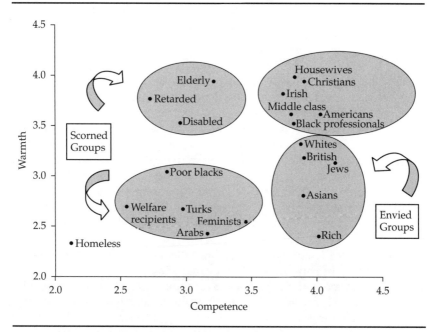

Source: Author's adaptation of Cuddy, Fiske, and Glick (2007).

tion that they are conspiring. All too often we assume that the powerful are in cahoots to carry out their dangerous intents, that they are all of one evil mind. Recall that canard, "the Jews control the banking industry." In one study, Eric Dépret and I simulated a situation in which those in power hold all the cards and they all hang together, so that one feels helpless to influence them. In this scenario, undergraduates came into a study where they could earn money for their performance under the distraction typically inflicted by roommates. The distracters had either more or less power (they could interfere a little or a lot), and they came either from one college major (they were in cahoots) or from several majors (they were unlikely to conspire). Faced with a uniform bunch of high-powered math majors, psychology majors felt more unhappy and threatened than they did when dealing with a motley high-powered group comprising a math major, an art major, and a business major.[106] They perceived high-status outsiders as having minds, but cold, calculating, threatening, conspiring minds. In the worst case, such a perception would justify the elimination of a high-status group as a threat to "us."

When envy entails anger and resentment, it harms the envied other. At a societal level, people who report both envy and anger toward privileged groups also report a greater tendency toward harming them.[107] At the individual level, envied out-groups are subject to schadenfreude (malicious glee at their misfortunes) and aggression.[108]

Envy Eats at the Envious

In daily life, we all too easily blame the powerful. To explain their financial challenges, low-wage workers blame powerful institutions, such as government (blamed "some or "a lot" by 74 percent) and corporate America (64 percent), at least as often as they blame themselves (63 percent) and far more often than they blame fate (29 percent) or discrimination (30 percent).[109] Many of us blame the political system for the gap between low- and high-income Americans (63 percent).[110] Feelings about inequality poison trust, and loss of trust, in turn, undermines participation in the local community.[111] Blaming the powerful arguably undermines our feelings of control, a loss that is well known to jeopardize health. Envy endangers the envious.[112]

Envy expert Richard Smith and his colleagues convincingly detail a "witch's brew" of ways in which envy may make us sick.[113] First, frustration is a component of envy, which is all about unresolved wanting, with an overlay of felt injustice. Giving in to the tendency to dwell on such grievances can undermine our well-being. Second, envy is self-destructive in that resentment, shame, and hostility can motivate us to hurt others, even at the risk of harming ourselves. For example, some people are willing to forgo personal profits if they can bring down the target of their envy. Third, envy damages close relationships that might otherwise provide an antidote to misery. Envy makes us feel inferior and probably prickly about receiving help or expressing gratitude.

Added to all these psychological risks is the totally scary low-status syndrome. Low status demands a vigilant attention to those with higher status, and this vigilance compromises health. Here's why. Single-shot, acute reactions to temporary threats benefit from the body's short-term stress responses, which ordinarily calm down after the danger has passed. If the body's stress system stays on prolonged alert, however, as it does for people who are constantly vigilant, mental and physical health are damaged.[114]

As it keeps the nervous system on alert, with downstream risk to the cardiovascular and immune systems, vigilance becomes costly. Low-status people incur the costs of vigilance for good reason. People are chronically watchful when their lives feel out of control. Indeed, this is the cost of being lower in the hierarchy and looking up all the time at those who control one's fate. Consistent with this analysis, men's social class predicts their heart disease risk; in pathbreaking work, Michael Marmot and his colleagues, surveying the Whitehall sample of British civil servants, show that the risk rises with the experience of not having enough control at work.[115] Besides lack of control as a risk factor, negative emotions are implicated in this finding, because resentment, hostility, anxiety, hopelessness, and cynicism (emotions related to envy) underlie the harms wrought by loss of control.[116]

Envy may be worse than other negative emotions because lack of control automatically comes with it. Keeping up with the better-off requires constant effort and attention. The novelist Richard Russo illustrates:

> My father had had a pretty good idea of our relative circumstances [compared with the neighbor family]. What had the Marconis acquired? How big were the economic strides they had taken? How much had those strides been offset by two more little Marconis? They were still renting, which meant something, but maybe they were saving for a down payment on a house. Were they close or still years away? My father had an inquiring mind.

Only peers doing slightly better are of interest:

> You don't identify with people worse off than you are. You make your deals, if you can, with those who have more, because you hope one day to have more yourself. Understand that . . . and you understand America.[117]

The upward comparison of envy stresses people more than downward comparison does. The social neuroscientist Wendy Berry Mendes and her colleagues paired undergraduates in a cooperative word game.[118] After meeting face to face, each participant completed the task alone; a random half of the participants then learned (falsely) that they had outperformed their partner, and the other random half learned that they had underperformed their partner. When participants had to work with their higher-ranked partner, their cardiovascular activity indicated an unmanageable threat, but when participants worked with their lower-ranked partner, their cardiovascular activity showed a more controllable challenge response.

Envy is more than upward comparison. The resentful vigilance of envy imports hostility, which, as noted, is a known risk factor in heart disease. Just as a specific type of hostility may explain the effect of scorn on health, so too a hostility subtype is likely to explain envy's corrosive effects on health.[119] Hostile submission describes someone whose felt inferiority simmers with resentment. This condition also carries cardiovascular risks.

Mental health as well as physical health is at risk when we envy another. Across laboratory and real-world work groups, lower status creates performance anxiety.[120] Low levels of power specifically impair the mind's executive control functions: updating, concentrating, and planning.[121] Thus, knowing that we sit below others—the situation conducive to envy—can impair our minds. In response, lower-status groups often specifically seek respect and care less about affection.[122] But their ability to earn respect is precisely endangered by the dynamics of resentment toward those on the rung just above their own rung on the social ladder. These dynamics undermine the very performance that might gain the desired respect. Envy eats the envious.

If Envy and Scorn Are So Toxic, How Prevalent Is Their Poison?

Status is everywhere, as the rest of this book will show. Creatures from orangutans to organizations arrange themselves in hierarchies.[123] This process is so basic that we automatically judge the dominance of another individual in a fraction of a second, using certain cues, such as physical strength.[124] Within close relationships, we compare and compete, ranking ourselves relative to each other, despite the damage this can do.[125] All known organizations gravitate toward status and power hierarchies because this structure makes them run more smoothly.[126] At the macro level, human societies stratify social groups by dominance hierarchies, especially social class.[127]

Despite Americans' insistence on egalitarianism, opportunity, and classlessness, "there is an un-American secret at the heart of American culture: for a long time it was [and is] preoccupied by class."[128] As this chapter suggests, we like to think that we minimize class distinctions in the United States, but we attend to class more than we think. We do not overwhelmingly identify as one big happy, homogeneous middle class. Instead, we are acutely aware of class distinctions, and we endorse the opportunity syllogism, which suggests that people attain the class status they deserve. We deride elites as out of touch, but we do not notice that we are the elites of the world. Comparison is a fact of social life.

> All men compare themselves with others. . . . Nature has ordained it, as a constant incentive to activity and industry, that, to acquire the attention and complacency, approbation and admiration of their fellows, men might be urged to constant exertions . . . to produce something.[129]

John Adams, as usual, was on to something about comparison. Social comparison, especially upward, is universal. Even dogs and chimps do it. Where there is ubiquity, there are arguments for evolutionary adaptiveness. Perhaps in the competition to survive and thrive, humans must notice and be motivated by gaps between themselves and others who are doing slightly better.[130] Sarah Hill and David Buss argue that we have a "positional bias" that shows us our rank relative to relevant others. From this, upward envy alerts us to our rivals' advantages and motivates us to compete. Most societies condemn envy, as a "disturber of the peace."[131] Nonetheless it persists.

Downward-directed scorn, likewise condemned, lurks on the other side of the comparison. "There is not in Human Nature a more odious

Disposition, than a Proneness to Contempt," according to the novelist Henry Fielding.[132] We spontaneously express but rarely admit to feeling contempt and scorn. In close relationships, contempt is a killer, as is fear of contempt. Outside the home, we distance ourselves from our underlings by ignoring them and discounting their full humanity. Societies urge pity for those who are worse off, and we do pity certain unfortunates, but only those who have landed at the bottom through no fault of their own. Otherwise, under meritocracy, they deserve their fate and are beneath consideration.

Where We Go from Here

Is this just a grim litany of the inevitable? Not if we understand that we cannot change what we do not understand. Pulling envy and scorn out from the untamed undergrowth allows us to recognize them in our society, in our relationships, and in ourselves. Human nature makes status distinctions, and comparison will never go away, so we are better off understanding it. Perhaps both individual lives and society as a whole will be improved by removing the taboo from these topics.

In chapter 2, a closer look will reveal the particular neural, emotional, cognitive, and behavioral signatures of envy and scorn. Both regular people and scientists have systems for detecting these revealing reactions and have, in effect, everyday working definitions of them.

Then chapter 3 explores the scope of envy and scorn. Who experiences them the most, and who does not? Which individuals and groups act out these comparisons the most? And where have people been most prone to comparison? What cultures most display these dynamics?

To explain *why* humans compare themselves, each of the next chapters focuses on one of the various practical consequences of comparison: We compare in order to inform ourselves about where we stand. We compare to protect our self-esteem. We compare to identify ourselves with our peer group, those others who are similarly situated.

All these dynamics tell us when we are likely to compare ourselves to others, envying up and scorning down. Envy and scorn both have warmer siblings, which hint at alternative scenarios. Understanding these dynamics can inspire us to be more self-aware, more socially aware, and more culturally aware. Perhaps we can harness this understanding to move beyond our affinity for comparison.

Chapter 2

Signatures of Envy and Scorn: We Know Them When We See Them

. . . But 'tis a common proof,
That lowliness is young ambition's ladder,
Whereto the climber upward turns his face;
But when he once attains the upmost round,
He then unto the ladder turns his back,
Looks in the clouds, scorning the base degrees
By which he did ascend.

—Brutus, *Julius Caesar*, II.1.21–27

T HE SIGNS of envy and scorn are everywhere because the vertical dimension is everywhere. The vertical dimension, "ambition's ladder," is a necessary part of any human system. Group-living animals all have hierarchies. Even chickens have pecking orders. Coordination demands it. Stability demands it. Adjustment demands it. Despite the corrosive side effects of envy and scorn, our social systems require status differences. So we know them when we see them.

Yet envy and scorn embarrass us. We hesitate to admit feeling them ourselves, whether privately or publicly. When I tell people at parties about this book project, they are intrigued, but they rarely volunteer a personal story about envying or scorning someone. Nobody wants to own these reactions. It is as if we define and conjugate the verb "to compare" thus: "I evaluate, we measure, you judge, and they obsess." What seems useful in the privacy of our own minds often seems pathetic or despicable in other people. So how do we detect these comparisons that none of us admit to making?

As chapter 1 shows, status-competence is one of two immediate priorities in first impressions (the other being cooperation-warmth). One of the first things we seek to know about other people is whether they can act on their intentions. Our research shows that competence-status is one of two fundamental dimensions of social cognition, and our research is not alone in this conclusion.[1] Data from Europe indicate that the status-competence dimension accounts for nearly one-third of the action in our first impressions of people.[2] So all of us are alert to the relative status and presumed (in)competence of other people from our first encounter with them.

Whenever groups gather, some people soon rank higher than others.[3] This happens because groups spontaneously award status.[4] The natural leaders seem best at representing the group's shared values, so they appear to be the most competent and expert, resolving uncertainty. Thus, they influence others and control incentives; they provide reassuring structure and predictability. This happens even in social groups, but more openly in work groups.

We seek to meet a variety of needs, besides earning a living, when we go to work. These needs include wanting to belong to a group and wanting some predictability and control over our lives within the group. These prediction-control needs arguably are best met in a hierarchical organization. According to Deborah Gruenfeld and Larissa Tiedens, status is crucial in all organizations, despite the easygoing management fashions of the twenty-first century.[5] As groups of groups, organizations cannot coordinate their activities or motivate their members without granting some groups and individuals more power and value than others. Every known organization has a vertical dimension, according to scholars who have searched for an organization without one. When organizations form, status spontaneously emerges. We tend to prefer organizations that have a consensus about who ranks above whom. What is more, once established, status systems perpetuate themselves, justify themselves, and legitimate themselves.[6] Hierarchy seems inevitable and even useful.

If we so relentlessly demand hierarchy, our brains must be wired for it. This chapter will explore our recognition of verticality in various venues: how our emotions signal it, our minds understand it, and our behavior reveals it. In each case, evidence comes from individuals, partners, groups, and societies, and these levels operate in tandem for everyone. All of us are everyday protocol officers, expert in the proper etiquette of up and down. We notice signatures of envy and scorn, though not always consciously.[7]

Wired for Status

Two tiny almond-shaped bits of brain alert us to the stuff that really matters. The amygdala activates when we encounter something emotionally significant, from a deadly snake to our own baby. The amygdala stores emotional memories, focuses attention, and links to the systems that prepare the fight-or-flight response.[8] People with a damaged amygdala do not

Figure 2.1   Social Group Members from the BIAS Map Space

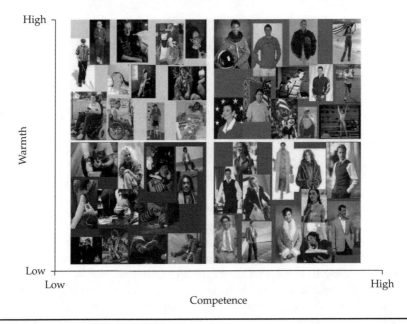

Source: Compilation copyrighted 2010 by Fiske and Harris.
Note: Groups elicit, from top right, clockwise: pride, envy, disgust, and pity. The disgust and pity groups together elicit scorn.

know enough to be afraid. People with an overactive amygdala are afraid of their own shadow. The amygdala allows rapid and automatic responses to salient events, marshaling attention and arousal. The amygdala is involved in instantly evaluating stimuli, especially unpredictable stimuli. Among the most unpredictable but most important stimuli we notice are other people.[9] In social cognition, the amygdala reliably comes on line when we encounter people who matter to us emotionally, for good or ill.

The amygdala activates in both kinds of social encounters that concern us here, that is, both occasions for envy (up the status ladder) and occasions for scorn (down the ladder). Social comparisons upward and downward both matter to us, as the amygdala responses suggest. Lasana Harris and I observed the activation of people's amygdalas in just these kinds of social comparisons up and down. In Princeton's brain scanner, undergraduates looked at forty-eight people in pictures that showed recognizable social groups across our BIAS Map's warmth-competence space (figure 2.1).

After viewing each individual for six seconds, participants indicated which emotion the picture made them feel. We predicted that students

Figure 2.2   Amygdala Location in the Brain

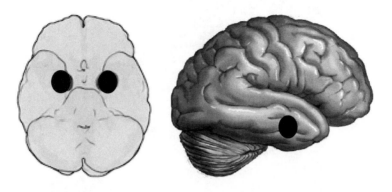

Source: Author's illustration.
Note: As viewed (left) in a horizontal slice and (right) from the lateral surface, outside where the amygdala lies in the interior. The amygdala typically activates to emotionally significant stimuli.

looking down the status hierarchy at homeless people and drug addicts would often report disgust (a close cousin of contempt and scorn). And we predicted that students looking up the hierarchy at rich people and businesspeople would often report envy. Indeed, they did report disgust and envy, respectively, down and up.[10] What is more, their amygdalas activated in *both* cases (figure 2.2).[11]

Other studies report the amygdala coming on line for both envied and scorned people. In another example of neuro-envy, amygdala responses to the faces of male CEOs predicted not only their rated leadership ability (the brain was signaling: this is someone to watch!) but also their company's profits.[12] In a completely different envy domain, consider this study: young women viewed photographs of slender female fashion models, under instructions (cruel!) to compare their own bodies to those of the models.[13] The participants' amygdala activation correlated with their reported anxiety while viewing those slim bodies.

For an example of the amygdala implicated in neuro-scorn, consider studies of white students' reactions to pictures of unfamiliar black students. The finding that the amygdala activated especially for white students who scored high on a subtle measure of racism is consistent with this neural response being more about their distaste than their simple discomfort with a racial out-group.[14] As a growing scientific consensus indicates, the amygdala is implicated in responses to emotionally important people both up and down the hierarchy.

Figure 2.3   The Anterior Cingulate Cortex, the Brain's Discrepancy Detector

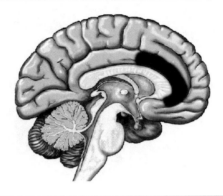

Source: Author's illustration.

Neural Signatures of Envy

Besides the amygdala alerting other parts of the brain, what brain systems activate specifically to upward comparison? Envied people, by definition, have what we would like to have. High-status people have prestige, and high-powered people control resources. Either or both of these assets would be nice to have, so we humans often set our minds to meeting this challenge. First, we have to notice the discrepancy between us and them—namely, the fact that they are better off. Second, we have to pay attention to them if we want to control our own fate. The neural systems involved with envy fit this two-step logic.

First, we notice the gap between ourselves and the person we envy. The brain's anterior cingulate cortex (ACC) is a discrepancy detector (figure 2.3).[15] When simultaneous inputs conflict, the ACC directs attention to the discrepancy so that higher-order systems can resolve the conflict. Perhaps it is a stretch, but upward comparison would seem to present such a potential conflict. Someone just like us is doing well, but that someone is not us. The neural evidence so far fits this speculation. Studies of envy as upward social comparison often report ACC activation. The young women looking at idealized female bodies activated the ACC.[16] Another study homed in on envy: asked to read about three other students, among them a same-sex peer who had superior credentials, popularity, possessions, and opportunity, students naturally reported being envious of this person.[17] What is more, the ACC also activated toward this envied peer more than toward the others. Better evidence yet, the ACC activation correlated with participants' reported envy. Still other ACC data suggest envy. Being treated unfairly can activate the ACC, among other neural signatures of pain.[18] Altogether, the ACC seems to be a plausible candidate for envy's neural network, especially for the first step of noticing an enviable person.[19]

After we notice that people we envy have what we wish we had, we think about them. At worst, we would like to take away their treasure. At best, we would like to figure out how they got it, or maybe we hope that they will share it. In each case, we have to figure them out. When we think about other people's minds, the neural signature includes the medial prefrontal cortex (mPFC). This marvelous swath of cortex, as mentioned in chapter 1, activates when we consider other people's minds.[20] We especially think about the minds of people who matter to us, and envied people matter. The women looking at slender models also activated the mPFC if they were anxious about the comparison. This is especially striking because the pictures excluded the models' faces, making it harder to consider their minds.[21] Apparently, just wondering how the models got their bodies to look that way was enough to cause participants to consider their minds.

In our lab, students looking at pictures of people they might wish to become (rich people, businesspeople) especially activated the mPFC, certainly more than they did looking at pictures of low-status people, such as the homeless or the disabled.[22] As chapter 1 pointed out, deactivation of the mPFC correlates with social scorn. Envy shows the opposite pattern.

The mPFC activates in pursuit of social rewards, that is, rewards controlled by another person.[23] One study compared juice given to a thirsty subject by a person versus by a computer; some mPFC regions activated more to the person-provided juice. A paired study also compared people's responses to disgusting versus enviable people (for example, homeless versus rich) and disgusting versus enviable objects (such as a dirty toilet versus a luxury car). The enviable people especially activated the mPFC.

Actual people who control rewards also activate the mPFC. People's pursuit of social rewards extends to teamwork with another person in charge. In our lab, Daniel Ames had undergraduate students work on a joint task with an education major, an expert in designing games to teach elementary school children using colorful windup toys; the students could win a $50 prize for designing the best game. In the scanner, the students read the teaching evaluations of their partner. Learning about this person's more unexpected characteristics, the most puzzling information activated the mPFC, consistent with its role in complex impression formation (see figure 1.6).[24]

All this evidence fits the envy signature that alerts us when another person possesses something we do not have (amygdala vigilance and ACC discrepancy monitor). Then the mPFC's mind reading comes on line to problem-solve about who controls that treasure and how we might get some too.

Figure 2.4   The Insula

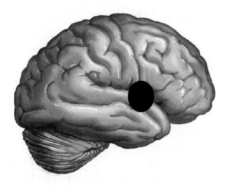

Source: Author's illustration.
Note: Figure shows the lateral surface, outside where the insula lies in the interior.

Neural Signatures of Scorn

On the downside of the comparison divide, the amygdala serves scorn by alerting us to someone who is emotionally salient. But obviously, the emotional salience of scorn differs from the emotional salience of envy. For one thing, envy approaches, but scorn avoids. People distance themselves from scorned others, to avoid real or symbolic contamination.[25] Consider why we avoid homeless street people: because of our expectations, we dread their dirt and disease, we fear getting involved with them, and we shun any association with them. The amygdala alerts us to these apparently tainted people.

Consistent with the disgust that people report feeling toward these lowest of the low, the brain's insula reliably activates when we see homeless people or drug addicts (figure 2.4).[26] The insula generally reacts to our experience of our own bodily states, such as feeling disgusted or feeling aroused. The insula's relation to disgust is among the most reliable neural indicators of any emotion.[27] Both the insula and the amygdala respond to various scorned outcasts, including those who are obese, pierced, or transsexual.[28] What is more, responding to other people's disgust expressions activates the observer's own insula, a sort of mimicked, shared disgust response.[29] To scorn another person is to view that person as inferior and potentially disgusting, so the insula findings make sense.

To scorn another person is also to view yourself as superior. Scorn requires the vertical fact of the self apparently doing better. Such self-congratulations apparently light up the brain's reward system. That is, positive social comparison activates the ventral striatum (VS) (figure 2.5).[30] The VS responds to our own advantages in reputation.[31] High-status

Figure 2.5   The Ventral Striatum

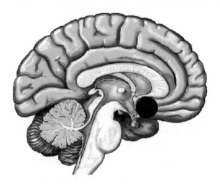

Source: Author's illustration.

people more often encounter ingratiating praise than lower-status people do. When we read others' praise of us, our VS lights up. The VS also activates when we give to charity, another reward of being high status.[32] To feel scorn, we have to stand above others, and narcissists that we are, elevating ourselves is rewarding.[33]

Neural Signatures of Schadenfreude

A potent mixture of envy and scorn happens when an envied person is brought down and becomes an object of scorn. Consider the guilty pleasure that people feel at the latest news of a billionaire's comedown. (From the last decade, Martha Stewart, Bernie Madoff, Tiger Woods, and countless politicians and entertainers come to mind.) People most often feel schadenfreude—pleasure at the misfortune of another person—when that person was once envied. Their seemingly deserved misfortune makes the person an object of scorn. For example, consider the Armani-suited, Blackberry-toting hedge fund manager who steps in dog poo while dashing toward his limo at the curb; he is laughable. But a homeless person or a disabled person stepping in dog poo is not funny. In Princeton graduate student Mina Cikara's dissertation showing exactly how rewarding it is to be able to scorn an envied person, the VS is implicated once again.[34] Similarly, in the envy study that made students compare themselves to an advantaged peer, the students later learned that the peer had experienced a setback. This misfortune not only activated the VS (rewards), but the VS correlated with the prior envy study's ACC (discrepancy monitor).[35] This suggests that schadenfreude depends on a discrepant upward comparison.

All these potential neural signatures—for envy, scorn, schadenfreude— bring on line the brain systems for vigilance, social problem solving, and self-relevance. Consistent with these useful neural activities, envy and scorn as emotions signal us to take care of our own interests.

Emotions Signal Status

Most of us do not think of emotions as useful, but in fact they can serve a practical purpose. Emotions send messages to us as individuals, partners, teammates, and citizens.[36] Emotions adapt us to fulfill our individual and social functions. Most people think of emotions as spontaneous eruptions, but emotions often work to facilitate our cherished goals. Emotions are adaptive, workaday tools of the mind, so emotions such as envy and scorn are perfectly predictable from their utility. We can see this concretely at all levels of analysis, from individuals to cultures.

Individuals Mind Their Goals Through
Envy and Scorn

Consider first our individual selves. Emotions inform our priorities by alerting us when a personal goal needs attention, and they help us maintain those priorities—by tracking not only our goals but our efforts to meet them. For example:

- Feeling guilty reminds us to make amends.
- Feeling jealous suggests that a relationship needs work.
- Feeling angry alerts us that we have been wronged.
- Feeling afraid focuses the mind on coping with a threat.
- Feeling happy signals that salient goals have been met.

Envy and scorn are no different from other emotions. Both envy and scorn identify a gap between what we have and what someone else has. "Envy is ever joined with the comparing of a man's self; and where there is no comparison, no envy," Francis Bacon observed.[37] Scorn likewise compares self to other, with self coming out on top. Feeling envious signals inferiority; feeling scorn signals superiority. In envy, we might wish to attend to the gap, either bringing the other down (malicious envy) or bringing the self up (benign envy). As an example of malicious envy, we show schadenfreude while watching the hedge fund manager's encounter with dog feces—or billionaires stubbing a toe or sitting on chewing gum (figure 2.6)—by the subtle activation of the smile muscles in our cheeks (figure 2.7).[38] Schadenfreude especially results from envy when the other is similar enough to us to offer a personally relevant social comparison.[39] Feeling resentful, angry, or wronged all predict schadenfreude.[40] We really mind the gap.

Figure 2.6   Sample Stimulus for Schadenfreude

Got soaked by a taxi driving through a puddle

Source: Author's illustration.

Conversely, to scorn someone is to confirm our own satisfactory position, so scorn signals not minding the gap, except to keep our distance from the apparently worse-off person. When we want to maintain our status, we know that we had better avoid "stigma by association." Steve Neuberg and his colleagues originated the term, applying it to how people stigmatize straight people who have a gay friend; Michelle Hebl and Laura Mannix show that stigma by association arises even when a normal-weight person is merely next to an obese person.[41] No surprise, then, that we tend to avoid other people with a bad reputation or simply an unattractive appearance—to avoid being tarred by the same brush.

Figure 2.7   Zygomaticus Major: The "Smile" Muscle That Reveals a Subtle Sign of Schadenfreude

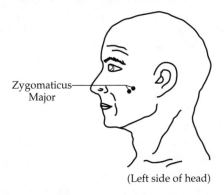

Zygomaticus—
Major

(Left side of head)

Source: Adapted and redrawn from Tassinary, Cacioppo, and Green (1989), figure 4.

In all these ways, emotions track how well we are meeting our personal goals, whether the goal is minding the frustrating gap between self and a superior or noting the satisfying gap between self and inferiors. The Nobel laureate psychologist Herbert Simon once described how one might build a doomed robot: an emotionless android would single-mindedly and reliably locomote to its next goal, remaining oblivious to all else; unwilling to change its operative goal, it would fatally fail to note an oncoming Mack truck.[42] A fear algorithm might be useful. In robots as in people, fear can be an emotion programmed to interrupt goal pursuit to reprioritize and adapt to changing circumstances. This is how emotions serve an adaptive function in humans.

Envy and scorn interrupt other ongoing activities to alert us to the risks we run by not living up to a salient standard (envy) or by surpassing someone else and needing to maintain that distance (scorn). Envy and scorn as emotions signal the importance of social-comparison goals. Emotions get more complicated when we move outside the mind to face the other person, but we are rigged to manage that as well.

Partners Coordinate Through Envy and Scorn

We are interpersonal comparison experts. When we encounter another person, we rapidly judge the other person's dominance or status.[43] This creates a face-to-face comparison; envy and scorn may follow. How could automatic comparison possibly be useful to the encounter? Would it be better not to rank ourselves all the time? Maybe. But social-comparison emotions do inform partners about each other's intentions, allow complementary behavior, and allow each partner to control the other's behavior.[44] The envious partner pays attention, and the scornful partner need not. Both envy and scorn allow the partners to make efficient assumptions that grease the social wheels. However, the coordination benefits differ on either side of the divide. What is good for the greater is not good for the lesser.

For the high-status person, both the comparison itself and its public nature generate pride.[45] Pride is a self-focused emotion that tends to ignore other people. (Inattention, remember, is an element of scorn.) As the research of Dacher Keltner and his colleagues on interpersonal power shows, most powerful people are confidently cheerful because one's own power feels good. For example, people express positive feelings in discussions with their romantic partner if that person recognizes them as powerful, or even when they are randomly assigned to be powerful.[46] When people have the advantage, they feel capable of overcoming challenges and are confident they have the inner resources to meet the demands of threat, uncertainty, or effort.[47] Henry Kissinger famously quipped that

Table 2.1   Personalities Associated with Certain Emotions and Traits

	Low Dominance	High Dominance
High affiliation	Fear, sadness	Happiness
Low affiliation	(No typical emotions)	Anger, disgust

Source: Author's adaptation based on data from Knutson (1996, figure 2).
Note: Anger implies a dominant, unaffiliative personality; happiness implies a dominant, affiliative personality; fear implies a submissive but affiliative personality; the fourth personality combination is not represented by any emotions. As with the dehumanization we show for people seen as low-status–incompetent or exploitative-hostile (Harris and Fiske 2006), observers have difficulty imagining any emotions characteristic of these lowest of the low. Note the similarity to the BIAS Map's status-competence and cooperation-warmth dimensions (Fiske, Cuddy, and Glick 2007).

power is the ultimate aphrodisiac, but because many people seek power and dominance simply because it feels good, perhaps power has benefits even beyond the bedroom.

Dominance not only allows us to have positive feelings about ourselves but also creates negative feelings in us against others. When high-status people feel on top of the world, they are more likely to express anger and disgust (cousins of scorn and contempt).[48] A furrowed brow indicates anger, and anger in turn signals dominance without any softening affiliation.[49] In one demonstration of this, undergraduates viewed three dozen photographs of faces expressing a variety of emotions (anger, fear, disgust, happiness, sadness, neutrality) and rated each one on thirty-two personality traits. The traits fit into two basic dimensions and certain emotions convey certain personalities. Expressing anger and disgust (scorn!) toward someone else, for instance, suggests a dominant personality devoid of affiliative orientation (table 2.1).

Expressing anger not only implies ruthless dominance but also gains the advantage in negotiation against a weaker partner.[50] Contempt subordinates, rejects, and excludes other people.[51] Scorn signals the freedom to look down on others, so in that perverse way it serves the power-holder.

What could possibly be useful about the other side, the envious feelings that come with disadvantage? Presumably, none of us like to come out on the bottom of a comparison in an everyday encounter. And videos of our facial expressions reveal that we especially mind someone else doing better if the arena is relevant to us and the other person is close to us.[52]

The litany of discomfort is familiar to us all. If we are low status, public comparison makes us ashamed, a feature of envy.[53] Similarly, we feel bad if our romantic partner has power over us,[54] and our self-esteem suffers as a result.[55] When we are at a disadvantage, we often feel threatened, which can make us judge that we have insufficient resources to meet the threat.[56] In light of all this, how can feeling hopelessly one-down in social-comparison encounters possibly be useful?

Apparently, even shame, envy, inferiority, and threat are better than uncertainty, chaos, and conflict. Interactions are predictable when one partner agrees to be subordinate and the other is dominant. Sometimes surrender is better than a fight, and one way we communicate our subordinate status is by the emotions we express. When we express fear and sadness we come across as subordinate, not just in the moment,[57] but as a character trait.[58] The subordinate emotions trigger several ways of giving up: doing nothing if we are sad, running away if we are fearful, or feeling small if we are ashamed.[59] All of these subordinate responses show how emotions can communicate lower status in a moment.

Emotions determine fates beyond the moment. Some facial expressions seem permanent, such as the face of someone who always looks innocent just because of having a face with the wide eyes and arched eyebrows of surprise (see figure 2.8). We are so sensitive to emotional cues of rank that we infer subordinate status even in people who are simply endowed with a sweet baby-face, regardless of age. We interpret facial immaturity, femininity, and weakness to mean subordinate status.[60] Thus, we pick up even unintended emotional cues.

We have little control over the fixed features of our faces, but we do somewhat control our emotional behavior. All these emotional communication channels tend to operate semiconsciously; the feelings that translate to rank are usually outside of conscious awareness. Although the emotional advantages to being dominant are obvious, the emotional advantages to being subordinate are less obvious. Presumably, even for the subordinate person, knowledge is better than uncertainty or conflict, so we excel at reading the cues that divide us.

Groups Organize Through Envy and Scorn

> First they ignore you, then they laugh at you, then they fight you, then you win.
>
> —Mohandas Gandhi[61]

Just as individuals track their goals through their emotions and partners track each other by reading each other's emotions, so do groups manage their collective goals, and their members, by using group emotions.[62] Gandhi notes that powerful groups scorn a rebellious minority by ignoring them and laughing at them before fully engaging them. In a more everyday example, we gossip not just to differentiate ourselves from the victims of our gossip but to connect with our co-conspirators. In social talk, group members bond when they share feelings about third parties.[63]

Through group-oriented feelings, the group extends the self. [64] As Eliot Smith, Diane Mackie, and their colleagues note, people incorporate the

Figure 2.8   Fixed Facial Features Mimicking Emotions

Nondominant: Fear   Dominant: Anger

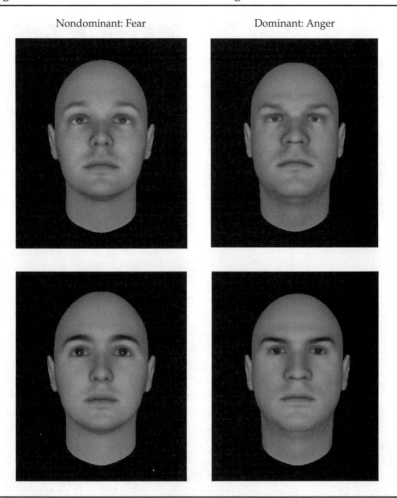

Source: FaceGen 3.1, face generation software; stimuli from Oosterhof and Todorov (2008).

group into themselves, so they react emotionally on behalf of their group. Maybe the group itself does not literally experience emotions, but people report emotions they feel as a group member. ("As an American, I feel proud." "As a Republican, I feel angry.") These group-oriented emotions, distinct from a person's feelings as an individual, depend on identification with the group and its shared values. If our cherished group is low status, we feel low status as a group member, and we experience the attendant emotions on behalf of our group. So, too, with high status. Our tribe's place in society determines collective emotions, including envy and scorn.

Figure 2.9   Activation of the Ventral Striatum in Baseball Fans

 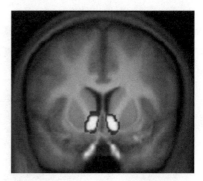

Source: Author's figure based on data from Cikara, Botvinick, and Fiske (2011).
Notes: (Left) Illustration only; the actual stimulus showed a dynamic video of a schematic baseball field and the relevant plays. (Right) Coronal view of ventral striatum, nucleus accumbens, and putamen, parts of the brain, implicated in feelings of reward.

Along these lines, in-group inferiority hurts. When our favorite team loses, for example, we envy the competition their victory. The social neuroscientist Mina Cikara recruited die-hard Red Sox and Yankees fans to watch a video game version of single baseball plays in which their team succeeded or failed against their longtime rival. Of course, people reported pleasure at their own team's success, as well as anger and pain at their team's failure. They also wished their rivals ill just as much: they were pleased at their rival's failure, as well as angry and pained at their rival's success. Then there is the malicious logic of schadenfreude: these fans reported pleasure whenever their rival lost even to *another team altogether.* As before, brain scans back up these self-reported emotions. Mere team loyalty made fans show brain activity that looked like empathic pain in response to their team's failures. Fans also activated part of the brain's reward network within the ventral striatum in response to own-team wins and rival-team losses to each other (see figure 2.9). What is more, the VS also activated in the schadenfreude case—rival-team losses to another team. Social identity as a fan is enough to get the neural reward networks going. And schadenfreude has consequences: this VS reward activation correlates with fans' reports of heckling, insulting, threatening, and hitting rival fans.[65]

Why do people even care about a rival's matchup with a third party? The philosopher Friedrich Nietzsche argued that the pain of own-group inferiority directs the mind to the substitute pleasure of out-group failure.[66] Maintaining loyalty to our own group, in the face of demoralizing low status, works better if the members of our group can share anger about our rival's allegedly illegitimate victory.[67] Shared resentments cement group membership. We understand each other because we all hate "them."

What is more, we are virtuous in direct proportion to the evil of our rival. Indeed, people who are highly identified with their group readily detect injuries to their group, reacting protectively and viewing group insults as self-relevant.[68] This fits the Smith-Mackie idea of incorporating the group into the self. Loyalists who feel that their group is downtrodden put down the out-group in turn and discriminate against it.[69] This can benefit the injured in-group, elevating collective self-esteem (members' feelings about the value of their group) as well as the individual self-esteem of its members.[70] For example, Jolanda Jetten and her colleagues studied people with multiple body piercings, a group whose members often feel stigmatized by mainstream society. The more a pierced person feels discrimination, the more strongly that person identifies with the in-group and the higher his or her feelings of collective self-esteem.

Besides organizing between-group relations, emotions also stabilize status within the group. Just as partners coordinate their relative status by expressing appropriate emotions, so people coordinate status within groups. Leaders are allowed to joke and laugh and to show anger and contempt, whereas followers may not show these emotions; however, followers may show shame, fear, and embarrassment.[71] When employees mock their employer in public, the enterprise is doomed. Well-functioning groups apparently favor the emotional certainty of shared goals, clear boundaries, and stable hierarchy, despite the negative emotions that may be experienced by those lower on the totem pole. Individuals join groups in the first place partly to feel more certain and secure.[72]

Cultures Regulate Themselves Through Envy and Scorn

> There is yet some good in public envy, whereas in private, there is none. For public envy, is as an ostracism, that eclipseth men, when they grow too great. And therefore it is a bridle also to great ones, to keep them within bounds.
> —Francis Bacon, "Of Envy" (1597)

Francis Bacon observed that the threat of public envy could contain high-status people. Cultures can also regulate people through the threat of scorn. In this sense, both scorn and envy are moral emotions, distinguishing the cultural right from the cultural wrong. Again, people usefully tune in to envy and scorn in the service of cultural regulation.

Psychologists have rarely studied scorn, but they have thoroughly studied its cousin disgust and, to some extent, contempt. Disgust is clearly a moral emotion.[73] When people break a taboo, other people judge them by saying, "That's disgusting," a real conversation stopper. In some circles,

Figure 2.10   The Most Common Disgust Motifs of Urban Legends

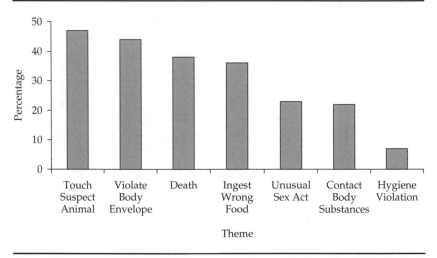

Source: Author's compilation based on data from Heath, Bell, and Sternberg (2001).
Note: The more disgusting the story, the more people pass them along, and the more often they appear on websites.

"nasty" implies either mean and cruel or gross and disgusting, so immoral behavior is nauseating. Disgust rejects, excludes, and repels. Our disgust toward some people signals that they have breached a sacred taboo, dirtying themselves, endangering sanctity and purity. When we admit feeling disgust toward homeless people and injection-drug users, we are reacting partly to the image of these people as contaminated, both morally and physically.[74] Disgust announces that the culture excludes such people from full humanity. Moreover, our desire to avoid disgusting other people is a powerful incentive to avoid disgusting, immoral behavior.

Gossip is a form of social control that capitalizes on disgust.[75] People are more likely to repeat disgusting stories, and no one wants to be the topic of such gossip. In one demonstration, students read a series of happy, sad, or disgusting anecdotes about another student; then they had to choose which story to communicate to their acquaintances. The most disgusting stories (for example, about gross public drunkenness) topped the list. Urban myths circulate selectively, to the extent that they are disgusting.[76] Chip Heath, Chris Bell, and Emily Sternberg scored the themes of disgusting web legends and found that all of them communicated what is disgusting and therefore taboo (figure 2.10).

Contempt also is a moral emotion; indeed, along with disgust, it predicts what will appear on urban legend websites. Contempt communicates that someone has offended community norms, and maintaining the proper hierarchy is one such norm.[77] That is, people risk contempt when they step out of line regarding their proper role, duty, honor, authority, and loyalty. Students in both Japan and the United States reliably pick contemptuous faces and the word "contempt" to describe their reactions to such norm violations as a child using obscenities to parents, an executive refusing to sit next to a laborer on a commuter train, a citizen burning the country's flag, or people not attending their own mother's funeral. Again, these emotions are useful, and in these instances they are useful to the culture, which can control people through scorn's cousins, contempt and disgust.[78]

As a cultural experience, envy expresses shared aspirations and attending to unequal others.[79] Envy may be bad, but through envy we do know what we value. Envy signals that someone has attained enviable status, but it also signals that the envied person has failed to act appropriately, respectfully, or considerately toward the rest of us. Envy entails feelings of injustice, which are based in cultural rules about what is just.[80] Although envy confers status on winners, they can suffer when they realize they are envied because they know that others resent them.[81] Being envied involves both competitive success (the sweet experience of victory) and fear (the threat of revenge or bitterness). When a situation sets us up to be envied, if we care about personal relationships, we will either downplay the difference or commiserate with the envier, both efforts to salvage the relationship. Just as scorn, along with contempt and disgust, are moral emotions, so too is envy because of its link to injustice. All of these moral emotions help us conform to cultural norms.

Moral emotions act as cultural controls both up and down the inevitable status hierarchy. To regulate behavior, some members of the culture have to express these emotions at least sometimes—though the mere threat of other people expressing scorn or envy is sometimes enough to make us behave. In either form, socially shared emotions are useful tools for cultures, groups, partners, and individuals. Emotions motivate us to coordinate with others, to consider their perspectives, and to treat them according to their relative status. When we recognize the emotions of envy and scorn, we maintain the social hierarchy, for better or worse.

Cognitions Explain Status

People routinely compare up and down, as we have seen, but why do we do this? One answer is that we also need status-related cognitions. All else being equal, thinking creates coherence and certainty. Chaos and concern yield to cognition. Not always, of course, but that is cognition's goal. When we are uncertain, we often look to others for lucidity. All meaning is social, cultural psychologists argue.[82] We especially seek out other people to make sense of status puzzles because status is always relative. As individuals, we compare upward and downward in order to rank our current and possible positions relative to others. We do this in groups when we represent someone as a prototypic leader. And we do this in society when we stereotype groups as higher and lower status. All these cognitive processes foster understanding our place.

Individuals Understand Their Standing As Relative

The signature of individual status comparison is uncertainty regarding one's own standing, which motivates a search upward, downward, and sideways. This theory goes back to the social psychology icon Leon Festinger, who was interested in how people evaluate their abilities and their opinions.[83] In both cases, he argued, people compare themselves to others to see where they stand relative to those others. Reams have been written about this theory, and later chapters will home in on the parts most relevant to status. For now, consider how we recognize and use these comparative cognitions. Festinger suggested that people compare themselves when more objective indicators are not available. For instance, determining your weight is simple if you have a scale. Determining whether you are heavy, however, requires comparing yourself to relevant others, probably people of your own gender, age, and perhaps class. But even then, how heavy is "heavy"? In the absence of other people and objective measures, none of us have set standards for weight, ability, beliefs, or—our concern here—status. Social comparisons strive for at least the illusion of accuracy.

We are so wired for comparative cognition that we do it automatically, as Diederik Stapel and Hart Blanton have shown.[84] Even subliminal exposure to a peer's face, flashed for a fraction of a second, primed participants in their study to think comparatively—they automatically thought about themselves. The experimenters measured participants' self-related thoughts by asking them to guess whether foreign-language pronouns were first person; those who guessed more first-person pronouns had self on their minds. Priming a peer caused people to think comparatively.

Comparing self to others involves what psychologists call contrast effects. For example, subliminal exposure to younger faces makes us feel old (and vice versa), and such exposure to attractive people makes us feel unattractive (and vice versa). A clown makes us feel smarter, and Albert Einstein makes us feel dumber. All of these are contrast effects, and they happen regardless of whether we rate ourselves overtly or covertly. Contrast effects are more likely to happen, however, when we are in a state of uncertainty, which readies us to receive comparative cues.

When we are practiced at any kind of comparison, we become efficient; like automated search engines, we immediately focus on the information most relevant to the particular comparison, fill in any gaps, speed our judgments, and then free up our minds for other tasks.[85] Operating on automatic makes us more prone to contrast ourselves with others, for example, in appearance.[86] We automatically contrast ourselves with a comparison person when we focus on our own self.[87] We automatically define ourselves by contrast to other individuals.

Figure 2.11   The Big-Fish–Big-Fish-Pond Effect

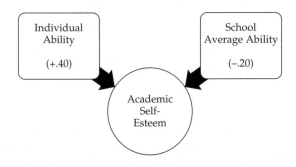

Source: Author's creation based on data from Marsh and Hau (2003).
Note: Comparison with equally talented students undermines academic self-esteem in more than 100,000 students internationally. Entries are average correlation across twenty-six countries.

When we are not thinking hard (that is, when we are operating on automatic), repeated upward comparisons make us devalue our own performance.[88] If we are practiced at comparing up, that comes to seem like our default status. Apparently, we automatically assume that frequency implies quantity. This heuristic could easily be wrong, as when an individual happens to be a big fish in a big-fish pond. Many high-achieving students at top-notch schools, for example, feel inadequate because of a warped set of comparisons (see figure 2.11).[89]

The same experience of inadequacy may plague someone who happens to be partnered with or related to a genius.[90] (Chapter 4 comes back to this idea.) Friends with an identical ambition or love interest may cease to be friends.[91] Chance circumstances determine our most immediate, automatic, personal comparisons, for good or ill.

Fortunately, when we bother to think, we can overcome these automatic biases. For example, the repeated upward-exposure effect is reduced when we bother to deliberate about our comparisons.[92] Perhaps we realize that we are seeing some of the same information repeatedly, so we discount the redundant comparisons. We can override our default inferiority complex when motivated to consider the opposite.

Groups Identify Comparative Rank

The better angels of our nature also emerge when we take the comparison less personally. So far, we have considered people as individuals ("I, me, mine") contrasting themselves with other individuals. When we compare up and down in a collective mind-set ("we, us, our"), we assimilate instead of contrasting.[93] That is, we rate ourselves as more similar to either the unattractive inferior or the attractive superior, depending on whom we encounter. Operating as a group member makes us think as if "we're all in this together." The collective self is more fluid and inclusive than the personal self.[94]

In adopting the group, we adapt ourselves to it. If the collective incorporates the individual, then the group provides certainty for those of us who are willing to assimilate. The groups researcher Michael Hogg suggests that we resolve uncertainty by identifying with groups that reduce uncertainty.[95] We choose or modify our groups to create certainty. Experiments can create feelings of uncertainty by asking people to write about times when they have felt uncertain; when an uncertainty really hits home (the self) but a group provides a clear resolution, we are especially likely to identify with that group.[96] In one study conducted by Hogg and his colleagues, Australian students, just before a national election, rated how much of a group their favored political party was and then, in the experimental condition, wrote about what made them feel uncertain about themselves, their lives, and their futures; finally, they rated a series of items about how much they identified with their party ("self-importance of and liking/familiarization for the party and its supporters, similarity and goodness of fit to the party, and identification, belonging and ties with the party"). When they first rated their party, the more well-defined they said it was, the more they identified with it. This makes sense—it is hard to identify with a vague, ill-defined, borderless group—but this tendency to identify mainly with well-defined groups holds only for people who have just been induced to feel uncertain. In contrast, people first induced to feel certain do not increase their identification with a group, even with a well-defined political party. Hogg and his colleagues have linked joining extremist groups (often well-defined) to a need for resolving uncertainty.[97] The groups that people prefer, in order to reduce uncertainty, are cohesive, solid groups with boundaries and homogeneity.

Such groups share defining beliefs and values, including what it means to belong and who is an ideal member. The most prototypic members become leaders partly because they make everything seem so certain. Leaders represent the group prototype; they are its icon. As a result, two cognitive processes are triggered. First, group members believe that the leader possesses the appropriate traits that represent the group. At a minimum, they believe that this individual is competent and able to act for the group's shared goals and values, whatever those may be. Different settings require different traits in effective leaders (consider the commander in chief versus a group therapist).[98] Naming someone a leader typically makes group members believe that the leader symbolically represents the group's shared characteristics.

The second cognitive process associated with leadership is attention: people attend up.[99] Attention follows power, perhaps partly out of admiration and emulation, but also out of need and envy. Attention provides details (accurate or not) about leaders. We view the powerful as fascinating individuals; they are somebodies worthy of our attention. Attention can increase our own sense that we understand what the powerful will do and how we might influence them.[100] Attention provides us with that sense of certainty.

Societies Bestow Status Stereotypes

Just as groups rapidly rank individuals within their boundaries, societies rank their groups.[101] Across the world, the rich rank above the poor, but other characteristics besides wealth determine status as well. First, work matters: professionals receive higher rank, as do businesspeople, even if they are minorities or immigrant entrepreneurs. Laborers, the unemployed, and welfare recipients have low rank. Second, education matters: college students have higher rank than dropouts. Third, fame matters: celebrities and royalty have higher rank than anonymous masses. Some of these status markers imitate the ways in which people identify their own social class, as mentioned in chapter 1.

Ethnicity also correlates with perceived status. People of color—especially people of African or mestizo Latino descent—rank below Anglo whites and Asians in the United States.[102] National debates about immigration focus on black and brown immigrants, not European, Canadian, or Asian immigrants. Ethnicity combines with social class partly because people see that they correlate in society. As they say in Latin America, "Money whitens." A wealthy or highly educated minority person receives higher status. More and more often, class can trump ethnicity.

Gender also predicts status, though race, education, profession, and social class can trump default gender status. For example, a nonworking mother has a different standing depending on her race. A white unemployed mother has more status than a black stay-at-home mother partly because race implies class in people's minds, and class confers perceived choice. That is, wealth implies that a mother is home by choice; poverty implies that she should be working but either cannot or will not. In Amy Cuddy and Cynthia Frantz's studies, people inferred that a stay-at-home white mother deserved a more expensive Mother's Day present and was a better person than a stay-at-home black mother.[103] Race makes no difference for working mothers. Presumably, racial stereotypes make the unemployed mother suburban if she is white, and ghetto if she is black. Overall, regardless of whether a group's status comes from social class, ethnicity, gender, or innumerable other attributes—such as age or disability—cognition follows to make sense of it all.

Across societal groups, even across artificially created simulations of intergroup perceptions, high-status groups see themselves as having superior attributes and low-status groups as having inferior ones. Low-status groups are less biased and if anything value themselves on the

Figure 2.12   Group Bias

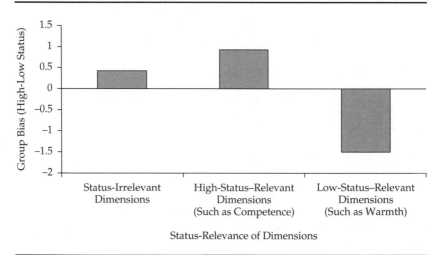

Source: Author's compilation based on Bettencourt et al. (2001) meta-analysis of eighty-seven studies.
Note: Group bias depends on status. High-status groups favor themselves and disfavor the out-group, especially on status-related dimensions, such as competence. Low-status groups favor themselves and disfavor the high-status group on dimensions relevant to their low-status identity—for example, warmth and other undervalued dimensions.

less-desirable, low-status-relevant dimensions.[104] So, for example, higher-status people view themselves, and are viewed by others, as competent (smart, capable), but lower-status people promote themselves as warmer (nicer, more honest). These are self-stereotypes, granted, but sometimes they spill over to the societal stereotypes held by high- and low-status people alike. Examples of this division of identity echo across stereotypes of racial majorities and minorities (driven versus easygoing), men and women (agentic versus communal), and upper and lower classes (elitist versus down to earth) (figure 2.12).

Altogether, our minds understand ourselves, our group-mates, and our societies by making sense of who is above and below whom. This pattern of cognition matters because our vertical thoughts and feelings predict our behavior, as the next section shows.

Behavior Puts Brains, Emotions, and Minds in Motion

We enact our status all the time. Everyday encounters follow status scripts, which we all recognize. Psychologists do not know how status affects behavior when people are alone, but we know a lot about how status works when people behave together, whether as individuals or as groups.

Individuals Embody Status

An individual can embody status, even in static snapshots. In all cultures, the higher, foremost, larger person has higher status.[105] Cues to authority ranking are often physical but symbolic, as in the placement of a throne on a dais ("Your Highness"). Status associates with physical cues, even for the placement of names on an organizational chart; greater height, more distance, and larger font all represent higher rank.[106] Something as simple as a heavier clipboard makes a candidate's petition seem more important. Being taller, heavier, or stronger than others also embodies power and status, especially for men. All these cues should enable envy, though no one has shown this yet.

Conversely, being lower, last, or smaller reduces a person's status. Distance has the effect of belittling people, making them appear smaller. Hence, keeping our distance should make it easier for us to look down on other people.[107] Indeed, it is easier to dehumanize someone at a distance. Scorn looks down and distances.

Partners Do the Status Dance

Apart from static comparisons that embody status, we also enact status whenever we meet. Status allows us in our daily encounters to coordinate with each other without fighting it out. Status uncertainty would make these interactions stressful. Instead, we implicitly agree on who is higher and who is lower, and that being settled, we can get on more effectively. Synchronized, reciprocal signals coordinate the status dance.

This kind of coordination is not unusual. We coordinate with conversation partners all the time, and we do it in two ways—one conveying warmth and the other status. We tend to imitate each other in conversation, unconsciously mimicking each other's body language and speech patterns and thus communicating warmth and solidarity. We like each other better when we do this.[108]

But when we communicate with someone who displays nonverbal dominance ("postural expansion"), we conveniently display complementary nonverbal nondominance. What is more, we both like it better when we nonverbally coordinate who is dominant and who is not.[109] This agreement helps us harmonize across ranks. At a minimum, we cannot both talk at once, at least not for long. So we coordinate by taking turns; for example, during our speaking turn, we fill gaps ("so . . . ," "well . . .") and make only intermittent eye contact. At the end of our turn, we drop our voice, pause, and extend eye contact to signal the end of the turn. Conversely, to signal listening, we maintain eye contact and remain silent.[110]

While talking, people use speech styles to signal dominance. Dominant speech is confident, direct, rapid, articulate, abundant, blunt, and standard speech.[111] In the movie *Matilda*, Agatha Trunchbull, the domineering headmistress, illustrates many of these features when she dresses down Matilda's father, himself no shrinking violet:

> WORMWOOD!!! You useless used-car salesman scum! I want you around here *now*, with another car! Yes, I know what *"caveat emptor"* means, you low-life liar! I'm going to sue you, I'm going to burn down your showroom, I'm going to take that no-good jalopy you sold me and *shove it up your bazooka!* When I'm finished with you, you're going to look like *roadkill!*[112]

Dominant people use other tactics besides verbal bludgeons. When given a chance to act, powerful people act more than they deliberate, and they make changes, especially toward personal goals.[113] Talking and acting indicate power. The lack of all these cues signals a willingness to be subordinate.

Finally, nonverbal posture can signal dominance. In another *Matilda* scene, when Matilda questions her father's order, he responds: "Listen, you little wiseacre: I'm smart, you're dumb; I'm big, you're little; I'm right, you're wrong, and there's nothing you can do about it!"[114] Powerful people are usually the "big" people. In a dynamic illustration, Larissa Tiedens and Alison Fragale put undergraduates into a conversation with an experimental confederate who expanded nonverbally, sitting with one arm draped over the adjacent chair and crossing one ankle over the other knee.[115] Over the course of this conversation, the participants literally took up less and less space, as measured later by a ruler against the video screen. Participants who were conversing with a constricted confederate— one who slouched, legs together, hands in lap—gradually took up more space over time.

Across studies, all manner of high-status people are expressive, relaxed, and intrusive.[116] Dominant expressiveness shows up in sheer facial activity and effectively conveying emotions. Dominant relaxation appears in an open posture and a calm, stable voice. Dominant intrusion emerges in a direct gaze, close proximity, interruptions, and a loud voice. A person can dominate a conversation by taking long speaking turns, being inattentive, using assertive speech, taking an expansive posture, and engaging in other dominant nonverbal behaviors. Anyone talking to such a person is no idiot: most of us can rapidly read these signals.

Indeed, a thin slice (only sixty seconds!) of a person's nonverbal behavior reveals social class.[117] In conversation, higher-class people disengage more, self-groom, doodle, and fiddle; they also engage less, failing to look, nod, laugh, or raise their eyebrows to indicate interest. These cues both reflect self-reported social class and predict perceived social class background. Of course, clothing reveals social class as well. Although the more obvious cues may be designer suits versus grubby denim, more subtle cues involve what Paul Fussell describes as "legible clothing"—T-shirts with writing or, slightly less low, anything that features the maker's logo. Another memorable low-class signal is what he terms the "prole jacket gape": an ill-fitting suit will have a gap at the back of the collar.[118] Money buys understated, tailored attire.

Higher-status people indeed are privileged, and as the nonverbal cues signal, they are also freed from the obligation to be excessively polite or attentive. One might call this scorn and question whether it is a benefit. Still, higher status also grants self-esteem, presumes competence, credits accomplishment, and—no surprise—prefers the status quo.[119] In a meritocracy, we are credited with our successes and blamed for our failures, so in most everyone's eyes, as well as in the mirror, we seem to deserve our status. The benefits of higher social class serve the self, not others, and so the stereotypes of high and low status carry a grain of truth.

Society Scripts Status

The shaggy underbelly of class-driven behavior is decidedly not classy. When social classes operate as a group, scorn down is neither elegant nor tasteful. In our surveys, people reported that lower-status groups are neglected, demeaned, and ignored.[120] This is what therapists call passive-aggression—that is, harming by *not* doing. Failing to attend to the needs of another person can be passively harmful if normally one would be expected to respond. The silent treatment is the prototype for passive-aggression between people who already know each other. Such person-to-person ostracism is painful.[121] People dislike exclusion so much that they do not like to be ostracized even by groups they despise.[122]

In society, we inflict one kind of passive harm on stereotypically pitiful groups, such as older people or those with disabilities. We pity them and help them because their afflictions are not their fault.[123] But we tend to help them by institutionalizing them; that may meet their survival needs, but it neglects their social needs because we segregate them from society. One might view this tendency to institutionalize as a form of passive harm even if it is a side effect of otherwise good intentions.

We inflict another kind of passive harm on stereotypically disgusting out-groups, the ones seen as having no redeeming features: people who are homeless, drug-addicted, or poor. Although in our better moments we pity them and act accordingly, these are the groups that society not only shuns but actively harms, according to our surveys. People report that the lowest of the low are attacked, and media accounts concur. Violence against homeless people on the street displays our worst behavior.[124] Apparently, those who attack the homeless are not the people at the top of the hierarchy but mostly youth on a rampage. Yet a more utilitarian kind of harm comes from the well-off when they decide that a homeless person's life is not worth as much as a middle- or upper-class person's life.[125]

Figure 2.13   Envy Affects Aggression by Way of Anger

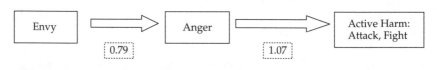

Source: Author's compilation. See Cuddy, Fiske, and Glick (2007) for details.
Note: Regression coefficients indicate the degree of influence; both are substantial and significant. (For statistical aficionados, the direct effect of envy on harm is 0.67, but adding anger reduces this path to a nonsignificant –0.18, consistent with complete mediation).

Social policies that scorn the needs of society's outcasts amount to this same utilitarian choice. Scorn is inattention where attention must be paid.

If scornful behavior is ugly, so too is envious behavior, which is sometimes provoked by the threat of feeling scorned. Aggression often stems from threats to fragile self-esteem.[126] Bullies indeed are insecure, as conventional wisdom has it. To them, aggression often feels like self-defense; aggressors readily interpret chance encounters as personally directed hostility. The malicious intent of upward envy is to bring down the powerful who threaten the self. Envy generates a wish to punish others for being better off; this is active harm, reported by our survey respondents to include attacking and fighting the envied (see figure 2.13).[127]

Society needs for people to feel what behavioral economists call inequity aversion, that is, to suffer envy from being behind or guilt at being ahead. Social psychology research indicates that we feel worse about being behind than we mind being ahead.[128] Society enforces fairness through individuals' reactions to unfair advantage. We worry about this more when we expect to see each other frequently, when we care about our reputation, and when we respect reciprocity for cooperation. That is, we care about inequity when we are socially connected. Aversion to unfair inequality predicts good outcomes like altruism but also altruistic punishment—the social reward for punishing norm violators.[129]

Society also requires that lower-status people cooperate with the higher-status people they may envy. Ongoing transactions demand that subordinates go along to get along, a kind of passive accommodation and association, according to our surveys. Higher-status groups control resources that lower-status groups need, so lower-status groups accommodate themselves to what they cannot change, when times are stable.

Nevertheless, envy produces mixed and volatile behavior. Consider the case of outsider entrepreneurs, such as Asians and Jews in diaspora. Historically, they have tended to set up successful businesses. In quiet times, lower-status groups put up with and even defer to these high-status groups, shopping at their stores, acknowledging though resenting their success. But when the chips are down, when society is destabilized, these groups are the first targets of mass violence, looting, and genocide. Examples of entrepreneurial outsiders turned into victims include the Koreans in the Los Angeles riots of the 1990s, the Chinese in Indonesia, the Indians in East Africa, the Tutsis in Rwanda, and the Jews in Europe. All were integrated into their host societies but were targeted for mass violence under social breakdown. Genocide often targets a formerly privileged out-group.[130]

Detecting Envy and Scorn

We know envy and scorn when we see them. As individuals, being wired for it, we automatically detect status. Our brains instantly process cues to dominance and subordination in face, posture, language, and gesture. We readily detect the contemptuous lip curl, the disgusted nose wrinkle, the gaze from the top looking down, as well as the placating, open-eyed gaze from the bottom up.

As emotions, envy and scorn are useful: they call our attention to status and its issues. We pursue our personal goals by noticing our own envy and denying our scorn. We coordinate with our partners, organize our groups, and regulate our society through envy and scorn. Along with our emotions, our beliefs explain our relative status—as individuals, as group members, and as societies. Status then dictates behavior.

Science has much to teach us about envy and scorn. We continue to be fascinated by verticality, as power, status, and prestige both attract and repel us. Although, as David Brooks notes, "we want our toffs to flatter us, and abase themselves," at the same time, "we want the bloodlines."[131]

Chapter 3

Who Cares About Comparisons?

[Status] anxiety is provoked by, among other elements, recession, redundancy, promotions, retirement, conversations with colleagues in the same industry, newspaper profiles of the prominent, and the greater success of friends. Like confessing to envy (to which the emotion is related), it can be socially imprudent to reveal the extent of any anxiety and therefore, evidence of the inner drama is uncommon, limited usually to a preoccupied gaze, a brittle smile, or an over-extended pause after news of another's achievement.
—Alain de Botton, *Status Anxiety* (2004), viii

C ONSIDERING THAT scorn is just as socially imprudent to reveal as envy is, evidence of our inner drama indeed is uncommon. Yet as the last chapter argued, we know these emotions when we see them, and they are everywhere. Unpleasant as they may be, we all share the experiences of comparison that give rise to them. We cannot help experiencing these comparisons—they are automatic. So we should not assume that we are somehow immune to them, and we should not believe people who say that they are immune.

Even if no one is beyond making comparisons, some people do compare more than others. Alain de Botton speculates that status anxiety derives from a variety of common experiences, such as feeling unloved, having unrealistic expectations, endorsing meritocracy, fearing snobs, and being dependent. For almost all of us, our well-being is contingent sometimes on other people's love, expectations, judgment, respect, and power, and this can make us feel insecure. Nevertheless, we differ as individuals, groups, and cultures in our obsession with comparison.

People Are Funny

Although comparison is an all-too-human preoccupation, some people do it more than others. Psychologists have developed one measure that

56

specifically tests this tendency, but a host of other personality traits also correlate with the tendency to compare self with others.

Social Comparison Orientation

How often do you compare how your loved ones are doing with how others are doing? Do you pay a lot of attention to how you do things compared with how others do things? Do you compare your accomplishments with those of others? Do you like to talk with others about mutual opinions and experiences? Do you often compare how you are doing socially (for example, in your social skills or popularity) with how others are faring? Do you often try to find out the thoughts of others who face problems similar to yours? These questions are sample items paraphrased from the Social Comparison Orientation Scale.[1]

Social comparison orientation (SCO) has two components: comparing our abilities (how am I doing relative to others?) and comparing our opinions (how much do I agree with others?).[2] These two dimensions—comparison of ability and search for others' opinions—are correlated, according to SCO researchers Abraham Buunk and Frederick Gibbons.

High-SCO people tend to think about themselves a lot, but they also tend to think about other people a lot because their selves are defined by others. Their selves come to mind easily and spontaneously, so they tend to be self-conscious.[3] They agree that they tend to reflect about themselves a lot (private self-consciousness) and to worry about making a good impression (public self-consciousness). When asked to guess the translation of foreign pronouns—a standard technique for measuring how self-oriented someone is—the guesses of high-SCO scorers include many first-person pronouns. Because their self is always at the front of their mind, their self pops up in ambiguous situations.[4]

But at the same time, high SCO keeps people interested in others and makes them empathic and sensitive to others. Being oriented to social comparison makes them realize their interdependence with other people. They are interpersonally oriented: "Other people are the source of my greatest pleasure and pain; I am greatly influenced by the moods of the people I am with; I am interested in knowing what makes people tick."[5] So high-SCO people are not necessarily competitive—just comparative.

Having your well-being too contingent on others is not good.[6] High-SCO people are more vulnerable to stress, and too much SCO goes along with being neurotic and feeling bad; neurotics, in turn, report feeling more anxiety, guilt, anger, and shame. Being SCO correlates somewhat with feeling bad, but not consistently. These associations with negativity, however, do remain a warning for the comparison-afflicted.

People high on SCO compare both up and down—that is, they specialize in neither envy nor scorn.[7] These individuals seek comparisons about everything—not just the obvious, such as their achievements, but also their health, their marriage, their depression, even their risk of dying from driving while drunk or getting HIV from unprotected sex. Any claim that such relentless comparison is adaptive behavior is hard to support. In the workplace, for instance, we know that this behavior can have bad consequences. The comparison-obsessed focus on the threat posed by their subordinates, who could take their place. The high-SCO scorers also look at subordinates in a sadder way: their supposed inferiors represent the high-SCOs' own worst-case scenarios, feared possible selves.[8] High-SCO individuals at work concentrate on other people who are doing badly and even identify with the worse-off ("There but for fortune . . . "). The comparison-obsessed have little feeling of control over their own success or failure, and they are especially vulnerable to these unhelpful downward comparisons when they are already stressed.

High-SCO people can fight their comparison-making tendency by mentally distancing themselves from hard-luck inferiors—for example, by assuming that anyone who is not succeeding is not really trying (*Unlike me,* they think). The Australian magnate Alan Bond opined, "I've always worked very, very hard, and the harder I worked, the luckier I got."[9] Unfortunately, he also bent one too many rules and landed in prison. In service to chicanery is not the only time when this self-justifying strategy does not work: comparison-obsessed people already inclined toward depression will become even more unhappy and discouraged when they encounter someone who is working really hard but still not making it. They can also find ways to be discouraged even by an upward comparison—"I'll never be as good as that winner"—unless they can distance themselves by viewing the superior achiever as a workaholic and therefore alien. Seeing others as working too little or too much is one form of cognitive distance.[10] We all make this judgment sometimes, but people high on SCO are especially prone to it.

Dispositional Envy

> Envy . . . consists in seeing things never in themselves, but only in their relations. . . . If you desire glory, you may envy Napoleon, but Napoleon envied Caesar, Caesar envied Alexander, and Alexander, I dare say, envied Hercules, who never existed.
> —Bertrand Russell, *The Conquest of Happiness* (1930), 71–72

Despite envy's futility, some people readily admit to resenting those other people who seem to succeed all the time or to have all the talent. Richard Smith and his colleagues devised a measure of people's vulnerability to envy.

Dispositional Envy Scale

1. I feel envy every day.
2. The bitter truth is that I generally feel inferior to others.

3. Feelings of envy constantly torment me.

4. It is so frustrating to see some people succeed so easily.

5. No matter what I do, envy always plagues me.

6. I am troubled by feelings of inadequacy.

7. It somehow doesn't seem fair that some people seem to have all the talent.

8. Frankly, the success of my neighbors makes me resent them.[11]

High-DES scorers are not just neurotic, hostile, depressed, or low in self-esteem, though they do tend to have these problems.[12] Chronic envy is bad for their mental and physical health, as the last chapter suggested. And it is no wonder: envious people are stressed, dissatisfied, irritable, anxious, and prone to unexplained aches and pains (what therapists call somatization).

Envy is also likely to undermine friendship. Who wants to spend time with someone who puts down other people's accomplishments? (*Not to mention belittling mine behind my back*, you wonder.) A disposition toward envy makes for schadenfreude (glee at the envied other's misfortune), which hardly encourages friendship; responding to a friend's good news with resentment can destroy the relationship.[13] What is more, the envious are gratitude-challenged. Being prone to envy deprives a person of the salutary effects of having a grateful disposition.[14] The online Urban Dictionary even has a term for the undermining effects of envy on a relationship: frienvy.[15]

Dispositional Scorn?

We know more about personalities inclined to upward comparison than about those predisposed toward downward comparison. Once again, scorn is the stepchild of comparison tendencies. Surely some people are more disposed to contempt and scorn than others. We all know these snobs! Narcissistic personality disorder involves pathological grandiosity, need for admiration, and low empathy, but this profile represents the fringe. What about the garden-variety scornful? Identifying them awaits a psychologist enterprising enough to develop a measure of dispositional scorn (maybe the SNOBB—Scorn: Not Our Business, Bud). In the nineteenth century, the novelist and essayist William Makepeace Thackeray was way ahead of us; in *The Book of Snobs*, he satirizes:

I have long gone about with a conviction on my mind that I had a great work to do—a Work, if you like, with a great W; a Purpose to fulfil . . . ; a Great Social Evil to Discover and to Remedy. That Conviction Has Pursued me for Years. It has Dogged me in the Busy Street; Seated Itself By Me in The Lonely Study; Jogged My Elbow as it Lifted the Wine-Cup at the Festive Board . . . and It Whispers, . . . "you ought to be at home writing your great work on SNOBS."[16]

Snobs seek to scorn others because they are insecure. The origin of the word is informative: "snob" comes from the Latin notation next to the names of Oxford and Cambridge students who lacked noble titles: "sin nobilitate," shortened to "s. nob." A student without a dignified title might indeed seek out others still less noble to scorn in turn. For instance, Thackeray ranks disgusting table manners as an excuse for snobbery.

Disgust, a cousin of scorn, has its own psychological test, but the items on the scale do not target whole persons but rather animals, food, body products, sex, hygiene, death, and violations of the body envelope.[17] People who are disgust-sensitive tend to be female and maybe a little neurotic, but are otherwise not too distinctive, and they are certainly not prone to scorn.

Dominant Individuals Prefer the Vertical

Machiavelli knew a thing or two about hierarchies, which reinforce the power of a prince to maintain his position and achieve greatness. He considered it a prince's highest "virtù" to have a flexible disposition capable of evil behavior without remorse, as circumstances might require.[18] Whether a dominant personality is necessarily evil remains an unanswered question because psychologists try to abstain from moral judgment.

We do know that the vertical dimension particularly appeals to some people—namely, those individuals who are dominant by personality. Dominance is a major dimension of personality.[19] Personally dominant people are identified by their outright agreement that they are dominant and forceful, as well as by their penchant for imposing their will on others and controlling conversations. They literally view the world in vertical terms: in a reaction-time test on a computer screen, they were faster to notice split-second flashes on the vertical dimension—above and below a midpoint—versus the horizontal dimension to the left and right of it (see figure 3.1).[20] Highly dominant people especially focus on the top of the vertical dimension.[21]

Dominant people are alert for competitors at the top. They criticize other high-status, assertive challengers and prefer subordinate behavior. Their vigilance for threat creates arousal, which is relieved only by putting down their opponents.[22] Dominant people like being around people who ingratiate themselves, though the dominant people remain unimpressed by the ingratiators.[23] Don Operario and I once designed a method for capturing this kind of self-serving dominant behavior toward subordinates. Undergraduates applying for a research assistantship learned that they could best impress the interviewer either by promoting their competence or by emphasizing their sociability. The ingratiators did win the dominant interviewers' liking, but not their respect. Being dominant may keep some people on top, but only at the cost of constant vigilance, which does not increase their own or other people's happiness.

Figure 3.1   Dominance-Submission Personality Score

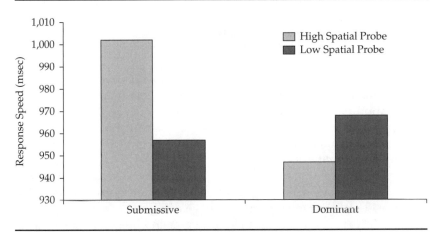

Source: Robinson et al. (2008). Copyright © 2008 Elsevier; reprinted by permission.
Note: Dominant personalities respond fastest (less time on vertical axis) to a stimulus presented at the top of the screen, compared with both stimuli at the bottom and with submissive personalities' response to the same high stimulus.

Comparison Malaise: Unhappy and Out of Control

Comparison creates malaise. In opinion polls, a comfortable 51 percent say that they earn about as much as they deserve, as opposed to fully 38 percent who say that they get less than they deserve.[24] That is a lot of disgruntled people. Who are they? Those disposed to social comparison are likely to be unhappy, to seek control, and to feel insecure and uncertain. The result is not a pretty picture for the comparison-obsessed.

Take the most general malaise first: some people are simply more unhappy than others, whether by temperament or by choice.[25] This shows up in people's self-reports of being a very happy (or unhappy) person, both absolutely and relative to peers, and then agreeing (or not) that they resemble people who "are generally very happy; they enjoy life regardless of what is going on, getting the most out of everything," versus those who "are generally not very happy; although they are not depressed, they never seem as happy as they might be."

In Douglas Adams's *The Hitchhiker's Guide to the Galaxy*, Marvin the Paranoid Android, a robot based on an unhappy personality type, is constantly informing everyone around him that he is more miserable than they are. Some examples:

> "The first ten million years were the worst," said Marvin, "and the second ten million years, they were the worst too. The third ten million years I didn't enjoy at all. After that I went into a bit of a decline." . . . "I got very bored and

depressed, so I went and plugged myself in to [the] external computer feed. I talked to the computer at great length and explained my view of the Universe to it," said Marvin.

"And what happened?" pressed Ford.

"It committed suicide," said Marvin and stalked off.[26]

Beyond fictional androids, unhappy people react strongly to upward social comparisons, feeling inadequate when someone outperforms them.[27] (Both happy and unhappy people feel good when they beat someone else.) Unhappy people are so sensitive to social comparison that they can take it personally when their team fails—that is, even a group defeat depresses their mood and self-esteem.[28]

Unhappy people are more likely to feel that their lives are out of control.[29] Comparisons make such people feel that their case is even more hopeless. That is, whether or not we have a sense of control determines how we react to comparisons. In Maria Testa and Brenda Major's experiments, undergraduates first learned that they had failed an essay test and then were told that it was either possible or impossible to improve their scores; this discovery made some feel in control and others feel not in control. They then encountered upward or downward comparisons, that is, the essays of students who had done better or worse than they had. The students who had no sense of control (because they had been told there was no chance of improving their failing grade) felt depressed and hostile upon being shown the better essays and gave up on a second task. In contrast, the students in this group who got to see even *worse* essays felt better and wanted to see more such comparisons.[30]

People who have a sense of control are less vulnerable to such comparison information, but people who generally believe that their lives are out of control may be especially vulnerable to both encouraging and discouraging comparisons.[31] Comparison and insecurity go hand in hand.

Marcel Proust's fictional account of the jealousy of Charles Swann, who compares himself to Odette's imagined lovers, illustrates the suffering obsession of the insecurely attached.[32] One night she tells him that he has arrived too late, and besides, she has a headache. Swann leaves, only to become obsessed with the possibility that Odette is expecting someone else. He returns and stands outside her shuttered window, listening to the murmurs of conversation and feeling "something almost agreeable, something even more than the appeasement of doubt and pain: the pleasure of information."[33] Although he is dying to see who his competitor is, and to show him that he knows, Swann reflects on the misery about to ensue from this discovery. The incident ends abruptly when he finally knocks and discovers that he has been standing at the wrong window.

To be sure, comparison malaise may have some benefits. If we cannot have dominance and control, perhaps we can have prediction, if only we can tolerate the malaise. The stress caused by uncertainty alone, however, is simply too unpleasant for some people, so they are unlikely to pursue social comparisons.[34] Yet everyone has to balance the comfort of certainty and closure, on the one hand, against the possibility of settling too quickly on the easy but wrong answer—that is, invalidity—on the other hand. People fall on both sides of this certainty-validity trade-off.[35] Those of us who are more motivated by certainty want to affirm ourselves as we are, even if the news is bad, whereas those of us who are more motivated by validity want to learn the truth, even if it takes a while and involves some uncomfortable comparisons in the process. People more tolerant of uncertainty do indeed seek all kinds of social comparisons, the better to assess their standing.[36] To do this, they have to be open to a variety of experiences, including malaise. Perhaps the chronic comparers are wiser but unhappier, like Marvin the Paranoid Android.

Groups Are Funny Too

Just as some people are oriented toward social comparison, even if it keeps them unhappy, some societal groups compare more than others. Just as individuals compare on what most matters to them personally, groups usually compare along the dimensions that matter to their group identity.

Men Compare More Than Women Do

Even though it is not the single most important source of their self-esteem, men's self-esteem hinges more on social comparisons than women's does (see the first columns in figure 3.2.).[37] Men are more likely than women to value "doing better than anyone else at something that is important," "thinking about how your skills and abilities compare to other people your age," and "thinking about how well people your age perform tasks you must also perform." Perhaps because men are—both stereotypically and in actuality—more openly competitive than women are,[38] men define themselves more than women do in terms of independence and agency, that is, being effective in the world.[39] The ability to be effective depends on knowing how others are doing, so it makes sense to compare. Men's tendency to compare and compete stems as much from internal as external ideals about what defines the male role.

As the stereotypical relationship experts, women care more than men do about so-called reflected appraisals—how other people view them (see the third columns in figure 3.2).[40] Women are more likely than men to value "having others think of you as a good person"; "getting praise from someone like a teacher, boss, parent, or older sibling"; and "having your friends, co-workers, or teammates recognize you've done a good job."

Figure 3.2   Sources of Self-Esteem

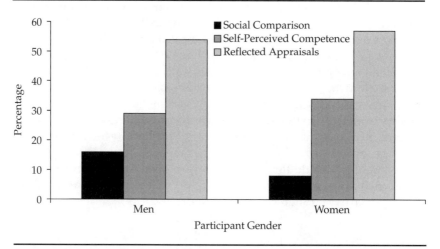

Source: Author's compilation of data from Schwalbe and Staples (1991).
Note: Both men and women assign first rank to reflected appraisals (what other people think of them), but women do this more than men. Both genders less often rank self-perceived competence first, but do not differ significantly. Both genders are less likely to rank social comparison first, but men do so much more than women.

Having your well-being contingent on others' opinions, as noted, undermines self-esteem. For example, an important dimension for women when they compare themselves to other people is appearance, especially their bodies. For women, this kind of social comparison predicts dissatisfaction with their own body.[41] An entertaining if tangential example comes from my experience with a visiting colleague known for his exceptionally tailored and elegant appearance. Feeling suddenly shabby, I retreated to the women's room, only to discover two female colleagues likewise repairing their appearance. The situation was especially odd because our colleague was gay; we were trying to meet the high standard he set, not trying to attract him.

Women tend to be more interdependent than men, so their concerns center relatively more on relational traits. Everyone hopes that other people will be trustworthy and warm (and secondarily that they will be competent), but women especially care about that first interpersonal dimension, trust and warmth.[42] Women, like men, self-stereotype, but their relational orientation makes them compare less and connect more. This orientation makes them better able to bask in an intimate's success rather than make invidious comparisons. Priming people to think interdependently has the same effect as gender, suggesting that the female-relational orientation is an even more plausible interpretation of gender differences. Wendi

Gardner and her colleagues primed interdependence by having participants in their study read a story in which the protagonist is motivated by
relational issues. These authors found that "when you and I are 'we,' you
are not threatening," a result they describe as self-expansion.[43] Perhaps for
women the key is including the other in the self.

Yet an overlapping, porous self has risks: downward comparisons can
evoke the "there but for fortune" empathy mentioned earlier. Women
more often identify with those who are doing worse—a possible self—
whereas men think of the downward performer as "not me." These forms
of comparison insulate men (who can buffer themselves) and depress
women (who endanger themselves).[44]

Wages make a useful case study. Women are still paid less than men,
on average, even controlling for relevant variables.[45] Yet women often do
not seem to feel entitled to their fair share, according to Brenda Major's
research program.[46] Women consistently compare themselves to other
women, not to men, so they do not focus on the gender gap. In fact, women
do not believe they personally suffer discrimination (though they think
other women do). Women's internal standards for their own pay are lower
than men's, and everyone's expectations for feminine jobs include lower
pay. Not feeling entitled means that women do not see their wages as
unfair or unsatisfying. The appropriate target for social comparison would
seem to be other people in the same job, regardless of gender, not other
women, regardless of job. But women appear to value connection more
than comparison.

A Note on Status and Comparisons

Other low-status societal groups may tolerate their lower pay using the
same kinds of mental gymnastics.[47] Comparing yourself within your own
low-status group, or your own history, reduces dissatisfaction, as opposed
to comparing yourself with a higher-status group doing better. Whether it
differs by ethnicity, class, or citizenship, the higher-status group may seem
simply irrelevant. Lowered expectations diminish the feeling of entitlement
to more than you get.

Social class may thus work the same way as gender. For example,
working-class adults act less as autonomous agents and more as collective, connected family or friends.[48] Perhaps class patterns mimic gender
patterns, with the lower-status groups being less scornful and more
empathic. Relative to high-income groups and whites, both low-income
and minority groups make downward comparisons that are more benign
(for example, when they note that people can be poor for circumstantial
reasons) and less blaming (by, for example, being less likely to say that
poor people are personally responsible for their poverty).[49] It may also be

that low-status groups (women, minorities, lower social classes) compare less because they especially support equality.

Socially Dominant Groups Prefer Hierarchies

How positively or negatively do you feel about each of these statements?

1. Some groups of people are simply not the equals of others.
2. Some people are just more worthy than others.
3. This country would be better off if we cared less about how equal all people were.
4. Some people are just more deserving than others.
5. It is not a problem if some people have more of a chance in life than others.
6. Some people are just inferior to others.
7. To get ahead in life, it is sometimes necessary to step on others.

These statements describe one's beliefs about social hierarchy: people who endorse these beliefs, and who say that they do not particularly value equality, score high on social dominance orientation (SDO).[50] On average, men, majorities, and higher social classes subscribe more to social hierarchy, which they often view as inevitable and perhaps even desirable. This is not just an American phenomenon. Across cultures, the most dominant societal groups endorse social hierarchy for the obvious reason that they have the most to gain from the status quo. Feeling advantaged relative to other groups makes people especially like their own group and dislike low-status out-groups.[51]

This kind of response is visceral. Being high-SDO makes people less responsive to another's pain, even on brain scans.[52] After viewing photographs of people in pain (for example, during a natural disaster), participants in one study who had higher SDO scores reported less empathy. What is more, for those with higher SDO, the neural networks that are normally implicated in pain (insula, ACC) activated less to others' pain. High-SDOs are willing to be disagreeable if necessary to maintain the hierarchy (see figure 3.3), because they view hierarchies as a social fact.[53] Social dominance is both competitive and comparative.

Because tough-minded high-SDOs view group hierarchies as only realistic, they succeed in hierarchical settings such as business, the military, and the police.[54] High SDO correlates with minimizing leisure and prioritizing work.[55] John Duckitt and Chris Sibley found in their research that this "dog-eat-dog" SDO worldview is based on the belief that some groups inevitably land on top and only the best survive; therefore, competition seems prag-

Figure 3.3   Social Dominance Orientation

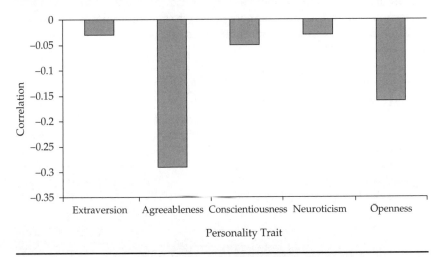

Source: Author's compilation of data from Duckitt and Sibley (2008).
Note: SDO correlates substantially with being disagreeable and, to a lesser extent, with being not open to new experiences, according to a meta-analysis of thirty studies on more than 10,000 participants.

matic. Competitiveness makes tough-minded, high-SDOs feel more negative toward even harmless subordinate groups, such as housewives and people with disabilities.[56] A cluster of attitudes shows that high-SDOs view these groups as competition and then both disrespect and dislike them. SDO often includes the belief that such subordinate groups consume resources, grab influence, and do not deserve support.

Socially subordinate groups themselves are usually lower on SDO, and they naturally prefer equality. Though they recognize hierarchy, they view it as unfair.[57] Low-status groups face a conflict between favoring their in-group and living within a system that devalues it, so they show more ambivalence toward their own group than high-status people show toward theirs. The more low-status groups view hierarchy as inevitable, the worse is this internal conflict between valuing their group and acknowledging society's contempt for it. SDO increases their ambivalence for their own low-status group because it increases this tension.[58]

Various other asymmetries distinguish low- and high-status groups because of their social dominance orientation. Regardless of group membership, however, people who believe in group hierarchies also endorse prejudices such as racism, sexism, and classism, as well as ideologies that legitimate them, such as meritocracy (see chapter 1) and status quo policies.[59] Nevertheless, it is high-status, socially dominant groups that particularly prefer hierarchies.

Social conservatives are not necessarily the only ones who endorse hierarchies. Left-wing extremists can also endorse hierarchy; Communist governments, for instance, usually believe in strong, undemocratic leadership.[60] So social dominance differs from social conservatism, though they are moderately related.[61]

Socially Conservative Groups Justify Hierarchies

Conservative ideology prioritizes control over spending and minimizing government intervention in social services. Conservative government policies tend to benefit high-income people. Liberal ideology, which prioritizes employment, income growth, and protecting vulnerable populations, tends to benefit low-income people. It is no accident that inequality increases during conservative administrations.[62] From 1948 to 2005, poor families at the twentieth percentile saw their incomes grow less than half a percent per year under Republican presidents but 2.65 percent per year under Democratic presidents. The rich who top the income distribution (the ninetieth-fifth percentile) showed no significant income differences under different presidential parties, but the hyper-rich (the top 1 percent) showed dramatic income growth, especially during Republican administrations. Republicans get elected when election years boast income growth, especially for the rich. Voters judge myopically, based mainly on the election year's economy and the richest people's incomes.

> Despite the superior historical performance of Democratic presidents in generating income growth for middle-class and poor families over the past half-century, American voters have shown a strong tendency to punish Democrats and reward Republicans based on the very unrepresentative sliver of economic performance that happens to fall within their narrow focus on [rich people's] "present advantages."[63]

The odd thing is that even middle-class and low-income people vote Republican more when rich people's incomes are going up. One possibility is that wealthy people donate more to election campaigns (especially Republicans) when their incomes are growing, so then rich and middle-income voters are swayed by election spending. (Poor people's votes demonstrably are not swayed by election spending.) Rich and middle-class people's views have a greater impact on their representatives, and rich people are more conservative than poor people, so election-year donations might favor Republican, more conservative voting.

Going beyond party ideology to another indicator of social conservatism, political psychologists have linked conservative values to justifications for hierarchy. As chapter 1 indicated, many Americans believe that people get what they deserve, and especially that poor people are responsible for their poverty. Belief in a just world correlates with the belief based on the Protestant ethic that hard work yields benefits and leisure is useless.[64] The people who most endorse this perspective tend to be politically conservative.[65]

Consider some opinions that certain kinds of conservatives tend to endorse:

- The established authorities generally turn out to be right about things, while the radicals and protesters are usually just "loudmouths," showing off their ignorance.

- Women should have to promise to obey their husbands when they get married.

- Our country desperately needs a mighty leader who will do what has to be done to destroy the radical new ways and sinfulness that are ruining us.

- It is always better to trust the judgment of the proper authorities in government and religion than to listen to the noisy rabble-rousers in our society who are trying to create doubt in people's minds.

- The only way our country can get through the crisis ahead is to get back to our traditional values, put some tough leaders in power, and silence the troublemakers spreading bad ideas.

- Our country will be destroyed someday if we do not smash the perversions eating away at our moral fiber and traditional beliefs.

- The "old-fashioned ways" and "old-fashioned values" show the best way to live.[66]

Bob Altemeyer's indicator of social conservatism, which he calls rightwing authoritarianism (RWA), focuses on attitudes toward authority.[67] High-RWA conservatives value conscientiousness more than low-RWA liberals do. High-RWAs endorse the work ethic of self-reliance, firm morality, and minimal leisure.[68] Faith in a work ethic predicts disliking poor people and holding them responsible for their own poverty.[69] As Alain de Botton notes, low status, in this view, comes "to seem not merely regrettable, but also *deserved*."[70]

Conservatives, by definition, prefer the status quo, or at least a desired past ("golden age"). Even when they advocate for change, they advocate the change of returning to an essential, pure period before particular progressive changes were made. The belief in order, stability, cohesion, and social control that reportedly characterizes all conservatives also correlates with the RWA kind of conservatism. RWA predicts negative feelings not only toward poor people, who allegedly do not conform to work ethic values, but also toward many groups seen as deviant and threatening to social control (for example, gay people or feminists). High-RWA conservatives personally dislike change and new experience.[71] They value social control, not comparison, which, by allowing people to focus on inequalities, destabilizes society.

Group Certainty Creates Individual Certainty

Because conservatives acknowledge and even endorse hierarchy, they need not make comparisons, and indeed they prefer not to, because comparison destabilizes. With its focus on who is worse off (scorn) and especially who is better off (envy), comparison just makes people unhappy, as we have seen. If social dominance is inevitable, and if both the rich and the poor deserve their fate because they earned it, then why bother to compare? Dwelling on the unpleasant reality of hierarchy is unnecessary and even unseemly. On the liberal side, if the social dominance system seems unfair, and if equality seems attainable and better, then social comparison is informative, even if it stokes resentment and uncertainty.

Accordingly, liberals and conservatives differ in their orientation toward certainty. Conservatives prefer assurance, and liberals like novelty. Conservatives are oriented toward known, trusted groups, and liberals value the experience of variety in groups. With these differences, more conservatives probably are long-term joiners, whereas more liberals are short-term experimenters. All kinds of people join groups to decrease their uncertainty and increase their sense of security, but conservatives apparently do this more than liberals do. For some people, knowledge of their group's place in society and a feeling of certainty about its value support the current order, as well as their conservative beliefs, and may eliminate any need to make comparisons. People who do compare themselves to others and end up feeling better off are more likely to subscribe to economic conservatism and work ethic values.[72]

As correlates of conservatism, both social dominance orientation and right-wing authoritarianism predict fierce in-group loyalty. Conservatism protects its own against threats from either competing out-groups (SDO) or deviant out-groups (RWA). The in-group comes first because conservatism cares about protection.[73] Conservatives protect the in-group, whereas liberals promote equality between groups. Conservatives seem to specialize in the in-group, avoiding risk, endorsing hierarchy, preferring tradition, supporting familiar values, and prioritizing family allegiance.[74] In *On Paradise Drive*, the neoconservative David Brooks describes the vision behind this lifestyle: "This common pursuit of the together life leads to the conformity that the social critics have always complained about. On the other hand, the pursuit of tranquility is also a moral and spiritual pursuit. It is an effort to live on a plane where things are straightforward and good, where people can march erect and upward, where friends can be relaxed and familiar, where families can be happy and cooperative, where individuals can be self-confident and wholesome, where children can grow up active and healthy, where spouses are sincere and honest, where everyone is cooperative, hardworking, devout, and happy. That's not entirely terrible, is it?"[75]

In contrast to conservatives' in-group orientation, which promotes certainty, liberals like adventure. As they specialize in group variety, liberals seem to value equality, engage risk, prefer new experiences, and support independence.[76] Hence, liberals are more likely to have both a motivation and a basis for comparison. Although no work to my knowledge shows that low SDO or low RWA predicts a focus on social comparison, by this logic liberals ought to be more interested in comparison. If liberals endorse independence, then they join groups only provisionally, but this fits their orientation to novelty and risk.

If conservatives are joiners, as noted, they join partly because identifying with a group supports personal certainty.[77] To categorize ourselves as group members is to have a mental image of the typical or ideal in-group member. This prototype confirms our identity as group members different from out-group members. Particular kinds of groups provide more certainty than others. Groups that are themselves certain make their members certain. A clearly defined group (such as campus Republicans) seems more real, concrete, and definite than a hypothetical, abstract, ill-defined group (such as middle-class Americans). Psychologists call this the group's entitativity—its property of being a distinct entity, which stems from having clear boundaries, shared goals, and strong norms. Groups that seem like entities have clearer prototypes, so they more effectively reduce uncertainty.

Other People's Cultures Are Funny (And Maybe Ours Is Too)

Cultural Collectivism Promotes Conscientiousness, Control, and Certainty

Some kinds of groups specialize in comparison (men, liberals), whereas others opt for stability, certainty, and connection (women, conservatives).[78] Cultures have a parallel distinction: individualist cultures, endorse comparing more than collectivist cultures do.

Individualism   Individualist cultures promote the autonomous person who is unique, separate, and private; individualists have independent selves that they evaluate through comparison with others.[79] Among the most individualist regions studied are the United States, other English-speaking cultures (for example, Australia), and Germany; among the least

Figure 3.4   Brain Activity of Individualist Americans and Collectivist Japanese

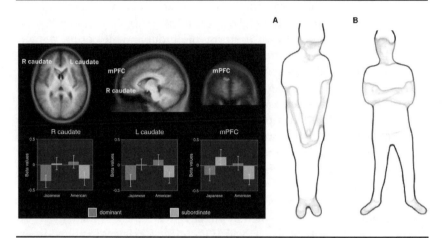

Source: Freeman et al. (2009). Copyright © 2009 Elsevier, reprinted by permission.
Note: The figure shows the activation of primary reward areas (left panel) to dominant and submissive stimuli (right panel), respectively, for individualist Americans and collectivist Japanese.

individualist are the East Asian countries.[80] In the United States, Asian Americans are the least individualist, Latino Americans are equivalent to European Americans, and African Americans are the most individualist. The American states that score highest on individualism are the mountain western, Great Plains, and northern New England states.[81]

Individualists belong to more groups, but looser ones,[82] a finding that correlates with loyalty but not with conformity to one's group.[83] Individualism is associated with general trust in people, which frees individualists to operate in a broad though uncertain social context.[84] In comparisons across states within the United States and across cultures in dozens of countries, individualists participate in many friendship groups and political activities.[85] In this freewheeling set of overlapping networks, upward and downward comparisons locate the individual in relation to other individuals. Differences are tolerated, and individuality rules. In social comparison, individualists contrast self with others.[86]

Individualist cultures may encourage envy through competition.[87] Especially if they are egalitarian, everyone can expect to succeed as much as anyone else. Even at a neural level, dominance is rewarding (see figure 3.4).[88] In an individualist culture that is also an "honor society," people prioritize reputation and fear shame, so upward comparison can be particularly humiliating, and envy especially dangerous. In honor societies, individuals use violence to protect their reputation.[89] Without a cultural authority to curb invidious comparison, envy can thrive, with its worst excesses.

Collectivism   In contrast, collectivist cultures promote the connected person who belongs, adapts, and performs; interdependent people define each other by relationships in context.[90] Among the most collectivist world regions are Africa, Latin America, and East Asia.[91] In the United States, Asian and Latino Americans are the most collectivist, and European and African Americans are the least collectivist. The American regions that are highest on collectivism include the Deep South and places with large Latino and Asian immigrant communities (Hawaii, California, New York, and New Jersey).[92]

Collectivism discourages individual prominence because fitting in matters more. Knowing one's place is rewarding.[93] Only a few in-group others are trusted, but those loyalties last a lifetime.[94] In return for secure relationships, collectivist cultures prescribe social control; people enforce norms as a social obligation.[95] For example, collectivists report that they would be more likely to indicate disapproval of someone who litters, spits, vandalizes, or commits other public incivilities. Maintaining the collective requires vigilance.

Collective selves live in relation to others, so the self is flexible, adapting to different contexts, roles, and relationships. The collectivist's contextual self ("I am assertive with my mother") contrasts with the individualist's general self, which stays more constant and abstracted across contexts ("I am assertive").[96] In one brain area that often activates to thoughts of self, individualists activate more to judging the general self, whereas collectivists activate more to judging the contextual self.

Collectivist and individualist tendencies need not be fixed by cultural residence. Everyone is capable of either orientation, and these tendencies can be instilled in a moment.[97] A two-minute task as simple as listing how we differ from (or resemble) our friends and family members can prime us to think about ourselves as an individual or a collectivist self. Circling "I," "me," and "my," as opposed to "we," "us," and "our," in a paragraph also primes the individual or collectivist self. Priming the individual self makes us differentiate self from others (think of the solo singer, the lone cowhand, the prizefighter). This self-differentiation ironically requires the social comparison that can plague us with envy and scorn.

Priming the collectivist self, on the other hand, makes us expand the self to include in-group others and assimilate any comparison into the inclusive self (think of choral singers, a barn-raising party, or football teammates). Interdependence makes us bask in the glory of those more accomplished people within our circle; upward social comparison can enrich the self when the self is interdependent.[98] Priming our collectivist self also makes us more relational, that is, more connected to others, obligated, supportive, sensitive, and helpful, and even physically closer. In collectivist, inter-dependent settings, emotions occur between people instead of within people, as they do in individualist, independent settings.[99] As a result, negative emotions such as envy and scorn need to be publicly suppressed because they can disrupt collectivist cultures more than individualist ones.

Envy and the Evil Eye

One new mother refuses to name her infant, dresses her newborn in rags, smears dirt on the baby, and hides from view. Is she ashamed? Does she hate her baby? On the contrary, she is just as protective and proud as the American mother who picked a name months ago, dresses up her infant, bathes the baby daily, and shows off her newborn at any opportunity. The difference is that the first mother is working to ward off the evil eye—the destructive envious encounter.

The evil eye represents the dangers of envy. In scores of cultures, both individualist and collectivist, the poison of envy contaminates the envied object through a wicked look.[100] Children, livestock, gardens, food, and even buildings are vulnerable to the evil eye. Certain malevolent people possess the evil eye and can direct it at those who seem too self-important or who simply make them envious. Even the gods and spirits can punish those with excess good fortune, balancing it with misfortune. In many cultures, well-meaning but careless praise can be so destructive that people suppress visitors' admiration of their newborns. The evil eye appeared in ancient Samaria as far back as five thousand years ago, and also in ancient India, Greece, and Rome, as well as Middle Eastern, North African, European, Latin American, and North American traditions.

However widespread, the evil eye is not universal. Indigenous Americans, both North and South, and indigenous Australians appear not to have believed in the evil eye, perhaps because hunter-gatherer societies require immediate sharing and individuals cannot hoard possessions.[101] East Asian societies also do not traditionally endorse evil eye beliefs, but being collectivist, they have other ways to discourage individualistic comparisons and the attendant envy. In some East Asian settings, the limited mobility inherent in complex hierarchies discourages envy because people do not expect to change their place in society. All over the world, as legal, economic, and bureaucratic systems have expanded to create modern industrialized societies, these modern cultures, too, especially the upper classes, do not hold evil eye beliefs.[102]

Nevertheless, the evil eye is remarkably widespread, even in other modern forms ("Whaddaya lookin' at?"). The provocative power of the gaze implies that attention can be aversive. Humans and other primates use gaze to infer attention and hierarchy; attention follows status.[103] High-status speakers are allowed to gaze directly at inferiors but not vice versa.

A monarch may stare down any subject. But high-status listeners need not attend closely. The monarch need not attend closely to others, though doing so signals noble courtesy. Control over one's gaze implies power. Gaze itself communicates a goal that implicates the other person; attention shows intention, for good or ill. The supplicant gazes at the monarch, but because royalty does not really need underlings so much as vice versa, the monarch may or may not meet the supplicant's gaze.

Given its importance, direct gaze itself demands attention and engraves memory. All this suggests that having someone stare at you is salient in the moment and may come easily to mind later to explain mysterious misfortunes. This could explain the wide appeal of evil eye accounts. Someone less fortunate who looks too long at your baby, your horse, or your house may seem to have a goal in regard to your treasure.

Attracting the wrong kind of attention worries people, even in modern societies. In the United States, a 1946 advertisement for *The Terrors of the Evil Eye Exposed* proposed that

> FEAR!! . . . MAKES COWARDS OF US ALL! SMASH THE FETTERS OF FEAR! Is there such a thing as the dreaded Evil Eye? Can it be possible that some people have the Power to cast strange spells on those they wish to destroy or is it just the figment of a tortured imagination or an unholy belief of the ignorant and the superstitious? . . . Once you understand the Mysterious aspects of this Evil Terror, and know of the many different Symbols, Talismans, Amulets, seals, etc. used to thwart it, all FEARS will VANISH as the clouds before the sun! If you believe you are a victim of this unspeakable MADNESS . . . Don't delay . . . Learn at Last the Truth about the EVIL EYE.[104]

And, at only $2, a bargain!

Social Ties Contain the Damage of Scorn and Ostracism

Although being seen by the evil eye can be unnerving, people are also concerned when they seem to be invisible to others. Being on the receiving end of scorn, disdain, or contempt usually means being ignored, and being ostracized amounts to a death sentence in most cultures, even now. In evolutionary terms, we survive best as successful members of our group.[105] Core social motives show our adaptive sensitivity to other people, who are, after all, our main evolutionary niche.[106] We avoid ostracism, social death, and physical death by fulfilling an intense need to belong, to get along with our in-group. We are motivated to endorse the in-group's understanding of the truth; the beliefs and norms of our group become our shared reality. To function effectively in our groups, we seek a sense of social control and contingency, some link between what we do and what we get from others. As social beings, we also seek to validate our self-esteem through the good opinion of others. And we are motivated to trust at least a core of in-group others in order to get along in our group niche. All these core social motives adapt us to live as social beings.

Social ties predict happiness and well-being better than almost anything else does.[107] People are so sensitive to ostracism that they immediately feel crummy even when strangers leave them out of a computer game.[108] The neural pathways for social pain parallel those for physical pain.[109] And physical pain diminishes when we make social connections, from looking at a partner's photograph to receiving social support from just about anyone.[110] Tylenol cures both physical and social pain.[111] As an improvised cure for social pain, people spontaneously engage in "social snacking" by seeking human images and surrogates. Even a volleyball on a desert island in the movie *Cast Away* becomes a friend named Wilson.[112]

People are no fools to fasten onto social connections. Social isolation endangers health, threatening the immune system, cardiovascular system, and health habits.[113] Negative emotions, including loneliness, may damage immune functioning by inflammatory processes often associated with cardiovascular disease, osteoporosis, arthritis, type 2 diabetes, certain cancers, frailty, and functional decline.[114] Social support helps people survive heart attacks.[115] Social ties also correlate with longevity, even controlling for physical health, smoking, alcohol use, obesity, activity, class, age, life satisfaction, and health habits.[116]

Cultures cultivate social ties for adaptive reasons as well.[117] In more interdependent cultures, people tend to emphasize similarity, avoiding overt comparison, as we have seen. This reinforces and protects relationships. Collectivists prefer quiet positive emotions and sympathize with each other's efforts to overcome admitted shortcomings. In more independent cultures, people tend to emphasize uniqueness, seeking overt comparison but also multiple social groups. People prefer exciting positive emotions and feel pride; their self-esteem reflects their standing in the group. These then are two routes for linking people to their social groups, both increasing well-being through connection.

How to Manage Comparison in Self and Others

When we are hyper-concerned about social comparisons, we make ourselves and others unhappy. If envy and scorn harm us, no wonder cultures seek to control them. No wonder, too, that we as individuals seek to control them. What do we do to protect ourselves from envy and scorn, besides wearing amulets and befriending volleyballs?

The book's last chapter will elaborate on this question, but for now, we could use some hope for the comparison-challenged. We protect ourselves from scorn by at least two routes.[118] Scorn most often seems passive and indirect, as when we are ignored or neglected. In this instance, we actively attempt to reengage, contact, and connect, all promoting ties. Failure leads to depression. Sometimes, however, scorn is more active rejection, and we respond with prevention rather than promotion: feeling agitated, we withdraw.

A subway encounter illustrates these two strategies, prevention and promotion. Waiting on a station platform one evening, I heard a guy coming from the far end, talking to himself, without benefit of cell phone. As he approached, I avoided eye contact until he asked me for some train information; I answered briefly, but when he pressed for details beyond my knowledge, I noted his disheveled clothing, felt nervous about engaging him further, shrugged, and looked away. He doubtless felt actively rejected and disappointed, maybe especially because of the race and class contrasts that would have been obvious to both of us, so he withdrew from me to prevent further unpleasant rejection. He then approached the woman on the other end of my bench. She appeared to be middle-class and black. She knew more about the trains and answered in some detail. The guy tried to continue their interaction, and although she soon ceased talking, she nodded without looking at him, while he proceeded to ramp up his account, complaining about people who avoided him, promoting his own sociable nature. His behavior toward me looked like a prevention strategy, while his behavior toward her looked like a promotion strategy.

Both strategies appear in Daniel Molden and Wendi Gardner's social psychology laboratory, where undergraduates volunteered for a study on friendship formation over the Internet, simulated by computer-based communication with two other students (actually preprogrammed confederates). In the active-rejection condition, the two other students insulted the participant's opinions and made disparaging remarks. In the passive-neglect condition, the two other students discovered that they were each other's neighbor and simply ignored the participant. Being ignored caused more dejection, but being rejected caused more agitation. Participants who were actively rejected focused on what they *should not* have done, a prevention focus, while participants who were passively ignored focused on their inaction and what they *should* have done, a promotion focus. In other studies, even people who simply recalled being rejected or ignored generated the same kinds of responses. These two types of responses match active and passive scorn with active and passive coping.

We may protect ourselves from envy either passively or actively as well—passively, by downplaying our good fortune to prevent envy, and actively, by inviting others to join us. In many cultures, people publicly minimize their good fortune, abundance, and fertility. They may conceal or deny having what others covet. When hiding fails, people may undermine envy by sharing their good fortune in an effort to placate other people or even the gods.[119] People may guard against the evil eye by using physical charms, such as amulets, but they also use social charms.

Conclusion

What do neurotics, men, liberals, and individualists have in common that makes them prone to comparison? Probably more than one thing motivates comparison obsessions, but all of these types, to greater or lesser degrees, want information to know where they stand. Besides particular individual, group, and cultural proclivities to compare, what about the normal but annoying preoccupation we all have with comparison up and down? To understand how to master our own comparison fixation, it helps to know what motivates comparison. The next three chapters outline several explanations for why we have this inclination.

Chapter 4

Why Do We Compare?
Comparison Informs Us

For me they normally happen, these career crises, often, actually, on a Sunday evening, just as the sun is starting to set, and the gap between my hopes for myself, and the reality of my life, start to diverge so painfully that I normally end up weeping into a pillow. . . . I'm mentioning all this because I think this is not merely a personal problem. You may think I'm wrong in this. But I think that we live in an age when our lives are regularly punctuated by career crises, by moments when what we thought we knew, about our lives, about our careers, comes into contact with a threatening sort of reality.

—Alain de Botton, "A Kinder, Gentler Philosophy of Success" (2009)

W E ALL need to know where we stand, especially in those "moments when what we thought we knew, about our lives, about our careers, [our relationships, our appearance, our health] comes into contact with a threatening sort of reality." Life requires that our self-view at least approximately fit our reality, not to mention our hopes. Psychologists know a lot about this. One major reason we compare ourselves with others is to gain information in order to evaluate and improve ourselves, functions that serve the twin motives of prediction and control. Comparison informs us.

Our need to understand (and perhaps control) our fate runs deep. We are healthier and happier when we think that we know who we are and where we stand. Self-knowledge adapts us to navigate our days, from the minor level ("Do I wake up easily?" "Am I a good tennis player?") to the major ("Do I get along well with my patchwork family?" "Do I reliably meet my work deadlines?"). Evolutionary psychologists argue that a self-concept serves our survival needs because it helps us not only in planning our own actions but also in coordinating with others.[1] How could we know whom to join and whom to avoid without knowing who we are?

How could we know what role to play when we do join others? How do we know what we can and cannot do if we do not compare our abilities to others? How well we get up, get by at tennis, get along with others, or get things done—all of these are relative judgments. Whether we should be the local alarm clock, tennis partner, family mediator, or group motivator depends on our abilities relative to those of others who are available.[2] Other people serve as a reality check on our abilities ("I may be better than most people at getting up without an alarm clock, but I know where I stand relative to others as a tennis player, and it's not good.").

Having information allows us to predict what will happen, and that is a comfort. By and large, we do not like surprises, at least not the ones that come without party hats. Even more, we would like to be able to control what will happen, or at least understand the contingencies between what we do and what we get. We like to know about upcoming parties, raises, lay-offs, proposals, and babies; also, we prefer to have some say in these events. What is more, the illusion of information and control—as long as it is not too far from reality—matters more to us than its accuracy.[3] That is, many of us tend to overestimate our own knowledge and influence, which reassures us that the world is not random and that what we do makes a difference. At a minimum, we like to believe that a trusted someone is in control, whether that someone is our president, our tech support, or our god. Indeed, some researchers suggest that our persistent religious beliefs stem from a need for at least vicarious control.[4] Our motives for seeking prediction and control are among the most basic to our survival as social creatures.[5]

Chief among our tactics for seeking information and control is social comparison with similar others. Even though we may deny that we are doing it, we do. For example, in interviews, women with breast cancer almost all spontaneously offered comparisons to how other patients were coping, and by comparing downward to women doing worse, most of them estimated that they themselves were doing better (see figure 4.1).[6]

Information helps us with evaluation, but it is not enough. Believing that we are in control (or that our doctor is) correlates with coping better than just having information, as seen in figure 4.2.[7] We need information to evaluate our relative standing, and we need a sense of control to improve it. Both prediction and control keep us going.

Comparison as a Need to Know and Control

Leon Festinger is one of the most famous social psychologists who ever lived.[8] His social comparison theory says that people seek information from others to validate their opinions and abilities when objective information is lacking. People compare with similar others because they are

Figure 4.1   Using Comparison As Information: Cancer Patients

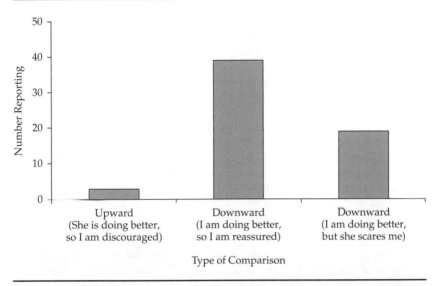

Source: Author's compilation based on data from Wood, Taylor, and Lichtman (1985).
Note: In seventy-three cancer patients, the majority reported making reassuring downward comparisons in evaluating their physical condition.

Figure 4.2   Believing in Own and Others' Control: Adjustment to Cancer

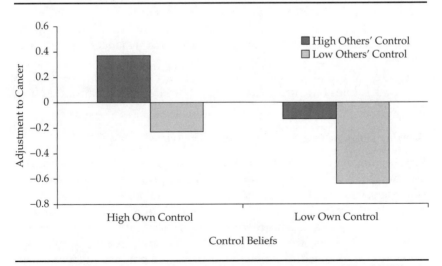

Source: Author's compilation based on data from Taylor, Lichtman, and Wood (1984).
Note: For breast cancer patients, thinking that both self and others can control their breast cancer helps adjustment, illustrating the importance of perceived control.

the ones who are most relevant and informative. As Alain de Botton put it in his 2009 TED lecture:

> I think it would be very unusual for anyone here, or anyone watching, to be envious of the Queen of England. Even though she is much richer than any of you are. And she's got a very large house. The reason why we don't envy her is because she's too weird. She's simply too strange. We can't relate to her. She speaks in a funny way. She comes from an odd place. So we can't relate to her. And when you can't relate to somebody, you don't envy them.

Not only do we not look up to dissimilar others, but we do not bother to look down on them either. For example, counting our blessings by realizing that we are better off than the panhandler down the street does not help us evaluate our standing. We have to pick someone within the realm of possibility. We compare with similar others because they are relevant.

Festinger emphasized that the information value of other similar people is that they can help us evaluate either the truth of our opinions or the standing of our abilities. He picks these two comparisons because they could have objective values; instead of fetching our tape measures and intelligence tests when we are uncertain, we compare ourselves with others. A distinctly asocial pair of judgments (truth and ability) falls back on distinctly social validation. We choose the subjective comparison when the objective one is ambiguous.

A cottage industry of social comparison research has employed social psychologists for decades, and we now know that people frequently use social comparison not only to evaluate their opinions and abilities but also to improve themselves (as well as for the other uses covered in the next chapters). Data support the role of comparison in meeting our needs for prediction (evaluation) and control (improvement). In short, we have a need to know and to control, and comparison meets those needs. This section describes how individuals cope; later, the chapter describes how groups cope with comparison.

Similar Enough to Be a Meaningful Proxy

People who are similar to us provide us with a proxy self.[9] If someone like you can climb this mountain, so can you. The proxy's relevant attributes (same age, gender, physical condition) make him or her diagnostic.[10] You can evaluate your ability relative to the abilities of the proxy, who resembles you enough to be informative. Sherpas are not invited to serve as proxies, but neither are couch potatoes. You are most likely to seek a proxy when you need to predict your own performance, such as deciding whether to join a hike. A quick ability assessment predicts your fate.[11] If the proxy is similar enough, you can project yourself into his or her boots and decide accordingly.[12]

Gossip creates a kind of virtual proxy: a group of people collectively try on someone else's shoes. Gossip is, in effect, collaborative social comparison. People often assess themselves by talking about others. In some estimates, most adult conversations concern someone who is absent from it.[13] People gossip with similar others about someone they agree is dissimilar. For example, an urban writers' colony filled with distinguished social scientists often spent their communal lunches discussing—not great ideas—celebrity sex scandals. Such gossip is evaluative talk about an absent but relevant other. The celebrities were relevant because everyone knew about them and because their failings were all too human. Groups use gossip to bond and to communicate norms—that is, prescribed and proscribed behavior.[14] And gossip is useful. Because gossip tells stories about people, we enjoy and absorb it better than we do abstract admonitions. Stories about people allow us to learn the easy way, by someone else's example. Gossip not only informs us but connects us. We feel close by agreeing about a third party.[15] The third party becomes a shared proxy for vicarious learning.

> The couples we knew were also aging . . . and paid rising taxes and suffered automobile accidents and midnight illnesses and marital woe; but under the tireless supervision of gossip all misfortunes were compared, and confessed, and revealed as relative.[16]

Expert Enough to Be Right

In an exception to the "similarity loves company" rule, we compare on belief-evaluation (opinions) differently than we do on self-evaluation (abilities). As already discussed, the mental puzzle for predicting our own performance is simple: we find someone similar enough to be a relevant proxy for ourselves and we predict our performance accordingly. By contrast, the mental puzzle for evaluating the truth of our beliefs often requires someone different: someone just like us might be prone to the same biases or be ignorant in the same ways, but someone different allows us to triangulate our beliefs.[17]

In this instance, the best comparison should be with someone who differs from us mainly in being more expert. To demonstrate this, Jerry Suls, René Martin, and Ladd Wheeler presented college students with a pair of (fictitious) past applicant files and asked them either to predict which applicants had become more academically successful (belief) or to decide which applicants were more likable (preference).[18] After making their judgments—based on grades, test scores, activities, hobbies, and goals—participants had a chance to see how another participant had reacted to the same applicants. They could choose among a student similar to themselves, a dissimilar student, a more expert student, or a less expert student. The researchers predicted that in evaluating their preferences the students

**Figure 4.3   Evaluating Self Automatically Makes a Best Friend
More Accessible**

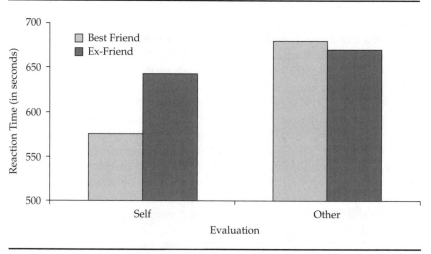

Source: Mussweiler and Rüter (2003), reprinted with permission.
Note: People evaluating themselves (versus another person) spontaneously bring to mind their best friend as a comparison. The evidence indicates that the friend's name is more easily identified: immediately afterward, the friend comes to mind in less time than does the name of an ex-friend. Evaluating another person does not show this difference.

would pick someone similar, but that in evaluating their beliefs they would focus on someone expert. As predicted, to evaluate liking, the students compared their preferences to those of someone similar, but to evaluate beliefs, they compared their choices to those of someone more knowledgeable.

Handy Enough to Be Fast

We compare so spontaneously that we do it automatically, and we use whoever is at hand. We do not necessarily have a choice: sometimes the environment imposes involuntary comparisons that we absorb, like it or not.[19] Thomas Mussweiler and his colleagues have shown in a series of studies that when people evaluate, for example, their own cheerfulness or passion, thoughts of their best friends come easily to mind as automatic standards.[20] They demonstrated this by measuring what was topmost in people's minds. After self-evaluations, participants in these studies could detect their friends' names faster from among a series of names and random-letter strings. They automatically activated knowledge about their friends as comparisons when they evaluated themselves, even if it was not required (see figure 4.3).

We are so ready to make comparisons that we use even strangers as standards. If we are reflecting, for example, on our own aggressiveness, subliminal exposure to the name of a relevant celebrity will affect our judgments.[21] We make social comparisons effortlessly and spontaneously when we self-evaluate. This may be useful if we can compare automatically and efficiently, without breaking stride. Indeed, we appear to be able to walk and chew all kinds of comparisons at the same time. When we engage information about ourselves, standards come to mind too. We automatically know that our realities are all relative.

Unfortunately, "automatic" can also mean "inadvertent." We may compare even when we know it is inappropriate. We automatically use friends, and even strangers, whether or not they should be our relevant standards.[22] In Daniel Gilbert's lab demonstration of this, undergraduates watched an instructional video of a woman judging pairs of photographs to decide which one was a schizophrenic.[23] Some learned that she performed well (getting sixteen of eighteen correct), but with training. Others learned that she did poorly (getting only four of eighteen correct), but that she was handicapped by misleading information. In both cases, then, circumstances could explain her performance. The students then performed the same task themselves and judged how well they themselves did at detecting people at risk from schizophrenia. Normally, people realize that someone who has been advantaged or disadvantaged is not a fair basis for comparison, and in the control condition, the students realized this and ignored the comparison person in judging themselves. However, half the students were distracted by having to keep an eight-digit number in their heads during the entire procedure. These cognitively busy students could operate only on automatic, and they inadvertently used the readily available comparison standard, even though that person should have been inappropriate (having been helped or handicapped).

People are famously cognitive misers: in our judgments, we go for fast, frugal, and good enough.[24] What comes to mind easily often determines our top-of-the-head decisions. In keeping with our mental efficiency, we rapidly judge whether another person supplies a similar or dissimilar standard.[25] If the person is generally similar to us, we assimilate ourselves to the other person. For example, people of our own age, gender, and ethnicity provide us with ready in-group standards. Assuming similarity as the default, we bring to mind ways in which we resemble a relevant other. A slightly more attractive but otherwise similar other makes us feel more attractive, as also happens with competence or any other flexible judgment. A man thinking of other men assimilates himself to the prototypical guy. In contrast, someone from an out-group makes us presume dissimilarity as a default, and we bring to mind all the ways in which this irrelevant person differs from us. This makes us contrast ourselves with the alien other. Whatever the person's competence or attractiveness, we feel different. A man, when thinking of women, contrasts himself with the prototypical woman.

People also assimilate and contrast depending on the gap between self and other. That is, if you asked me whether, as a professor, I am intelligent, I would assimilate to other professors and say, sure. But if you asked whether I am as intelligent as Einstein, I would have to contrast myself to him as an outlier and respond more modestly. We assimilate to moderate comparisons and contrast to extreme ones. And we do all this by rapidly and automatically reviewing the evidence that comes to mind. Measuring the accessibility of this evidence, psychologists usually find that it comes to mind in a matter of milliseconds.

In fact, we use mere ease of access to inform our comparisons.[26] What comes to mind easily implies similarity; what comes to mind with difficulty implies dissimilarity. Consider Michael Häfner and Thomas Schubert's inventive experiment. Women viewed a moderately attractive or unattractive female model's photograph, which was either blurry or not. When they saw the photo in focus (the easy comparison), they assimilated: they felt more attractive after viewing the attractive photo than after looking at the unattractive photo. But this pattern exactly reversed when they saw a blurry photo (the difficult comparison): the attractive model made them feel less attractive, and the unattractive model more so.

Just because it is automatic does not mean comparison is not flexible. When we focus on ourselves as individuals we tend to contrast, spontaneously and unconsciously, whereas when we focus on ourselves as group members we tend to assimilate, again spontaneously and unconsciously.[27] That is, what is automatic depends on the immediate situation, and our groups provide important contexts. We are drawn to our groups partly because they provide models of our own possibilities. Hart Blanton and Diederik Stapel directly tested this idea by priming people's possible selves ("who I might become") versus their actual selves ("who I am"); the possible self allowed people to assimilate as well. They found that a possible self has flexible boundaries and that its shifting potentials are easily influenced by suggestions of someone else's fate, either good or bad.[28] In so many ways, judging ourselves inevitably activates other people as comparisons, in a process that is fast but flexible.[29]

Near Enough to Inspire

The focus here so far has been on prediction—on our need to locate ourselves, to self-evaluate. But what about the role of information in our need to go beyond mere prediction and to control our fates? The work on possible selves suggests that we can assimilate to a potential proxy, if our mind-set is open to considering our prospects. We use a proxy to imagine how we could get there from here.

Self-improvement—our efforts to control our position for the better—can thrive under upward comparison, if it is attainable.[30] In Penelope Lockwood and Ziva Kunda's research, undergraduates intending to pur-

Figure 4.4   Superstars Inspire Those Who Can Still Emulate Them

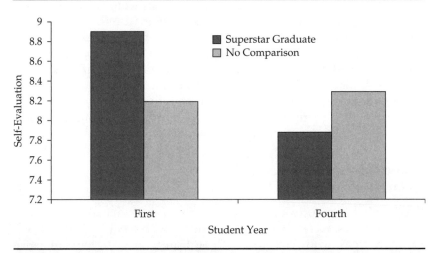

Source: Author's compilation based on data from Lockwood and Kunda (1997).
Note: Self-evaluations of first-year students are boosted by an inspiring graduate, but fourth-year students are discouraged because the level of performance is no longer attainable.

sue careers in accounting or teaching were inspired by a relevant role model who won an award, and they rated themselves higher as a result of merely reading about the award.[31] Attainability matters: first-year students were inspired by a superstar graduate, whereas fourth-year students were deflated because it was too late for them (see figure 4.4). Similarly, people who believe that intelligence is flexible are inspired by upward comparisons because they believe that success is controllable, but people who believe that intelligence is fixed are discouraged, presumably because they believe that success is not controllable.

A Comment on the Need to Know and Control

We make sense of ourselves by finding other people who are similar enough to us to be meaningful, expert enough to be right, handy enough to be fast, or near enough to inspire. All of these comparison tools make us sound supremely reasonable. Are we really that efficient and effective? As info-bots, we are in fact deeply flawed by the very strategies that usually make us good enough for everyday purposes. Being fast and frugal has its advantages on the fly, but its quality does not always hold up to closer scrutiny. Considering that we make sense of ourselves by recruiting information, assessing it, and comparing it, there is plenty of room for error.[32]

Generally, in seeking and using information, we know more about ourselves than we do about other people—and we know it better and faster. So information about ourselves is likely to carry more weight.[33] We also tend to focus on ourselves as the anchor in any comparison, so again, we loom larger than we should in our own comparisons. And when we compare ourselves to an abstract category (for instance, people in one's own profession), concrete information is hard to use—so once again, our own selves matter more. Lots of other glitches come into our comparison processes—for example, available attention, selective standards, differential confidence—and make us less than objective, and not even for any murky Freudian motives. We just process information about self in special ways because our selves are special to us.

When Groups Compare: Relative Deprivation

Even as we compare to others who are sufficiently similar, nearby, handy, and sometimes expert, individuals compare with other individuals, and groups compare with other groups. These distinctions go by the old-fangled terms "egoistic" and "fraternal."[34] Walter Garrison Runciman, Third Viscount Runciman of Doxford, professionally known as Garry or WG, noted the difference between feeling deprived on your own (so much better to be a full-fledged count than a mere viscount) and feeling deprived on behalf of your group (modern British nobility do not fare as well as the American nouveau riche). Although ordinary people certainly suffer when they feel individually deprived, that feeling, as we have seen, rarely drives their political and social action. We do not vote our wallets so much as our neighbors' wallets.[35] Mostly, of course, this conclusion applies to those of us who experience the relative deprivation that sometimes leads to working-class or disadvantaged group uprisings.

The idea of feeling deprived on behalf of your in-group (us) and against the out-group (them) first appeared in the peculiar findings of Samuel Stouffer and his colleagues on military morale during World War II.[36] Soldiers who were objectively better off (African Americans stationed in the North, or air corpsmen with a good chance of promotion) were less happy than those who were objectively worse off (African Americans stationed in the South, or military police with a poor chance of promotion). In each case, it was not the objective situation that made for unhappiness, but the relative comparison. Northern black soldiers felt worse off than local black citizens, but the situation was reversed for black soldiers in the South; air corpsmen got their hopes up for promotions, which never come as fast as hoped, whereas military police did not expect promotion. Also relatively deprived were less educated soldiers, married soldiers, and older soldiers, all of whom were more likely to feel that they should have been excused from service, as many of their peers had been, and so their sacrifice upon being drafted was unjust.[37] These comparisons were individually made, but collectively they all relied on similar, handy, nearby collective comparisons. So far, the messages from relative deprivation echo social comparison.

It's the Injustice That Really Gets to You

What the relative deprivation idea uniquely pinpoints is the reaction of groups to collective deprivation, which, experienced as injustice, predicts social movements. Individual and group experience differ a lot—for example, group-on-group interactions are more competitive and vicious than one-on-one interactions.[38] Feeling individually deprived (for example, being unemployed) may alert a person to feeling collectively deprived ("People like us are in trouble"); when this collective feeling leads to blaming out-groups (immigrants, rich elites, the party in power), the way is paved for collective action.[39] Action counts as collective when people feel they are acting on behalf of their group to improve its standing.[40]

The key to collective action is feeling that our own group is unjustly deprived, relative to other groups.[41] Heather Smith, Thomas Pettigrew, and their colleagues meta-analyzed 207 studies totaling 142,176 respondents. When people reported how they actually felt about the difference between "us" and "them" or indicated that their relative disadvantage was undeserved or unfair, it was these feelings—not the sheer difference—that predicted collective action. Frustrated, deprived groups may take unstructured or structured collective action and may approve political violence. For example, although Asian Americans made up only 4 percent of Philadelphia's population, they were 20 percent of the hate crime victims in 1988; non-Asians' feelings of anger, frustration, hostility, resentment, and threat most likely predicted this kind of group-based violence.[42] Besides violence against minorities, other collective action targets the dominant group (such as whites), which other groups (minorities), feeling frustrated and angry, often blame for their relative deprivation. Again, it is the feelings of injustice that drives people to support all of "us" sticking together and working as a group to change things for "our people."[43]

People's cognitive appraisals of the in-group's situation join with their deep caring about the group to produce these feelings of injustice. So, although information is necessary, it is the feelings that drive action. The important information, however, is not about the objective differences but the relative differences, derived from comparisons with other groups that seem most relevant.

Getting Down to Cases of Comparison

Love and work . . . work and love, that's all there is.

—Sigmund Freud[44]

We experience comparisons in the domains of our lives that matter most—namely, love and work. Not surprisingly, these areas preoccupy psychologists as well. The best arenas for this chapter's focus on how people get comparison information have been school and work; in both of these achievement domains, people need information to assess their standing, and knowledge is power. In other domains, such as health and home, people have other priorities, which the next chapters will address. Here, let's look at what should be relatively objective comparisons in achievement settings.

School

In my experience, one of the tragedies of college teaching is watching the freshman deflation. No matter the prestige of the college, new students will rank lower in college than they did in high school. At Princeton, not everyone who was a high school wunderkind can keep performing at the A+ level in college. At a state school that admits the top half of its applicants, not all incoming freshmen can be in the top half of their college classes. In mentoring my graduate students, my academic protégés, I feel sad that most of them will not get jobs as good as their graduate alma mater. They cannot, simply because there are not enough top-notch university jobs for all the graduates of the top-notch universities. There are not even enough academic jobs in general for all the would-be professors graduating with academic training. The numbers just do not add up, given the pyramid shape of any career progression. This merciless math of selectivity can deflate dreams and collapse confidence. It is hard for students not to take it personally when it happens as they move up the ladder, yet somehow most of them survive this change in status. The key is choice.

Students do suffer when they have been a big fish in a little pond and they move to a bigger pond where they become just another high achiever in a selective setting. In one of the most convincing demonstrations of this experience, the survey of more than 100,000 students in twenty-six countries described earlier, students in selective schools showed lower academic self-concepts than those in nonselective schools.[45] In defiance of reality, these students' ratings of their academic ability, skill, and interest—all of which should have been higher the more selective their school—reflected academic self-esteem that had suffered by comparison with other high achievers. This happened in part because the outliers, representing off-the-scale standards, were all right there, ready at hand for comparison. Like it or not, the comparisons that these students experienced were invidious.

But what about their role models? Students manage to aspire where they admire. Students who compare slightly upward, who observe a peer doing well, do in fact perform better. Admiring someone doing slightly better ought to discourage students, given all those depressed big fish, but it does not. Students who compare upward can improve their academic performance,[46] mainly when they are optimistic[47] and perceive that they have some control over their performance.[48] As a strategy for self-improvement, we can choose to compare ourselves to someone doing just a little better. The key lies not only in who we pick but in our deliberate decision to compare. An imposed comparison, as when the big fish moves to a bigger pond, is just depressing.[49]

To be sure, students are no fools. They acknowledge the meaning of tracking into high-achievement groups, and they recognize their own personal high achievement accordingly.[50] But their learning goals determine how they cope with relative comparisons. Students with interdependent selves can benefit from either upward or downward comparison. In contrast, those with isolated, independent selves are happy only in downward comparisons and vulnerable to being discouraged by upward comparisons.[51] Overall, students can use social comparison for inspiration, but mainly when they intentionally choose a possible-self role model for themselves. When role models are imposed on them by a high-achieving environment, especially if they already feel pessimistic and not in control, upward comparison can damage self-esteem as it begins to look more and more like envy of those who are doing better.

Work

In Dostoyevsky's *Notes from Underground,* the narrator describes his coworkers:

> Needless to say, I hated all the members of my department from the first to the last, and despised them, and yet somehow feared them as well. At times I would even rate them above myself. This quite often happened to me at that time; at one moment I despised them, at the next I felt they were superior to me.[52]

At work, as in the rest of life, we stumble into comparisons.[53] Modern organizational innovations can create unavoidable comparisons. For example, team-based pay makes coworkers confront each other's relative effort-reward ratio, leading to resentment of free-riders. The currently fashionable 360-appraisal, whereby everyone relentlessly evaluates everyone else, from above, below, and sideways, forces comparisons.

To judge our standing at work, we have to ask, "Compared to what?"[54] Pay is not the only issue. We compare ourselves with others at work on an array of factors:

- Procedural justice: being evaluated fairly ("Is my appraisal process equitable relative to my peers?")
- Interactional justice: being treated well ("Do I receive the respect that relevant others do?")

- Distributive justice: getting paid enough ("Are my pay and benefits comparable to the compensation of similar others?")

These comparisons lead us to conclusions that make us feel envy and scorn (among other emotions, but these are our focus here). Comparison can cause stress, depending on our perceptions of control, that is, whether our resources are adequate to the challenge.

In receiving performance appraisals from our supervisors (a stressful but common work experience), we unfortunately often deflect comparative feedback. Shown a model employee at work, we may deny the comparison by raising ourselves in our own eyes ("I'm not so different from Ms. Perfect") or lowering the other ("Mr. Wonderful is not as great as the boss thinks"). In a pinch, we may reject the comparison if the model is too far ahead or otherwise irrelevant ("Mr. Ideal is just an alien; he works all the time").

We delude ourselves despite the best efforts of HR specialists—even given the full treatment of a 360-appraisal, which ought to be harder to deflect. When we compare our own performance with that of a peer, our biases depend on how well we did ourselves.[55] If our own performance is exceptionally good or poor, this suggests that the performance of most other people will be less extreme—that is, more average—than ours. This much is rational. But we fail to take into account the possibility that we aced the task because it was easy, or blew it because it was hard, not because we ought to be taking extraordinary credit or blame. We tend to think that we are better than others even on easy tasks and worse than others even on hard ones. The net effect is that we are not always the best judge of our own performance—or of other people's, for that matter.

Even if we are not accurate in our judgments of ourselves and others at work, we still do it. Such judgments are major topics for water-cooler conversations. Envy at work (or jealousy of anyone favored by a supervisor) causes bad feelings; specifically, it lowers job self-esteem and feelings of control.[56] Envying is worse than being envied. Envy at work makes employees withdraw or aggress, either of which undermines the workplace.[57]

Employees cope with their envy at work by either engaging or disengaging, and both can be constructive or destructive.[58] For example, we can constructively engage our envy by trying to make ourselves more valuable or by praising the successful person. We can constructively disengage our envy by seeking support from friends and family or by affirming ourselves. On the more destructive side, we can engage our envy by interfering with or criticizing the successful person and even trying to provoke him or her into an emotional outburst at a meeting. Less devious, more disengaged, but also destructive strategies would include seeking solace in drugs, alcohol, or a new job.

How to Get the Best Information from Comparisons

To evaluate how you are doing, choose similar, relevant others who are handy enough to provide sufficient standards. Leon Festinger was right in saying that when we lack objective standards we seek subjective ones. Performance at work and school is all relative, so inevitably we compare ourselves to our proxies to know where we stand. This is not only a natural way to evaluate ourselves but a smart one.

To improve your performance, choose expert others who are knowledgeable but close enough to you to be informative. People who are too similar to you will not provide new information, but people with somewhat more experience or a slightly higher performance can teach you something. Avoid people who are too far away: they will not provide an obvious road map for how to get where they are from where you are.

Self-improvement is not just a matter of getting the right information. To some, it resembles the endless task of Sisyphus, forever pushing his rock uphill, only to have it roll back:

> Society is a long series of little uprising ridges, which, from the first to the last, offer no valley of repose. Wherever you take your stand, you are looked down upon by those above you, and reviled and pelted by those below you. Every creature you see is a farthing Sisyphus, pushing his little stone up some Liliputian molecule. This is our world![59]

All of us try to self-improve, and even someone as illustrious as Baron Henry Lytton Bulwer, Esquire, Member of Parliament, could feel looked down upon, as well as reviled and pelted from below. This chapter moved away from envy and scorn to focus on our "need to know" as the motivation for a lot of social comparison. But what about our need to control? Didn't this discussion show us that the human search engine can be a little biased? The next couple of chapters admit that we are not invariably so careful, and they take a look at our need to feel good about ourselves and our groups. Envy and scorn depend on what and who is at stake.

Conclusion

People need information to evaluate and control their fates, to handle the times when, as Alain de Botton put it, "the gap between my hopes for myself, and the reality of my life, start to diverge so painfully" (2004). Sometimes we cannot close the gap with information, so we become skillful at the mental gymnastics of protecting self-esteem (chapter 5) or take refuge in our most comfortable and familiar in-group (chapter 6). Comparison operates in accord with the dictates of both the rational mind and the emotional gut.

Chapter 5

Why Do We Compare?
Comparison Protects Us

I'm bored to extinction with Harrison.
His limericks and puns are embarrassing.
But I'm fond of the bum,
For, though dull as they come,
He makes me feel bright by comparison.
            —Anonymous, quoted in Greenberg,
            Ashton-James, and Ashkanasy (2007, 22)

S OMETIMES WE want to know where we stand, but sometimes we just want to feel "bright by comparison." Besides evaluating and perhaps improving ourselves, we would like to feel good.[1] Self-esteem is a less lofty goal than being informed, but we all need to feel good enough to get out of bed in the morning.

We are so oriented to the subjective that we often prefer it to the objective—but only if it makes us look good.[2] In Bill Klein's study showing this, undergraduates were asked to judge the quality of artworks. They learned that they had scored absolutely well or badly according to the objective standards set by professional artists. They also learned that they had scored subjectively well or badly compared with other undergraduates. Only their relative score affected how they felt about their aesthetic abilities and their choices to compete for a prize, confirming that most of us use the subjective, relative standing only if it makes us look good; otherwise, we pay no attention to it.

To be sure, people are no fools: if an objective situation is too extreme to ignore, their absolute standing does trump their subjective, comparative standing.[3] But still, self-enhancing is as natural as eating.[4] Americans and Europeans reliably feel that they are better than average, have more control over their lives, and are more optimistic about the future compared

94

with other people. Ironically, they also believe that they are less prone to errors of judgment in these matters than other people are.[5]

Motivated Maneuvers

We practice some Olympic-caliber emotional gymnastics to protect and promote our fragile selves. That is, we choose our comparisons—self now to self earlier, self to other—in ways that protect our self-esteem.

Oh, That Old Self

One strategy is self-comparison. We compare the new, improved self with our old, discarded self. As Anne Wilson and Michael Ross put it, we go "from chump to champ," at least in our own stories.[6] In one typical study, undergraduates described themselves at age sixteen and at their current age, then rated each statement as positive, negative, or neutral. (Observers agreed with their ratings.) Although positive self-descriptions won over negative and neutral ones for both past and present selves, the difference was exaggerated for the shiny new self compared with the tarnished old one. To avoid selective reporting, and to show that it can happen at any age, another group that included both students and middle-aged adults rated their past and present selves on a series of personality traits (socially skilled, self-confident, dull or boring, and dishonest). The same story of personal growth emerged.

Moreover, we do not tell such stories about our friends improving with age (see figure 5.1). I may have once been a jerk and a fool, but at least I improved with age, while you have stayed your same old lovable, flawed self. As far as each of us is concerned, our own old chump-self seems a distant memory.

For our autobiography, we imagine desired self-concepts.[7] Our motivation is limited by the facts available, so most of the time we are not totally making things up, as Ziva Kunda showed in her careful review.[8] Rather, we craft our history by locating, constructing, and valuing events to minimize the awkward and accentuate the flattering. The past is our personal historical fiction that gives a pleasing but plausible account of who we are.

For the self at center stage, the future looks lovely. We fully expect ourselves to go from winner now to even more wonderful ever after. Our cheery optimism about ourselves qualifies as a positive illusion.[9] Optimism motivates, persists, improves, and encourages, at least in the short run.[10] Of course, unrealistic optimism, fantasies, and downright narcissism are not helpful. Pleasant fantasies, for instance, allow unproductive daydreaming, whereas optimistic expectations motivate effort, which makes them a self-fulfilling prophecy, in Robert Merton's felicitous phrase.[11] In life domains as varied as pursuing a crush, acing an exam, seeking a job, or enduring hip replacement surgery, we do indeed do better when we concentrate on the

Figure 5.1   Past and Present Evaluation of Self and Acquaintance

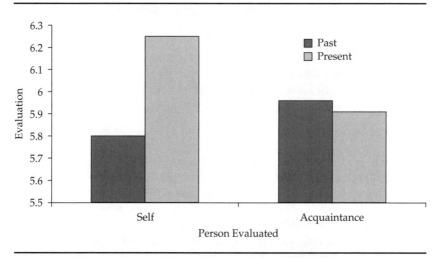

Source: Author's compilation based on data from Wilson and Ross (2001).
Note: Self-evaluation is negative for a past self, but more positive for the present self; evaluations of an acquaintance do not change with the time frame.

odds of doing well. Fantasies promote inaction, but high expectations motivate action.

The future self motivates us, and we value the future more than the past.[12] Self-esteem depends on the future self more than on the past self because the future is elastic, while the past is rigid.[13] In Neil Weinstein's classic study, Rutgers students reviewed forty-two positive and negative future events and estimated the comparative chance (relative to their same-gender classmates) that they would experience each of them.[14] They felt 50 percent more likely to enjoy their first job than other people, 44 percent more likely to own a home, and so on for the positive events, but even more, they felt immune to the negative events (alcoholism, suicide, divorce) relative to their classmates (see figure 5.2). They tended to focus on desirability and probability for the positive events: the more desirable and probable the goal, the more certain they were about their plans to achieve it for themselves. For the negative events, accordingly, they tended to focus on being preventable and stereotypic: the more these events were allegedly controllable and applicable only to certain victim types, the less participants had to worry for themselves. For example, if only losers are unemployed, then as a hardworking person, I am protected. Thus do we easily imagine all the personal factors that would make our future selves exceptions to the challenges faced by everyone.

Daniel Gilbert, Timothy Wilson, and their colleagues have amassed a mountain of evidence that we forecast our futures to be decidedly different from the shabby present.[15] Besides our hopeful prediction that good

Figure 5.2   Likelihood of Positive or Negative Events in the Lives of Self and Others

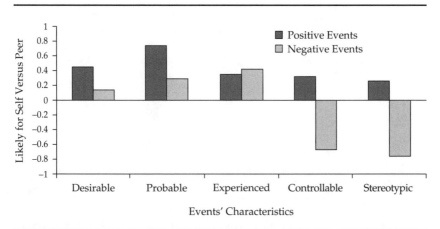

Source: Author's compilation based on data from Weinstein (1980).
Note: More desirable and probable positive events are seen as especially likely for self rather than for a peer. More controllable and stereotypic negative events are seen as more likely for a peer than for self. Personal experience of both positive and negative events makes them more likely for self.

events will prevail over bad ones, we expect more sheer drama than we get. That is, we expect our future windfalls to delight us more and our future tragedies to devastate us more than they actually do. We overestimate both the intensity and the duration of our emotional reactions to events. We do this mainly by focusing on the anticipated event and neglecting everything else that will be going on at the same time—that is, the simultaneous events that will tend to dampen the main event. If we break a bone, it will indeed be horrible, but our partner, our job, and our friends will distract us from the mishap. Also, we will cope better psychologically because we will adapt faster than we expect. We especially exaggerate the expected devastation that will be caused by negative events; in fact, most of us are more resilient than we would expect. In short, we adapt faster than we expect especially to misfortune.[16] Overall, when we compare our present self to our past self and our future self, we are motivated, more than the facts justify, and in spite of our admission that the past was cloudy, to forecast sunny if variable days ahead.

Triangulating on Me

Although we tend to compare our current self to our past or future selves—which gives a lot of leeway for constructing comparisons that favor the current self—sometimes we take a baby-step outside of ourselves to create a comparison fantasy. American teens are especially prone to compare themselves with their image of the kind of person they want to be, a form of

Figure 5.3   Self, Other, and Comparative Performance

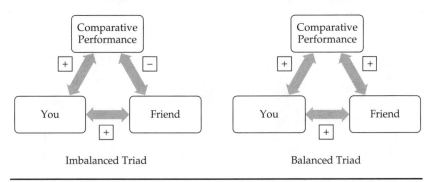

Imbalanced Triad   Balanced Triad

Source: Author's illustration.

upward social comparison, but using an abstract ideal instead of a real person.[17] They want to do what they imagine is the prototypical thing, whether it is smoking, drinking, reckless driving, or unsafe sex. Social comparison norms shape health habits, both good (exercise) and bad (smoking). People who socially compare a lot are especially prone to parrot the prototype. But this kind of comparison is of course entirely in the mind.

Comparison, like sex, is better as a social pursuit than a solitary one; we usually prefer an actual other to a fantasy other. Although our autobiographies reliably portray the growth of the main character, we seem to prefer stories with more than one character. Perhaps we are more likely to opt for solo self-scrutiny when no one else is available.[18] Admittedly, such scrutiny comes easily considering that our pathetic past selves especially enhance our near-perfect present selves because the old self cannot protest the comparison, and our even-better future selves do not have to prove themselves yet.

Having a more objective vantage point when we are outside observers of someone else, we view peers as a better basis for comparison than the same person over time.[19] For example, to judge another person's current absolute standing, would you rather know this person's rank relative to peers or whether his or her own performance had improved or deteriorated over time? Relative rank, of course. Exactly. Only the expressly social comparison influences objective observers because even striking change over time says nothing about where the person started, let alone landed. Despite the soothing ascent stories we tell ourselves in private, we would be wiser to rely on our peers as proxies.[20]

Moving out of the privacy of our own minds makes comparison complicated by creating a triangle, comprising self, other, and some area (see figure 5.3). For example, you may compare yourself with a friend on fitness. Whether up or down, the comparison is problematic for the friendship because it could result in reciprocal envy and scorn (left side of figure 5.3). Unless you and your friend are perfectly matched (right side of figure 5.3), one of you is going to feel bad and one of you is going to feel superior. Fritz Heider, a grandfather of social psychology, noted that such triangles comparing the lots of two people enhance or undermine the self-concept of each, with social fallout.[21]

One study illustrates this problem among 121 award-winning real estate agents in the United States from the Northwest and Southeast, compared with 118 of their randomly selected coworkers.[22] The coworkers reported their feelings, both external (irritated) and internal (embarrassment), in relation to the awardees. The award winners rated what, if anything, they did to cope with the threat they posed to their peers. And indeed, they reacted in self-protective ways. Award winners behaved more modestly when others resented them, mitigating a negative response that otherwise could damage social relations in the workplace. And the award winners avoided the topic if their coworkers felt embarrassed or ashamed, even though the coworkers' private misery was less likely to cost the awardees. Mere children know that it is not nice to brag. In any case, underperforming—the ultimate sacrifice to avoid bad feelings—was simply not an option for these real estate agents. Ultimately, they stayed focused on the business, tried to neutralize the award's impact, and did not take personally their coworkers' responses to them.

People do care about being stuck in a triangle—or in Julia Exline and Marci Lobel's apt acronym, STTUC (Sensitivity to being the Target of a Threatening Upward Comparison).[23] Thomas Powers put it well in a thought experiment:

> How would you tell an old friend that you understand why he is tongue-tied, that failure has sometimes infected your spirit too, but you like him anyway, and you don't care a damn whether he's done the vast things he wanted to do, that you sympathize with his disappointment and understand the shrinkage of his ambition? This would be such an affront, such a condescending insult, such an unmanning attack on a friend's effort to maintain his own dignity that it is (to me at any rate) unthinkable.[24]

Caring about the feelings of your discouraged friends requires a certain kind of empathy. To feel STTUC, you must be aware of being enviable, believe that this threatens another person, and feel concerned about the fallout.[25] The first part seems automatic: we have seen repeatedly that people know where they stand relative to others and cannot help but know when they are envied. And people are well aware of the politics of envy. But what does it take to feel concerned? We are built for empathy; our social survival depends on it. Empathic pain and guilt over another's suffering help to preserve relationships, reining in runaway self-interest. What is more, even the selfish want to avoid the burden of contagious distress, which is caught by experiencing someone else's pain.

Like the award-winning but modest real estate agents, we groom our image, if only to avoid potential resentment. Peer hostility is real. Malicious envy punishes the standouts with gossip, backlash, and revenge. High performers know this and often feel ambivalent about their awards. Psychologists used to call this feeling "fear of success," one explanation for which is the tension between getting ahead and getting along with others.[26]

Besides genuine fears for self and other as separate individuals, enviable people worry about their relationships. More than one academic superstar has recounted not wanting to share their success stories at home for fear of straining rapport or escalating conflict. At class reunions, most people do not start conversations by reciting their résumés, and not without reason: a swelled head ensures retaliation by or ostracism from work teams and friendship networks. Our cultural axioms record these tendencies: "Tall poppies get mowed down" . . . "Nails that stick up get hammered" . . . "Pride goeth before a fall" . . . "Putting on airs invites puncture." Moreover, cultural rituals enact these beliefs—for example, in an American celebrity roast. Under older Japanese business norms, a salaryman could disrespect his boss without consequence when both were drunk. In Hottentot traditional culture, the hunters could urinate on the most successful.[27] American summer camps symbolically do the same in a skit that mocks counselors (preferably in late August). Social comparison creates interpersonal tensions that high achievers manage as best they can. People get STTUC on the upside. Being one-up is not all it is cracked up to be. Here are some of the likely concerns and emotional reactions of the STUCC person.

My Concern About Being STUCC	So I May Feel
I am responsible for your distress	Guilty
I identify with your distress	Sad, anxious
I should manage your feelings	Anxious
I can't help you	Anxious, frustrated
You might be hostile	Afraid, angry
I will look bad	Embarrassed, anxious
People will reject me	Ashamed, afraid, sad
Our relationship will be damaged	Anxious, sad, dissatisfied[28]

Envy Cries, "Foul!"

People also get caught being one-down. When we find ourselves looking up from the bottom side of social comparison, our envy mixes with resentment and shame.[29] Living on the downside makes us see the injustice of our situation, but we also experience shame at our possible collusion in it. The shame of envy can paralyze us, but the anger of envy can energize us, as we have seen. Although paralyzing resignation doubtless occurs on the downside of envy, most evidence points to active hostility as the more common reaction.

We feel hostile, malicious envy mainly when the stakes are high—namely, when someone else beats us at our own game, in something important to our self-definition.[30] Otherwise, why bother? We protect ourselves against threats when it matters to us. The father of psychological science, William James, famously mused that he was content to be outdone in an irrelevant domain, but not in his own field:

> I, who for the time have staked my all on being a psychologist, am mortified if others know much more psychology than I. But I am contented to wallow in the grossest ignorance of Greek. My deficiencies there give me no sense of personal humiliation at all. . . . With no attempt there can be no failure; with no failure no humiliation. So our self-feeling in this world depends entirely on what we *back* ourselves to be and do.[31]

Self-relevant failure rallies us to protect ourselves by shifting the standards—for example, we may shift from comparing ourselves with superior others to comparing ourselves with an earlier, less adequate self. Even if forced to compare with others, we may act on our disappointment by lowering our standards, no longer comparing so much, or even changing domains: academics suddenly matter less, for instance, and athletics suddenly matter more.[32] Who wants those sour grapes anyway? Our motivation to repair our self-esteem can even make us perform better in the alternative domain. The athlete may run faster after a failure in the classroom.

One way to disengage from envy's bitter pill is to decide that the winner is an alien; not even on the same planet, that person is obviously not relevant for social comparison. Deciding that the winner is a genius works just as well.[33] In Mark Alicke's lab, participating students who took a difficult perceptual intelligence test scored only about 30 percent but learned that another student had scored 70 percent. Naturally, they viewed that person as more perceptually intelligent than themselves. More important, compared with neutral observers, they even exaggerated that student's skill (see figure 5.4). This judgment made them respect themselves more than did a control group who never had a chance to rate the "genius." Unable to dismiss the high scorer's relevance, the control group could not repair their self-respect.

The opposite of dismissing someone is to merge with that person. Envy can transmute into inspiration. A superstar becomes a role model if two conditions are met. First, we must believe that we have the opportunity to follow the person's success, and second, we must believe that talent can grow, that it is not fixed.[34] When we hope to resemble someone better off, the upward comparison is inspiring.[35] We mostly compare at the same level or slightly above, so all these processes are common. Altogether, the social comparison victim uses several strategies to cope.

Scorn Cries, "No Harm, No Foul!"

So far, to understand how we defend our fragile selves, this chapter has looked at the fears of the better-off that the worse-off will envy their good fortune, as well as the types of envy that the worse-off do and do not feel.

Figure 5.4   Exaggerating the Superior's Ability Allows Self-Respect

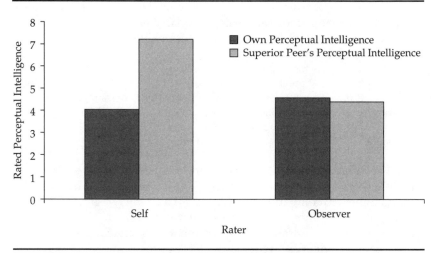

Source: Author's compilation based on data from Alicke et al. (1997).
Note: Compared with observer ratings, participants exaggerated the perceptual ability of a peer who outperformed them. As the text explains, having explained their lack of perceptual intelligence, people then rated themselves higher on *general* intelligence than did a control group not given that opportunity.

Now we come full circle to the better-off looking down with scorn on the worse-off. Thomas Wills has proposed that when our well-being declines, we do precisely this, in order to feel superior.[36] Human behaviors from aggression to scapegoating to prejudice to humor all feature downward comparison.

Common sense suggests that scorn is the privilege of those who securely inhabit the top of the heap, but research suggests otherwise. Those who are sliding down the heap are more likely to make downward comparisons in an effort to arrest their descent. Frederick Gibbons, Meg Gerrard, and their colleagues have examined downward comparison in the classroom (see figure 5.5). They find that students who perform poorly try to protect themselves from the implications of their failure by lowering their standards and expressing a preference for downward comparison over upward aspiration.[37]

People who are feeling low (depressed, low self-esteem, bad mood) can especially benefit from downward comparison.[38] Downward comparison reduces regret, for example, among older people.[39] Considering "what might have been" also improves mood and motivates us to try again, if we can.[40] In these ways, downward comparison can encourage some of us, some of the time.[41]

To be sure, downward comparison can also be a bummer. Our worse-off peers could be possible selves, so feeling vulnerable to their fate can

**Figure 5.5   Interest in Downward or Upward Comparison Depends on
One's Own Performance**

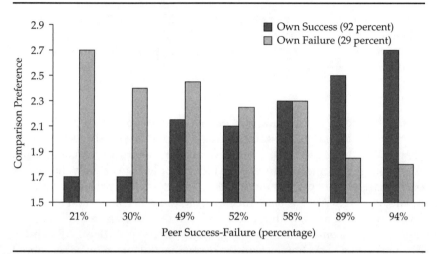

Source: Author's compilation based on data from Gibbons et al. (2002).
Note: Success seeks upward comparison; failure seeks downward comparison.

deflate our own self-esteem (although it may also engage prevention strategies).[42] With low self-esteem spiraling out of control, a downward comparison can have negative implications for us.[43] Also, sheer emotional contagion can make downward comparison depressing, if the peer seems similar to self.[44]

The point here, however, is that the people at the top do not derogate others nearly as much as those who are trying to distance themselves from the heap into which they fear falling. Downward comparison is at best a short-term coping process, not a long-term strategy.[45] Better long-term strategies maintain optimism, feelings of control, and adequate self-esteem. These strategies, in turn, encourage us to cope actively, seeking support from friends and family and not avoiding the issues.[46] These personally oriented strategies rely less on social comparison—which typically preoccupies people with vulnerable self-esteem—and more on personal standards, which aid self-improvement as well as self-enhancement.[47]

To go back to the section title, scorn's "no harm, no foul" happens in two ways. True scorn (self-protective downward comparison) says, "If I am feeling threatened, I am doing this to help myself, not harm you, so why do you care?" Neglect scorn (simple inattention) says, "No offense, but I've got my own work to do, and I am not actually busy looking down on you, so relax." Either way, personal scorn may be less of an issue than worse-off friends fear it is.

Defensive Comparison Close to Home

Viewed as merely a way of gaining information, as in the prior chapter, social comparison is most obvious at work and at school. Defensive social comparison, the fount of envy and scorn, appears in more personal domains: our bodies, our health, and our relationships.

The Gym

A full 80 percent of American college women are dissatisfied with their bodies.[48] According to 170 studies, comparison is the culprit. As we saw in chapter 3, women compare their appearance to others more than men do. Also, younger people do it more than older people do. Normally the targets of comparison are similar enough to be relevant—that is, people of the same gender and age. We compare our bodies to those of friends and strangers and to media images, with the same ill effects. Comparing our bodies to more attractive ones makes us dissatisfied with our own bodies. By "body dissatisfaction," psychologists mean dysfunctional, negative beliefs about the body, not just ordinary monitoring of weight, exercise, and calories.

People are more likely to compare their bodies with others if they read a lot of magazines and are depressed.[49] And these conditions are especially likely to make women feel dissatisfied with their bodies. A study by Debra Trampe, Diederik Stapel, and Frans Siero shows how this happens in both directions.[50] Women who are dissatisfied with their bodies are more self-evaluative in the first place, so they tend to compare their bodies along with everything else. Because they are so primed to compare, body-dissatisfied women are negatively affected not only by exposure to attractive women—even if they are fashion models and so perhaps less relevant—but also by exposure to a fat (versus thin) vase (figure 5.6).

Because body-dissatisfied women do differ in other ways, in another study the researchers came at the issue by making some women dissatisfied, rather than relying on naturally occurring individual differences. Undergraduates had to write an essay using the words "I," "attractive," "beautiful," and "thin" (or "I," "unattractive," "ugly," and "fat"). Next, in an apparently unrelated exercise, they were shown a fat or thin vase. And finally, they were asked to rate their own attractiveness and satisfaction as well as the beauty of the vase. The experimentally dissatisfied women responded the same way as the temperamentally dissatisfied women. When dissatisfied with their bodies, for whatever reason, even a chunky vase reminded women of how fat they felt. Though men may not find vases this relevant (inverted triangles, maybe?), they are not immune to the discouraging effects of seeing perfect physical specimens.[51]

Of course, we compare both up and down, even at the gym. Seeing someone more out of shape than we are makes us feel better.[52] Also, when

Figure 5.6   Body Satisfaction in the Presence of Fat or Thin Vases

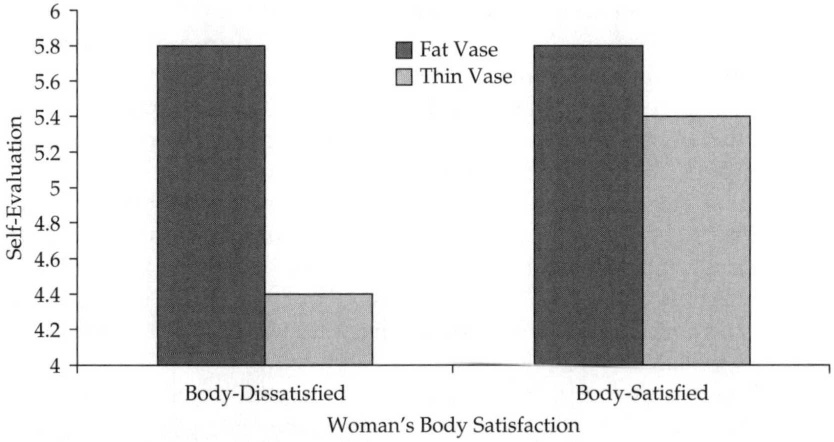

Source: Author's compilation based on data from Trampe, Stapel, and Siero (2007).
Note: Individual body dissatisfaction makes even a thin vase depress self-evaluations.

women consider a fashion model on non-appearance dimensions (such as brains and personality), suddenly she does not seem so intimidating, and with that in mind, they report feeling better even about their own bodies.[53]

The Hospital

The ultimate body comparison involves survival. People who are severely ill compare both up and down because each direction provides potential protection. People can imagine themselves as better off than the worst-case scenario of their illness, and healthier people inspire best-case scenarios.[54] Patients seem to prefer comparing themselves to whoever has the most information, notably someone whose treatment is a little more advanced. For example, someone about to go into surgery can get information from a postoperative patient who has recently undergone the same procedure.[55]

Of course, coping is not just about seeking the best information. In matters of life and death, a reasonable sense of optimism and control, even if illusory, helps people cope with cancer, HIV/AIDS, heart disease, and other ruinous diagnoses. In Shelley Taylor's pathbreaking research interviews with breast cancer patients, the women proved both remarkably resilient and remarkably unrealistic. They believed that their cancer was under control (either their own control or their doctors') even as the illness progressed, and they selectively compared themselves to women even worse off. Both strategies helped them cope, and their illusions did not damage their adaptation.[56] Squarely facing all the facts seemed to confer fewer benefits than maintaining a rosy illusion. Illusory control reduced anxiety and depression.[57]

Illusions also benefit physical health.[58] In particular, optimism predicts immune response, and even unrealistic optimism protects health.[59] Relatedly, finding meaning in illness can slow disease progression as people compare their past self with their present and future selves. The acutely ill frequently report that their diagnoses set their priorities straight, making them cherish their closest relationships, appreciate their advantages, and value each day for itself. Several physical health benefits result from such realizations. Emotional well-being improves immune function and reduces other medical complications. Hope and calm raise the odds of maintaining healthy habits, and pleasant, upbeat attitudes attract support from friends and family. (Misery may love company, but company does not love misery.)

As Glenn Affleck and Howard Tennen's research program shows, the health benefits of meaning-making endure as long as eight years later in cardiac patients.[60] Seven weeks after their heart attack, a slight majority of men reported that the heart event had produced some benefits, such as better health habits, a change in lifestyle that had increased their enjoyment of life, and the development of personal or spiritual values. Those men who rearranged their priorities to produce these benefits in the first weeks then looked better eight years later. As it turned out, not just any meaning-making would do: men who blamed their heart attack on stress or on someone else did not do well. External control (blame) is not helpful, but internal control is.[61] Certain kinds of feeling in control—specifically, over one's medical care and treatment—also benefit those suffering from another chronic condition—arthritis.[62] Coping emotionally pays off not only for mental health but also for physical health.[63]

The health benefits spill over even to our close friends and family. Parents whose at-risk newborns must spend time in a neonatal intensive care unit nevertheless often find benefits in the experience. If they have positive expectations and find meaning in the experience, their child is better off eighteen months later, by both well-being and developmental measures.[64] Long-term adjustment, even to permanent conditions such as spinal cord injury, correlates with satisfying social relationships and reported well-being, which are often comparable to the relationships and well-being reported by uninjured people of the same age.[65] A sense of personal control is key here as well.

Ronnie Janoff-Bulman wisely notes that our assumptions about the world are shattered by trauma.[66] Most of us believe that the world is generally meaningful and benevolent and that we ourselves are worthy. Random injury and unexpected illness endanger those ground rules. Our psychological work as victims of these events requires that we rebuild our positive assumptions. To survive and thrive, we need to believe that the world is somewhat predictable and controllable, that we ourselves are basically good, and that we are securely attached in our relationships.

Home and Heart

In the adversity of our best friends we always find something that is not displeasing.
— La Rochefoucauld, *Réflexions* (1665)[67]

Every time a friend succeeds, I die a little.
— Attributed to Gore Vidal[68]

We need our relationships, and we like to think that we are big enough to celebrate the successes of our friends and partners, but human nature interferes with the best ideals. Envy and scorn especially plague us when we are already downhearted. And when we are insecure in ourselves or in our relationships, we make ourselves more miserable by making intimate comparisons. As we have seen repeatedly, people who are unhappy or suffering from low self-esteem are more likely to seek comparison—downward comparison in particular. This does not bode well for relationships, but the plight is not hopeless.

Competition in the service of self-esteem does make for miserable friendships, especially among college men.[69] Interviewed about the meaning of friendship, students described their closest friendship and how much they competed with their friends in games, grades, arguments, and in general. Students competed less as they progressed through school, but more as their roles expanded (for example, to include not just being friends but also sharing activities, teams, classes, a dorm room). Competition created conflict that undermined friendship, whereas their opposites—intimacy and companionship—strengthened friendship.

How do we manage—or fail to manage—relationships that are caught in the bind of unequal comparison? Although we naturally compare with others, Fritz Heider observed that "envy is not a necessary consequence of the inequality of the fortunes of people who are close."[70] Go back to Heider's triangles to understand how this works. Every comparison includes self, other, and some arena, with links—three in all—from each to each (see figure 5.3). Each link changes the meaning of the overall comparison.

As Abraham Tesser has explained, in any relationship where partners' interests overlap (and how else do we get together?), each still has self-esteem to maintain.[71] We react not only to our own outcomes but also to each other's outcomes. For any given triangle (you, your partner, and your overlapping interests), the comparisons matter more if they are relevant and the relationship is close. For starters, self and other can be more or less close: closeness magnifies the effects of comparison. Who cares

Figure 5.7   Three Responses to Comparison Threat in a Relationship

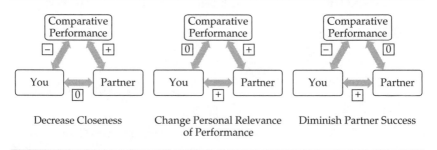

Source: Author's illustration.

about the accomplishments of some stranger in the street? The accomplishments of our near and dear, however, pressure us to react. To escape the tension, we could dissolve the relationship (see left side of figure 5.7). Although we are reluctant to discontinue our relationships over unequal successes, sometimes we choose our friends to be nonthreatening in self-defining domains.[72]

Second, how we respond depends on the personal relevance of the particular arena. The more relevant the domain is for us, the more magnified the comparison: I may not care about our relative ability to hurl a curling stone, but I will care deeply about our relative ability to write a book on envy and scorn. We maneuver the emotional minefields created by comparison primarily by changing how we interpret the self-relevance of other people's accomplishments (see middle panel of figure 5.7). For example, if you and your friend are both ice-fishing aficionados, you could admit that your partner finds more fish than you do, but claim that you get better results from studying their habits when dormant. (Depending on your relative accomplishments as ice fishers, you might be well advised to adjust the self-relevance of hooking hibernating fish in February.)[73]

Finally, we can diminish our partner's success in the domain (see right side of figure 5.7). Some of us will even sabotage the performance of a close friend if the task is really self-relevant. In one classic Tesser study, students participated in a word identification task with friends and strangers. When the task was framed as measuring important skills (rather than presented as a game), students apparently interpreted the task as more self-relevant. Given the opportunity to provide clues to others, they gave harder clues to their friends than to strangers for the most personally relevant tasks. When the task was not personally relevant, they helped their friends more than the strangers.[74] Similarly, students sometimes provided helpful hints to their friends, to improve their grades, but they reported doing this less for familiar than for unfamiliar others.[75]

Depending on the importance of the relationship and the domain, emotions may run high.[76] On a low-relevance task, we can afford to be generous and are actually pleased when our friend outperforms us, but not when a stranger does. On a high-relevance task, we are more self-protective and happier when we beat a friend than a stranger.[77]

To be sure, we do not always compare: we can also be proud of those close to us ("my friend the Olympic curler") as long as the domain is irrelevant. As with comparison, we are most likely to appreciate reflected glory in domains that are personally irrelevant. As Robert Cialdini and his colleagues have shown, we bask in the reflected glory of accomplished close friends and family, but our basking diminishes as closeness and success diminish.[78] We cannot brag as much about a distant cousin as about a sibling, and we cannot brag at all about a loser.

Married couples can overcome comparison and bask in their partner's successes, even when they are self-relevant, owing to the empathy and shared future assumed by the marital state.[79] In one particularly poignant study, each participant was given a device that beeped six times at two- to three-hour intervals each day for two weeks. In this experience-sampling method, participants reported any spousal comparison they had made since the last report. (They had to be well paid for their participation.) In their accounts of their everyday comparisons with their partners, participants reported feeling good when their partner outperformed them, even in personally relevant domains. When they reported that their identity included their partner and that they felt like a unit together, they were more likely to bask in their partner's success than to suffer by comparison. In other studies from Penelope Lockwood's group, the closer the participants, the more they coped with awkward comparisons by affirming their own strengths that were relevant to the relationship.[80] In other words, they felt better by valuing themselves as a warm, caring, affectionate partner. This strategy is not available to spouses who are less close. Affirming your own strengths eliminates the need to distance yourself from the relationship or from the performance domain.[81]

Some partners actively empathize and try to accommodate each other's egos, attending to the inevitable reflections and comparisons. This bodes well for a marriage.[82] Indeed, a partner outperforming the other inevitably worsens the rifts and the avoidance in a troubled relationship, but increases empathy and appeasement in a healthy one.[83]

Marriages also work well when couples divide up the expertise. Couples show less negativity when they balance each other by excelling in domains relevant to themselves but irrelevant to their partners, complementing each other's strengths.[84]

People protect their marriages when they are threatened by social comparison in ways similar to how they protect themselves when they look individually bad by comparison in any other circumstances. Just as we feel better by seeing ourselves as improving over time, couples see their relationship as better than it used to be. In unsatisfying relationships, the partners tell themselves that things have been improving lately.[85] But when marital problems are severe and the chips are down, Nancy Frye and Benjamin Karney find, people protect their marriage by seeing improvement where there is in fact none.[86]

Couples also protect their marriage by seeing it as better than the marriages of other people—that is, by downward comparison.[87] They use this strategy when they can, and they are often accurate about their relative standing. Even in Asian cultures, where people are relatively modest about their personal successes, people view their close relationships (with friends, family, and partners) as better than other people's.[88] In this strategy, we can connect with close others by admiring them. When we are dissatisfied and uncertain about our relationships, we also may seek upward comparisons to learn from those doing better, especially if we are gregarious types.[89] Looking down on other couples can make us miserable if our own doubts and uncertainty make us wonder whether we could suffer an even worse fate.[90]

How to Control Comparisons

On hearing about her college classmate's "moment of fame . . . her friend experienced what she described to me as part jealousy, and part self-contempt because she had done so little herself."
—Thomas Powers, "Can Friendship Survive Success?" (1972)

Everyone on both sides of toxic comparisons dreads those moments of envy and scorn that threaten our own or another's integrity. But we can get past our defensive comparisons.

Strategies for the Envied

Let's take envy first, since psychologists have worried about it more.[91] Viewed through a self-protective lens, how does an enviable person avoid malicious envy ("I want you not to have what you have")? Let's move from the least to the most constructive responses.

For the envied, being clueless is one option that prevents the painful awareness of being envied; this response probably works in the short run, but not over the long term. Powerful people who choose to look the other way risk neglecting their subordinates as they focus on their own goals, so they may not notice all the resentment simmering around them.[92] Indeed, the envied may think that their subordinates worship them. Magical thinking runs eventually, however, into reality.

The enviable in many cultures downplay their success, concealing it or denying it.[93] Women with a fear of success sometimes worry that success would undermine the possibility of finding a close heterosexual relationship, and women are also more likely to worry about others envying them (to feel STUCC). So people trying to avoid the glares of the envious may hide their light under a bushel.

Taking the moral high ground might also work for the envied. The envied one can claim innocence ("I lucked out"), conspiracy ("My friends arranged it"), or legitimacy ("Fair fight—I don't make the rules"). In any of these ways, the envied person aims to show that his or her success was not intended to destroy the loser, who merely suffers collateral damage. This strategy may absolve the successful self, but it does not repair the feelings of the slighted. Besides, discounting responsibility for one's own success undermines justifiable pride.

Turning malicious envy ("You shouldn't have it") into benign envy ("How can I get it too?") is a more plausible strategy, although in attempting to inspire the downhearted ("You, too, can succeed"), the envied person could end up delivering a condescending insult. Still, as the last chapter showed, most of us are motivated to compare slightly upward, in the service of self-improvement, and so the envied person can try to persuade the envier to switch from a social comparison (you versus me) to a temporal comparison (your current self versus your future self).

Affirming the other is probably the most effective strategy, if it is sincere. Someone suffering by comparison can learn to accept that feedback after having a positive self-concept affirmed in another domain.[94] People who are told that they have tested high on social skills and ambition then readily admit that an extremely attractive peer is in fact more attractive than they are. Because people can also control their own defensive responses by affirming themselves as a good and worthy person, perhaps the envied can mimic this by affirming the envier's value.[95]

Our perceptions of our relative standing are easier to shift when rank is subjective. Convincing someone that success is in the eye of the beholder is easier in a beauty contest than in a footrace, easier in lifestyle matters than in salary or GPA. Nevertheless, this is another workable strategy if it does not come across as manipulative or condescending.

Also open to interpretation is self-relevance. How much a comparison hits home depends on how much the envier cares. We can change some identities more readily than others. A lifelong career choice is harder to deny than a casual hobby.

Probably the most effective way to defuse envy is to become one with the other. If self and the enviable other overlap, the comparison evaporates. Close relationships researchers Art and Elaine Aron and their colleagues show that relationships thrive when people incorporate the other into the self.[96] Overlapping the self with the other also facilitates empathy, of both the cognitive sort (understanding the other's pain) and the emotional sort (feeling the other's pain).

But we cannot merge with everyone. Simply trying to be likable as well as enviable undercuts the competition and encourages mutual cooperation.

Sharing, as in holding a fiesta to spread the wealth, eases the tension. Claiming, as one award-winner did, that the individual recognition is "good for our tribe" places self and other on the same side, a topic for the next chapter.

Strategies for the Scorned

Before leaving defense mechanisms, let's defend the loser: how do we avoid being scorned? Magical thinking is the subject of story and song, as Bertolt Brecht's Pirate Jenny knew:

> You people can watch while I'm scrubbing these floors
>
> And I'm scrubbin' the floors while you're gawking
>
> Maybe once ya tip me and it makes ya feel swell
>
> In this crummy Southern town, in this crummy old hotel
>
> But you'll never guess to who you're talkin'.
>
> No. You couldn't ever guess to who you're talkin'.
>
> . . .
>
> There's a ship, the black freighter with a skull on its masthead will be coming in.
>
> . . .
>
> By noontime the dock is a-swarmin' with men comin' out from the ghostly freighter
>
> They move in the shadows where no one can see
>
> And they're chainin' up people and they're bringin' 'em to me
>
> askin' me, "Kill them NOW, or LATER?" Askin' ME! "Kill them now, or later?"
>
> Noon by the clock and so still by the dock
>
> You can hear a foghorn miles away
>
> And in that quiet of death I'll say, "Right now. Right now!"
>
> Then they'll pile up the bodies
>
> And I'll say, "That'll learn ya!"[97]

Magical thinking is one satisfying option, but it is ineffective in the long run. Revenge fantasies, daydreams of success, controlling the rich people's fate—all make for good song lyrics, but weak coping in the long run. And magical thinking is best suited to the envious who already feel scorned.[98]

When we are in danger of being scorned, we can capitalize on empathy and try to persuade the scornful to sympathize with our lesser status and to help us as a result. Edward Jones and Thane Pittman call this underappreciated strategy *supplication*.[99] It requires portraying oneself as weak—a move we could call strategic incompetence ("Won't you just move that little ol' grand piano for me?" "I have no idea how the dishwasher works. You're so much better at loading it.") The downside of this strategy is being seen as manipulative or in fact useless. But the upside is sympathy.

Self-promotion is another Jones-Pittman strategy for self-presentation, but in this case the goal is perceived competence, despite any apparent failures ("Let me tell you about the time I won an award like that . . . "). The downside is the risk of being seen as an arrogant narcissist. If it works, however, the upside is that it readjusts the attitude of the scornful.

The one-down person can also strive for the moral high ground, a strategy termed *exemplification* but perhaps better termed *self-sanctification*. By shifting the dimensions of comparison, the holier-than-thou can gain ground, but they do risk seeming insincere or phony.

However vexing a problem it might be to avoid being scorned, one puzzle nonetheless remains: how does scorn ("please go away") fit with downward comparison ("your lesser status makes me feel better")? The next chapter takes us to group-on-group encounters, where scorn can make us feel good, even as we send the scorned away.

Conclusion

We compare partly to protect our fragile selves. Most of us compare our flawed past self to our new improved present self. Some of us maintain relationships by being sensitive to how we threaten others with our superior accomplishment. We change our own envy to inspiration, we shift our standards, and we use downward comparison to emphasize how much worse it could be. These are the self-protective mental gymnastics we practice with our comparisons, both up and down, to maintain our health and our homes.

Chapter 6

Why Do We Compare?
Comparison Helps Us
Fit into Our Groups

Man is by nature a social animal; and an unsocial person who is unsocial
naturally. . . . is either unsatisfactory or superhuman.
—Aristotle, *Politics* (1253a)

A RISTOTLE WAS among the first to tell us that we are profoundly collective beings. We prefer to be included: "We'd love you to join
us" may be one of the most compelling human appeals. As chapter 3 noted, we have good adaptive reasons to be with others: we survive
and thrive better if we are social than if we are isolates. Exclusion literally
pains us, so to avoid being shunned, we aim to fit in with our own in-
groups.[1] Comparison facilitates our belonging because it shows us where
we stand both within our groups and where our groups stand relative to
other groups. Comparison between groups can be especially vicious, so
envy and scorn between groups can be correspondingly brutal, as examples in this chapter will show. As group members, our first loyalty lies
with our own group because we need it so much.

We may want to be individually distinctive, but not at the price
of sacrificing membership in at least one worthwhile group that will have
us, so we go along to get along.[2] Our attunement with our own groups
shows up in social contagion of all kinds, most immediately in emotions
and perceptions.[3] We imitate each other's nonverbal behavior.[4] Especially
if anxious, we copy each other's facial expressions and emotions.[5] In fact,
we unconsciously mimic even politicians' facial expressions on television,
which explains the electoral success of more than one warm, expressive,
incompetent doofus.[6] Not just our emotional contagion but our conformity to our groups is legion. We will even distort the evidence before our
eyes, objective perceptual judgments, to fit in with a group.[7]

Figure 6.1   A Chain of Health Comparisons, Part of a Network of Norms

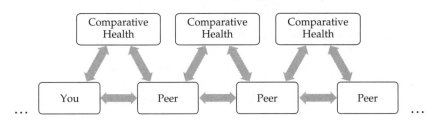

Source: Author's illustration.

Conformity also shapes life-or-death decisions and outcomes, including those that affect our health. For example, binge-eating spreads through
sororities: sorority sisters compare themselves with each other to gauge
just the "right" amount of bingeing that correlates with popularity.[8]
Networks spread health habits and health standards across three degrees
of separation; the obesity of your friend's friend's friend correlates with
your own.[9] In the decades-long Framingham Heart Study, investigators
asked participants to nominate someone who would know how to reach
them if they moved. Their nominations, the nominations of their nominees, and so on down the line, created networks of health influences.
Perhaps it is not surprising that as your best friend gains weight, you feel
permission to add a few pounds yourself. But your friend's friend's friend,
whom you may not even know? Other people in our network form the
most relevant comparisons, which set standards for our health habits.

Though social scientists believe that we are indeed fundamentally social
beings, they are not totally sure how this network of contagion happens.
Social support by family does not explain the spread of conformity because
networks extend well beyond family. Indeed, friends increase a person's
odds of becoming obese by 57 percent, even more than do spouses and siblings (about 40 percent each). Merely observing your fat neighbor on his
riding mower or your skinny neighbor out running does not explain social
contagion, because neighbors do not necessarily make neighbors fat.

Rather, "the strength of weak ties" probably operates through trusted
but indirect connections, communicating ideas, information, norms, and
influence across social distances.[10] Remember the social triangles—linking
you, me, and some shared experience—from chapter 5. Now imagine a
chain of triangles. The series of weak ties extends beyond tight social
groups to strings of acquaintances, creating a sense of what is normal (see
figure 6.1).

Network norms guide health habits such as smoking, drinking,
weight-watching, food preferences, and cancer screening. Health networks probably also radiate stress, mood, self-esteem, and self-efficacy,

and these psychological states make health habits contagious too.[11] Networks serve many functions—supporting, influencing, engaging, providing—so it is no wonder that social belonging affects our choices. Networks influence even fraternity membership (arguably a health hazard but also a support system): randomly assigned roommates and even dorm-mates influence college men's decision to pledge.[12] Belonging in a loose network causes us to belong to close groups. Networks cause conformity, as we compare ourselves with others and try to fit in with those who matter to us.

The Need to Belong—Just to Be Me

The "sociometer" is not the latest science-fantasy golden compass, but Mark Leary's invention to explain how groups shape our self-esteem.[13] Our sense of worth depends on our social acceptance: if our group helps us survive and thrive, we need to gauge how securely we belong to the group, and self-esteem may serve this function ("I feel bad about myself—have I offended someone?"). Study after study shows that our self-esteem closely tracks feeling included or excluded. Randomly assigned ostracism makes us miserable, even when we know that the meanie was just a computer programmed to exclude us.[14] We are defined by belonging, so good standing in a group ranks as a fundamental human need.[15] To be ourselves, we must identify with some groups. Our intense need to know where we stand within our groups sets the stage for envy and scorn, which are mitigated by shared membership and group norms.

What is more, our quest to understand and value ourselves as social beings benefits our groups. Self-knowledge develops through the groups we join. We know ourselves because we associate with certain groups, play some special roles, feel effective in specific group activities, and sustain certain social commitments.[16] All of this individual involvement strengthens group cohesion and coordination because groups need to claim committed, differentiated, cooperative members within their bounds in order to persist and to benefit those members. Group belonging provides information about our identity.

Groups and their members do not benefit from knowledge alone. When we enhance ourselves through in-group pride, this also strengthens the group. We respond to personal injury by devaluing out-groups (thereby elevating ourselves and, indirectly, the in-group). In an illustrative study by Steven Spencer, Steven Fein, and their colleagues, undergraduates at Williams College learned that they had performed poorly on an intelligence test, a sure self-esteem threat to these elite students.[17] In an allegedly separate study, they read about Greg the actor, who was implied to be either gay or straight. After experiencing the self-image threat, the students rated gay Greg as stereotypically gay. They did not derogate him without the self-image threat; when they were feeling affirmed rather than threatened, they stereotyped less. Under threat, putting down an out-group improved damaged self-esteem, and the students seemed to do it spontaneously.

Prejudice maintains self-image by allowing us to ally ourselves with an in-group that seems better by comparison.[18] We are especially likely to reaffirm our in-group belonging when we experience a specific threat of social exclusion (someone saying, "you can't join us"), not just any generic threat to self-esteem ("you're stupid").[19] In this case, in-group comparisons are muted and the out-group becomes an envied or scorned scapegoat.

How Do We Know Me?
Let Us Count the Ways

Whether we understand ourselves as individuals or whether we understand ourselves as group members determines how we go about comparing up and down. As an individual, we prefer to compare within our in-groups, because it is our peers who are most relevant and similar to us, as this chapter will explain. As we will also see, group-to-group comparisons are a whole different game, so by and large they are more vicious. Let's begin by considering the immediate impact on the comparison game of self-construal as an individual versus a group member.

All that is needed to prime an individual "I" or a group "we" is to get people to word-search a text for the relevant pronouns.[20] Then trigger comparison up or down by giving them an article about a successful or unsuccessful peer. As individuals, our self-esteem feels threatened by the successful peer and enhanced by the unsuccessful one. In other words, we contrast ourselves with an individual peer, having an "I"-self focus. But as a group member, we do the opposite. "We"-primed group members feel proud of the successful peer (their own self-esteem increases) and disappointed by the unsuccessful one (their own self-esteem decreases). A group "we"-self assimilates to a fellow group member's success and failure. This reliable phenomenon—individual contrast but group assimilation—then boosts or lowers later test performance, so it could be automatic behavior.[21] Level of self-construal (as an individual or as a group member) thus determines self-esteem because it determines social comparisons. We have flexible selves—now a group member, now an individual (figure 6.2).

The Europeans invented a name for this multiple, shape-shifting self: social identity. In any given encounter, we can act as individuals or as group members. If we act as group members, whatever is salient in the context may dictate a shared identity. For example, if you meet a casual acquaintance when you both are traveling, suddenly you feel like you have

Figure 6.2   Social Comparison As Individuals and As Group Members

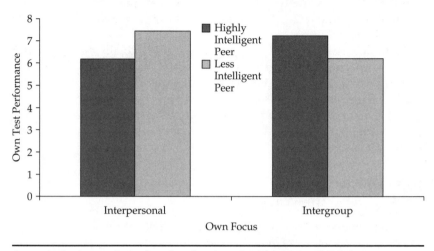

Source: Author's compilation based on data from Gordijn and Stapel (2006).
Note: Test performance after upward or downward comparison with an interpersonal (contrast) or intergroup (assimilation) focus.

more in common (say, as Americans) than when you merely nodded on the street back home. Or salience may determine contrasting identities (for example, one black, one white), as when someone "plays the race (or gender or class) card," suddenly making contrasting group memberships relevant.

We do not constantly think about ourselves in terms of our group identities. The same two people can relate in an interpersonal way or an intergroup way. After the 9/11 attacks, many Americans noticed that racial identities became less salient as shared American identity prevailed, at least temporarily. On a bus or a subway, people will studiously avoid eye contact, operating as individuals, until some bizarre public behavior makes everyone exchange glances, uniting in contrast to the deviant. Similarly, even a person alone at a computer can identify as an individual or as a group member, depending on which identity is relevant to what the person is doing. We all have multiple, flexible identities that depend on context.

Volumes of research and theory have studied this crucial multicultural phenomenon, but here the focus is on the continuum from interpersonal to intergroup.[22] In an intergroup mode, we identify with our own in-group (either a group we claim as a member or an admired reference group) in contrast to some out-group. In the intergroup context, we consider other in-group members to be more relevant, so we compare mostly with others in our own group.

Just Between Us

We prefer to compare with in-group ("my group") others because they provide the most relevant frame of reference.[23] That much is sensible, but in-group peers are also salient because they happen to be nearby. Like fish, we tend to be aware mainly of the others in our own frog pond. It is those immediate, spontaneous in-group comparisons that consistently matter to our feelings and self-esteem. We use out-group comparisons only when no in-group peers are available. In experiments capturing this phenomenon, Ethan Zell and Mark Alicke call it "contextual neglect"—that is, not noticing that the pond we happen to inhabit makes all the difference to our comparisons.[24] These researchers gave undergraduates a verbal reasoning test, after which they learned that they personally had performed at the fortieth or eightieth percentile (the controls received no feedback); they also learned that their school had performed at the fortieth or eightieth percentile (again with a no-feedback control). Personal feedback affected all of the students, regardless of what else they heard, and it changed their estimates of their own abilities and their feelings of pride, satisfaction, disappointment, and so on. Group feedback made a difference only when they had nothing else to go on. The importance of individual feedback resides in its concrete, immediate nature, as compared with the abstract quality of the in-group's standing. But the in-group is more immediate than out-groups are.

Even beyond its immediacy, the in-group is useful as a form of "social capital," as the economists might say, describing it as an asset. Joshua Correll and Bernadette Park explain why the in-group is a social resource.[25] In-groups provide for people in a variety of ways, including self-knowledge, self-worth, belonging, security and continuity, power and control, and sheer survival, as the last several chapters have shown. Their idea of the in-group as a social resource homes in on the features of an in-group that supply its unique utility to the individual: public value, identity, and entitativity—that is, its concrete reality (about which more in a minute).

Our Public Value

An in-group's recognition as having merit, power, and reputation makes it a valuable commodity. For example, when the university football team is winning, suddenly more students don sportswear boasting the school's name, logo, and colors.[26] They also use "we" to describe their team's wins, more so than with losses ("*we* won today, but sometimes the *team* loses"). Robert Cialdini and his colleagues have found that people bask even in the glow of trivial in-groups; for example, people will announce their birth date if they share it with a successful peer but not if they share it with an unsuccessful peer.[27] Clearly a winning sports team has more public

Table 6.1   Collective Self-Esteem and Related Subscales

Subscale	Sample Item
Private collective self-esteem	In general, I'm glad to be a member of the social groups that I belong to.
Public collective self-esteem	In general, others respect the social groups that I belong to.
Membership esteem	I am a worthy member of the social groups I belong to.
Identity importance	The social groups that I belong to are an important reflection of who I am.

Source: Luhtanen and Crocker (1992). Reproduced with permission.

value than a shared birth date, but this shows how much we delight in any publicly shared merit.

The reverse is not true. People from publicly devalued groups do not necessarily feel terrible about themselves. Jennifer Crocker explains that people actively construct their self-esteem depending on their situation.[28] Even people from groups that society stigmatizes—minorities, obese women, the mentally ill—can separate out their own private evaluation of their group and the public's evaluation of it. Crocker and Riia Luhtanen have a scale that distinguishes collective self-esteem, both public and private. Roughly, public and private self-esteem is the difference between how we see our group and how we know society sees it.

Crocker and Luhtanen also separately measure how good we think we are as a group member (membership esteem), as well as the importance to us of this identity; all four (public and private collective self-esteem, membership esteem, and identity importance) are distinct from individual self-esteem (see table 6.1).[29] People high in private collective self-esteem—that is, they value their own group, regardless of what others may think—also favor their in-groups and disfavor out-groups.[30] In other words, valuing their own group, they will do what they can to benefit it. Thus, although public value goes a long way toward making group membership useful, belonging to a devalued group does not make the in-group emotionally useless by any means. A variety of human rights movements show this: black power, feminism, gay rights, and disability alliances offer at least private collective self-esteem to each group member.

Another individual strategy used by stigmatized group members is downward comparison within the group. Downward comparison allows people with cancer, arthritis, mental handicaps, physical disabilities, or responsibility for ill infants to imagine others who share the same affliction but who seem even worse off.[31] For example, people with schizophrenia see themselves as individually better off than others with schizophrenia, and even many others without it.[32] They may feel that even if they suffer from

Figure 6.3   Spontaneous Comparisons by People with Schizophrenia

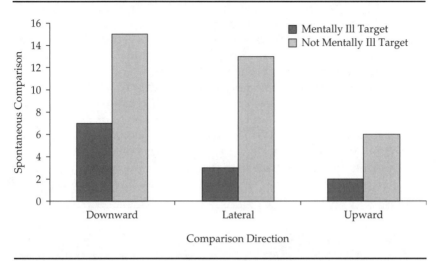

Source: Author's compilation based on data from Finlay, Dinos, and Lyons (2001).
Note: People with schizophrenia make mostly downward comparisons with other schizophrenics, but especially with nonschizophrenics.

mental illness, they have a better perspective or a more solid character than someone who does not (figure 6.3). Even with stigma, we prefer to compare downward, showing our advantages. And for the majority of us who are not part of a stigmatized group, the public merit of our group increases its value.

Our Shared Identity

Besides their public value, in-groups also play an important role in identity—that is, its self-relevance to members who claim it as part of their self-concept. In-group identity multiplies the effects of its value, according to Correll and Park. For nonstigmatized groups, as we have seen, the reliable comparison effect mostly shows in-group assimilation and out-group contrast. The psycho-logic runs like this: an in-group comparison spontaneously brings to mind the details of how you resemble your peer, so your self-evaluation tends to be based on those accessible ideas, resulting in your assimilation to the in-group comparison person. On the contrary, comparison with an out-group member brings to mind the stereotypic categories that distinguish groups from each other, so that person seems to contrast with yourself.[33]

The more relevant the in-group, the more comparison makes us contrast with the out-group.[34] William James and I (how nice to claim him in my in-group as a psychologist) find economists to be another species entirely. And as people who both value summering in New England, we cannot imagine what is in the minds of people who go to Timbuktu. The more relevant the in-group (psychologist, New Englander, writer, scientist), the more we include the in-group in the self, and thus the more the fate of in-group members matters to our own experience. As noted earlier, we sympathize with unsuccessful in-group members and feel bad about them if we are oriented to the collective rather than the self. (Those Boston Red Sox, for example, for decades just couldn't get a break.) Sometimes we literally feel our group's pain.[35] For example, with a strong group identity, you will experience your group's emotions regardless of your personal feelings.[36] We feel angry or proud as Republicans or Democrats, in shared solidarity with fellow party members. A local election outcome on the other side of the country may not mean much to our own personal life, but for a party loyalist, it may be an encouraging or devastating omen.

Our Group Entitativity

A final feature of the value of the in-group for comparison is expressed by that million-dollar word "entitativity." A psycho-neologism invented by one of our field's icons, Donald Campbell, it means the property of being a coherent *thing*, a unified and meaningful entity.[37] This gets interesting when we consider how aggregates of people become recognizable as named social groups. Proximity, similarity, and a common fate all contribute to "groupiness." As mere acquaintances, you and I may share our building's elevators, but if someday we are trapped in the same car, we suddenly become part of a close, similar, interdependent group, at least for the time being. In a longer-term way, if all of us in the building have to take turns emptying the office trash can during a maintenance worker strike, we become more of a group. If we form a recycling collective, we are even more of a group. More entitative, "groupy" groups have more utility for their members. As Correll and Park note, groups can provide a feeling of consensus and acceptance only if they cohere. We tend to believe that entitative groups share a fundamental essence, such as blood, genes, spirit, or talent. An ineffable but natural essence makes group membership seem not just arbitrary but rooted in reality.[38]

We find groups most useful if they provide structure and meaning. The recycling collective is more of a group than the garbage-hauling group because recycling has a value-laden meaning (saving the planet) and more structure (organizers, fund-raisers, volunteers) than a simple rotation group that handles turn-taking with the garbage. Groups provide useful coherence and identity, helping their members avoid feeling completely at sea. We reduce uncertainty by assimilating ourselves to an in-group prototype, itself an entity furnished by a relevant, cohesive group. The ideal recycling collective member is easier to imagine than the ideal trash-hauling coworker. Reducing uncertainty through proto-types is adaptive and makes us feel good, including feeling better about ourselves.[39] We compare ourselves with other group members, then adjust to fit the prototype; this makes group attitudes more homogenous over time.[40]

We thus gain a great deal—value, identity, coherence—from belonging to groups. As already discussed, we prefer to compare within our in-group of similar peers. So upward assimilation (identifying with a successful peer) protects our self-esteem. Within the in-group, the collective "we" can turn the disheartening experience of being individually bested—otherwise a discouraging upward comparison—into "yes, we can," instead.[41] In a study by David Marx, Diederik Stapel, and Dominique Muller, undergraduate women read a newspaper article portraying a female student like themselves who was either brilliant or mediocre at math. Then they took a twenty-item math test, described as diagnostic of math ability and designed to identify a person's mathematical strengths and weaknesses. This presentation would generally threaten the per-formance of groups stereotyped as defective in a given domain (such as women in math), but it also makes the individual acutely aware of being a member of that group (identifying as female instead of, say, as a student). Normally, performance suffers accordingly. Despite this potential threat, after the female students read about another in-group member excelling in math, their performance and self-efficacy both improved. Apparently, they were inspired by identifying with the tal-ented in-group member and worried less about how they came across themselves (see figure 6.4).

We have some choice in these matters. We all belong to several entita-tive groups—based on gender, ethnicity, generation, school, profession—so we also can avoid a painful upward comparison by picking a different identity.[42] Women do not necessarily compare themselves to everyone in their profession (perhaps because on average they earn less than the men), but they do compare themselves with other women, perhaps because other women seem like a more coherent entity. We can avoid downward assimilation by reverting to our individual identity. On the whole, how-ever, we seem to prioritize within-group comparisons that are "just between us." We work around the potential self-esteem issues because belonging to the group is useful in so many ways.

Us Versus Them

Although we generally compare with in-group peers, we do sometimes compare across groups, as part of defining our in-group identity. Henri Tajfel, the founder of social identity theory, of course put it well: "All

Figure 6.4   Female Students Exposed to an In-Group Comparison

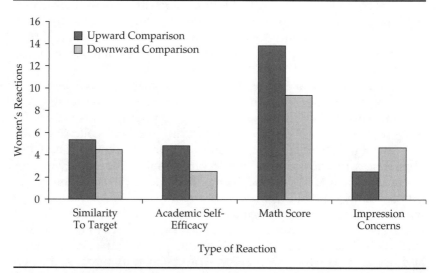

Source: Author's compilation based on data from Marx, Stapel, and Muller (2005).
Note: When their gender identity is salient, women feel more similar to the superstar role model, feel more efficacious, perform better, and worry less about the impressions they convey.

groups in society live in the midst of other groups . . . [and] only acquire meaning in relation to, or in comparison with, other groups."[43]

Group identity therefore depends on the intergroup comparison. What is our specialty? Is our group good or bad at a particular task? Are we nice or not nice? Compared with which other groups?

A basic principle of social identity theory is that groups typically favor their own. Social beings that we are, we consistently enhance our in-group, showing the typical pattern of favoring and valuing our own group. So just as social comparison often reveals individuals enhancing themselves (chapter 5), so too in group comparison people enhance their in-group.[44] Indeed, the utility of downward comparison—individuals feeling better by looking down on other individuals—was anticipated by social identity work that showed groups looking down on other groups.[45] Each wave of immigrants, for example, famously scorns the next wave of newbies. Italian Americans, once scorned, can look down on Chinese Americans, who can look down on Latino Americans. On the basis of such comparisons, we feel group emotions, experience group attitudes, and justify group prejudices.[46] To be sure, each immigrant group fights its own unique battles. At their worst, Italian immigrants were viewed as untrustworthy, whereas Chinese immigrants were viewed as untrustworthy but competent; Mexican immigrants are currently seen as neither trustworthy nor competent. Over time, each group joins the American in-group as trustworthy and competent, but at first each group starts as an outsider.[47]

Comparison comes out better for high-status insider groups than low-status outsider ones. We saw earlier that high-status groups generally display more intergroup bias and more in-group love than do low-status groups.[48] They have more public prestige, so this makes sense. Ironically, those same proud (arrogant) insiders can especially afford to act as independent individuals because they need their group less, having already gained its resources.[49]

Although, on average, everyone assimilates to their own in-group, members of lower-status groups (for instance, women and minorities) seem especially likely to include their in-group in the self. This might seem odd because, by virtue of their lower status, subordinate groups can only suffer by emphasizing their group in comparison with higher-status groups. How can the low-status groups maintain self-esteem as group members? We already saw that stigmatized group members emphasize their personal regard for their devalued group and also compare within that group as individuals. Minority individuals such as African Americans feel pride more than humiliation as members of a subordinated group. But what about the group as a whole? Several creative strategies work for subordinate groups to salvage their group-esteem within society.

Instrumental Versus Expressive Strategies: Getting It Done Versus Getting It Out

First, consider the position of the low-status group. Its members must be practical if they want major change. While the high-status groups can afford symbolic identity expression ("people like us are simply superior"), the lower-status groups have to focus on what works; in other words, they have to be instrumental (getting the job done), especially if the status quo is firmly in place, rather than expressive (getting their identity out).

When all of the comparisons make them feel relatively deprived, they have nothing left to lose. Daan Scheepers, Russell Spears, Bertjan Doosje, and Antony Manstead suggest that if low-status groups are among the worst off in society, they may, as desperately subordinate groups, try to topple the hierarchy, bringing down the high-status groups.[50] Speculating about what motivates low-status groups stuck in a rigid hierarchy, these researchers predict that stuck groups will be desperately instrumental— as tragically illustrated by the numerous real-life examples of terrorist attacks and other extreme strategies undertaken by groups that view their situation as hopelessly oppressive.

Imagining the motivations of terrorists in no way defends their actions, but consider an analogy that might help us get inside their heads. The

American Revolution was the outcome of an oppressed people confronting what was then the world's greatest military power. The American revolutionaries were more invested in taking extreme actions for change than were the high-status British soldiers they were fighting. Even under less desperate circumstances, providing instrumental, practical aid for the in-group (for instance, the isolated rebellions leading up to the Revolution) works to prepare them for long-term collective action but also motivates them. High-status group members (the colonial-era British) have no such need because they already have resources by virtue of their privileged position.

An experiment simulates a far tamer version of these conditions. Participants take a test that supposedly categorizes them into synthetic thinkers or analytic thinkers. Each group then does a task separately and learns that one group has outperformed the other (status manipulation). They also learn that later on they will have a chance to improve their group position or they will not (stability manipulation). Then they rate their own and the other group. Praise of their own group ("a superior group") and put-downs of the other group ("a bunch of losers"), as measures of their symbolic expressions of bias, may be satisfying but have no practical utility. Giving points to anonymous in-group and out-group members, however, provides participants with tools for the second round—an indication of instrumental favoritism.[51]

Low- and high-status group members respond in opposite ways to stability. Under stable circumstances (no change possible), high-status group members celebrate themselves, scoring the highest on symbolic in-group favoritism under stability; they can afford to enjoy themselves. Low-status group members focus on a different kind of favoritism, but only under unstable circumstances (improvement possible): they score the highest material benefits to their own side under instability because they need the tools for change. Evidently, they want to motivate their comrades: in another study, for instance, low-status group members score high on material benefits only when they can communicate with in-group members. Under stable conditions, in contrast, when low-status group members find that they can do nothing, they resort to derogating the out-group. Name-calling is the best they can do.

This admittedly artificial simulation gains support from a paired study of soccer fanatics. Given a scenario in which a critical goal is scored by the rival (threat) or by their own team (secure), soccer fans choose cheerful, celebratory chants to express their identity when they feel secure, but derogatory, team-motivating songs when their team is under threat. Instrumental strategies prevail when underdogs think that they can change things; otherwise, they and the top dogs enjoy putting each other down, even if it accomplishes nothing.

Individual Mobility

If the in-group cannot hope to improve its position as a whole, an uncommitted individual may abandon the sinking ship and strive for upward mobility alone, where permeable boundaries make that possible.[52] Immigrants routinely do this. As a study by Maykal Verkuyten and Arjan Reijerse shows, some Turkish guest workers in the Netherlands reported that the ethnic hierarchy was stable and legitimate; those system-supporters identified less as Turkish if they also viewed group boundaries as permeable. That is, if they could easily become Dutch, they placed less value on being Turkish.[53] For the lower-status Turkish-Dutch in general, the system seems more legitimate if it is potentially unstable and permeable, whereas for the higher-status ethnically Dutch, the system seems more legitimate if the status quo—stable and impermeable—prevails.

More than anyone else, Naomi Ellemers has elaborated on the importance of group identity to individual mobility.[54] One study simulated society in microcosm: based on ambiguous computerized tests, participants were classified into allegedly inductive and deductive thinkers. (Assignment to these apparently important but actually arbitrary groups was random.) After undergoing an apparently unassailable array of measures—another bogus computer test, an assessment of their supposed style of group participation, and contact with some intimidating skin-conductance electrodes—participants learned that they supposedly identified with their group much more or less than average.

Randomly assigned to believe that they did or did not identify with their group, they then found out that their group scored poorly and was therefore low status (see figure 6.5). The bottom line of this elaborate procedure was telling because the random assignment allowed a causal inference: individual in-group identification (manipulated) decreases a person's reported group commitment, which in turn affects his or her stated intent to abandon the group—that is, defection.

In the real world, women scientists in the Netherlands and Italy exemplify this individual mobility strategy. Science faculty in both countries reportedly believe that female graduate students are less motivated than male ones, although the students themselves do not agree: men and women rate themselves as equally motivated students.[55] However, women faculty especially hold this stereotype of female graduate students; the successful women make themselves the exception to the rule and also distance themselves as not typical of other women scientists. The queen bee syndrome describes individual mobility out of a low-status group.

Figure 6.5   Group Identification, Group Commitment, and Individual Mobility

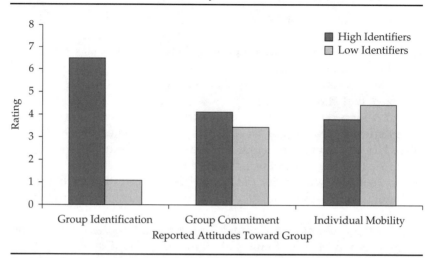

Source: Author's compilation based on data from Ellemers, Spears, and Doosje (1997).
Note: Low status as an individual or as a group? Experimental manipulation of group identification (confirmed here by self-reports) also increases group commitment and decreases individual mobility out of the group.

Challenging the System

Besides attempting group mobility through collective action or individual mobility through defection, low-status groups sometimes contest the legitimacy of the entire status system. Groups may choose which dimensions make relevant comparisons in order to come out on top. For example, although high-status groups favor themselves in status-relevant domains (such as competence), low-status groups often switch to status-irrelevant domains, a creative maneuver to achieve self-respect.[56] Both the Dutch and the Turkish-Dutch see status-irrelevant dimensions (hospitable, tradition-minded, family-oriented, faithful, respectful toward the elderly) as more characteristic of the Turkish, but only those of Dutch origin think that status-relevant dimensions (efficient, achievement-oriented, disciplined, successful, persevering) are more characteristic of the Dutch.[57]

In a parallel case, competing schools carve up the achievement landscape in similar ways, according to status, and they salvage the group-esteem of the lower-status school by handing over some status-irrelevant crumbs. The more selective school is admitted by both schools to be the more academically elite—this being the status-relevant characteristic—but the lower-status school is allowed to be nicer.[58] In research conducted with Julian Oldmeadow, students from two local colleges rated themselves and each other on traits related to competence (smart, capable, intelligent, efficient) and warmth (sincere, friendly, trustworthy, likable). Then they allocated points to anonymous in-group and out-group members, separating academic and sports abilities, these representing domains of intellectual competence and interpersonal teamwork, respectively.

All participants recognized the status differences and the rivalry, both academic and athletic. The lower-status students identified more strongly with their school, as in other research showing ironically that higher-status groups do not bother as much with their identity group (because they do not need it). But both groups implicitly agreed to trade identity domains. Both ceded more competence than warmth to the high-status school, but more warmth than competence to the low-status school. What is more, the high-status students emphasized the competence differences and rewarded themselves accordingly for academics, while the low-status students emphasized the warmth differences and rewarded themselves for sports teamwork ability.[59]

Each group sought to define a positive distinction for itself. One view is that competence is more verifiable than warmth.[60] The more subjective warmth dimension is therefore more serviceable to a low-status group as a flexible option for challenging the hierarchy. For example, stereotypes often paint women and minorities as warm but not so smart, and these societal subordinate groups may even endorse these stereotypes of themselves.[61] Another view is that appeasing low-status groups with a low-cost giveaway—warmth—pacifies them and stabilizes the status quo.[62] The patterns go even further: warmth and competence do more than justify or challenge the system, as the next section indicates.

Mapping Society

> No society is complete without some victim, a creature to pity, to ridicule, to scorn, to protect.
> —Honoré de Balzac (1855/1975, 324, translated by the author)

Four Kinds of People: Friends and Foes, Able and Unable

Balzac was describing society's combined reactions to one type of person, but he was uncannily right about how society distinguishes four kinds of people—the pitied, the ridiculed, the scorned, and the protected—and he could not have known that they spring from the combination of the warmth and competence dimensions so important to groups. We make sense of each other in predictable ways, a subject introduced briefly in chapter 1. Just as any individual in a dark alley wants to distinguish friend from foe as a stranger approaches, so too do we size up new groups, such as immigrants. To figure out a stranger's intentions or to locate new groups

Figure 6.6   BIAS Map Showing Emotions Toward Social Groups

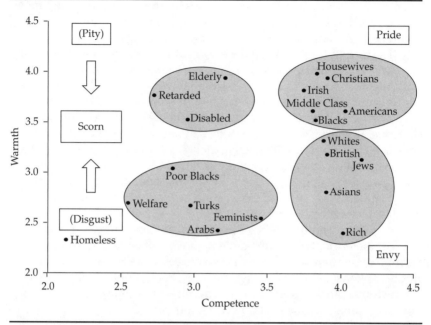

Source: Adapted with permission from Cuddy, Fiske and Glick (2007).
Note: Because this book focuses primarily on the status-competence dimension, for present purposes the pity and disgust clusters most often combine into overall scorn toward low status, as shown on the left.

in society, we need to form impressions. We need to know quickly whether the individual or the group comes as an ally or an enemy (warm or hostile), and next we need to know whether they can act on those intentions (competent or incompetent).[63] These simple assessments combine to powerful effect—they construct a social map that distinguishes all of those people toward whom we feel pity, envy, scorn, and pride (figure 6.6).

When people map out society as a whole, regardless of their own group membership, they believe in the same warmth-competence trade-off that low- and high-status groups use when they barter in their specific rivalry. That is, when we compare any two groups, we believe that one is likely to be nicer but dumber, while the other is likely to be smarter but colder.[64] This belief is truly strange, because normally valuing a person on one dimension spills over to praise on another dimension. This "halo effect" is as old as psychological science.[65] But comparison changes everything. Somebody has to be better and somebody worse; usually, each side is better in particular ways and worse in others, that is, distinct domains: high on either warmth or competence, but not on both.

Granted, societies select a few reference groups that set the norm for being both warm and competent. In the United States, these standard-bearers are the middle-class citizens—people who are not only society's default reference group but also all-around good, worthy folks.[66] In European cultures, the default good guys are also their own citizens. And in both cases, the "best" people of all may just happen to be those filling out the scale (in most cases, students are the in-group).[67] Latin American samples show similar patterns.[68] We are proud of these reference groups and in-groups, and we want to protect them more than other groups.[69]

Each society, of course, also has its really bad guys. In the United States, by far the most extreme out-group is homeless people, but drug addicts, welfare recipients, and immigrants, especially undocumented ones, are also among society's default bad guys.[70] In European countries, the extreme out-groups are also the poor, the unemployed, and immigrants. To a very similar list, Australia adds its aboriginal people. Latin American countries correspondingly focus on the poor, the illiterate, the indigenous, and immigrants from neighboring countries.[71] Asian samples show no change in this pattern: Hong Kong identifies the poor, the unemployed, immigrants, maids, and janitors as out-groups; South Koreans put the unemployed, the poor, and illegal immigrants in extreme out-groups; and Japanese consider the homeless, the poor, and odd-jobbers their default bad guys. Malays name drug addicts and criminals. These seemingly untrustworthy, down-and-out exploiters are among the most scorned across cultures, and our samples report both contempt and disgust toward them.

Apart from those few groups that societies nominate as their default best and worst, attitudes toward every other group are mixed. Indeed, most societies rate the majority of groups ambivalently—as being at least warm or competent, though not both. The ambivalent clusters contain about 80 percent of the groups across the United States, Europe, Latin America, and Asia.[72] Most social groups score higher on either warmth or competence. What is more, most societies agree about which groups land where in the ambivalent sectors of the map of society.

Take the first ambivalent combination. Who seems stereotypically nice but dumb across cultures? Older people and those with disabilities allegedly appear warm but incompetent across the globe, and they are sometimes joined by children and hippies. Oddly, many northern societies view southerners as warm but incompetent.[73] These stereotypically harmless groups seem not so well off, through no fault of their own (except maybe the hippies, whom some probably perceive as too naive and stoned to pose a threat). These alleged unfortunates are the ones pitied by society.

The second ambivalent combination captures the inverse: all the seemingly smart but cold groups. People everywhere concede that rich people seem to be competent, but they win no points for warmth. Other smart but not very warm groups include managers, professionals, entrepreneurs, the upper class, and northerners—all cold but efficient automatons. The only ethnic groups that consistently appear in this cluster across cultures are two that have endured diaspora by becoming entrepreneurs: Jews and Asians. All these allegedly competent but cold groups are envied.

Envy Up, Scorn Down

But wait, the reader says. This book is about status, which is just one dimension. How does the two-dimensional map square with vertical envy up, scorn down, social comparison up and down, status hierarchies, and all the comparisons discussed in the rest of the book?

Envy Up   Envy up fits both the two-dimensional map and this book's focus on comparing up and down. Of the groups we respect, those on our side are our warm and cozy in-group and society's reference groups; we do not envy these groups because they are us. But other respected groups are not us. Others at or above our place in the hierarchy are rich people and those scheming to be rich, and we envy them, if anyone. They have status, but they are not us. They are the resented elites. As William Faulkner put it:

> You only envy whom you believe to be, but for accident, in no way superior to yourself: and what you believe, granted a little better luck than you have had heretofore, you will someday possess.[74]

Envied groups would be peers in status, except that they are not our kind. As evidence, consider how the lucky ones differ from us. Mainly, they are "in no way superior" to us, just lucky this time, but as competitors they are rivals. Competition differentiates us from them, at the level of peers.

Consider a famous baseball rivalry, perhaps the best known in American sports: the New York Yankees versus the Boston Red Sox. For her dissertation, recall that Mina Cikara, along with Matt Botvinick and myself, showed that competitive social identification acts like physical pleasure and pain.[75] Baseball fans of these roughly same-status competitors naturally showed that they cherished their own team, but even more so, they acted as if they envied the rival, wishing them ill (schadenfreude). Merely identifying with your favored team makes you respond to their outcomes neurally as if they were your own group—with vicarious pleasure and pain.

Avid fans watched a series of baseball plays in the scanner. Own-team calamities—our losses, their wins—activated the brain regions (the insula and the anterior cingulate cortex) associated with physical punishment, such as bitter tastes, pinches, and electric shock. Own-team wins activated part of the brain's reward network (ventral striatum). Relevant to malicious envy, fans relished their rival's losses to another team altogether, also showing reward activation to an outcome that did not directly concern their own team. This schadenfreude-type response correlated with the fans' reports of heckling, fighting, or otherwise harming rival-team fans. Group identity explains envy toward competitors who happen to be doing well but whose downfall would cause pleasure.

Why, then, call it "envy up"? When those "in no way superior" happen to win, they are in fact doing better, so they have higher status, even if not for long, and even if wholly undeserved. In personal encounters, people report envy and jealousy toward a rival peer arbitrarily assigned to be their boss in a competitive online game.[76] Viewing photographs of individuals from various identifiable groups, people rate envied targets—for example, rich people—as competent but not warm. The competence ratings are even higher than for the in-group and societal reference groups, as if the rich are indeed not like us—they are supra-human.[77] They seem more than human, as though they are above regular humans in some ways (such as sheer intelligence), but inferior in the ways that make a person a regular human. The rich are seen as failures at being warm, as though they are incapable of experiencing complex emotions, being self-aware, having ups and downs, and being typically human. Envy up, toward the unsympathetic winners (rich people), is thus clearly established.

Scorn Down   Scorn down encompasses both disgust toward the lowest groups and pity toward the nice-but-dumb ones. We said scorn was disrespect, inattention, lack of consideration ("you might as well go away"). It is obvious how disgust and contempt are like scorn, but what about pity? Where is the scorn in pity? Lumping disgust and pity together under scorn makes sense because all of these feelings demean, neglect, and ignore the lower-status other. Pity and disgust both look down on the other.[78]

To be sure, pity and disgust are not identical: disgust blames the low-status for being lazy and stupid, whereas pity spares them in its view of them as downtrodden. This contrast between blame and pity certainly describes our more considered reactions to poor people. For her dissertation, Ann Marie Russell tackled these polarized reactions to low-income people.[79] Undergraduates first read about a friend's roommate, who apparently was from a very low-income family and seemed like either a very hardworking person or a very lazy person. An alleged beneficiary of a new university initiative that recruited low-income applicants, the roommate supposedly had priority in admissions and now in other centers of undergraduate life (for example, class space, room draws, food points, and discounts at the campus store). In this resource-threatened atmosphere, undergraduates polarized their views of the hardworking versus lazy low-income roommates: the one with a good work ethic was admired, pitied, and helped, whereas the one with a poor work ethic was resented and judged to be exploitative and deserving of harm (criticism, confrontation, attack). A parallel story about a lazy or hardworking rich roommate elicited no such polarization. Similar effects appeared in an online study that asked adults to rate rich and poor job candidates who were either hardworking or not. These studies show what happens when people learn about an out-group member.

Otherwise, the common reaction to poor people is to assume that they are incompetent and exploitative, in the United States and elsewhere, over a relentless parade of findings.[80] Even individual poor people are expected to be incompetent in a face-to-face encounter, absent personal knowledge to the contrary.[81] It is this default assumption about poor people that merits describing them as scorned, given the contempt and disgust directed at them.

What about groups that are pitied by default, such as older people and people with disabilities? How does scorn encompass reactions to them? Rachel Farnsworth's senior thesis combined our societal map with a classic moral dilemma.[82] Imagine that you are standing on a footbridge, minding your own business, when suddenly you see a runaway trolley car beneath you speeding down the track, where it will certainly kill five people in its path. You have a split second to decide whether to push someone off the footbridge, thereby stopping the trolley and saving five lives but sacrificing the one person. (Assume that you cannot sacrifice yourself.) Would this decision to "push one, save five" be acceptable? When push comes to shove, the overwhelming majority of people say no.

Suppose now that the five people endangered on the track are all-American middle-class citizens and the person near you on the footbridge is a homeless bum. Would pushing that person seem less unacceptable, more okay in a pinch? Respondents find not only that trade-off more acceptable, but any trade-off that sacrifices even a pitied out-group individual—say, an older or disabled person—for either in-group people or businesspeople. In other words, participants find it acceptable to value some lives (high status) over others (low status). This decision activates a brain network previously involved in complex moral decision-making, consistent with this being a deliberate choice. Scorn downward devalues pitied groups (older, disabled) as well as stereotypically disgusting groups (homeless, drug addicts).

Help and Harm in the BIAS Map

Mapping society up and down matters because doing so predicts help and harm. For her dissertation, Amy Cuddy measured the prevailing winds and created the BIAS Map of Behaviors from Intergroup Affect and Stereotypes (figure 6.7).[83]

Consider the friend-foe warmth dimension, the first and fastest judgment we make to ensure our survival. That judgment readies us to act: to

Figure 6.7   BIAS Map of Behaviors from Intergroup Affect and Stereotypes

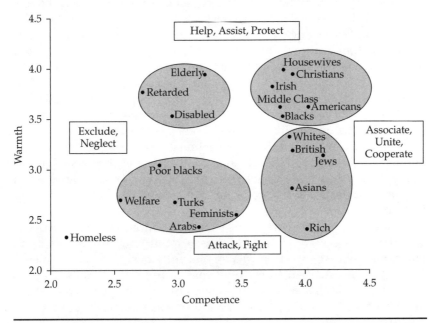

Source: Adapted with permission from Cuddy, Fiske, and Glick (2007).

give direct, active aid to friends (assisting, helping, protecting) or to do direct, active harm to foes (fighting, attacking, sabotaging). We aim to facilitate the goals of our side and block the goals of the other side. Consistent with the readiness to act immediately on the friend-foe warmth dimension is the U-shaped response of the (left) amygdala to trustworthiness. That is, both extremes (extraordinary untrustworthiness and trustworthiness) spur instant vigilance.[84] Judging trustworthiness tells us whom to approach and whom to avoid, who is good for us and who is bad for us.

After we make the friend-foe decision, we must next determine significance (effectiveness). The status dimension, remember, assumes someone else's apparent competence to enact goals. This competence judgment intensifies the initial appraisal of good for me/us versus bad for me/us. A competent, effective friend or foe matters more than an ineffective, incompetent one. As such, this judgment follows the warmth-trustworthiness judgment, and the relevant behaviors are less urgent. Because being competent to enact goals is a secondary judgment, we engage in passive but positive behavior with competent, high-status people, essentially going along to get along (cooperating with, uniting with, associating with). In contrast, scorned, low-status people merit passive harm (excluding, ignoring, neglecting).

The combinations of the two dimensions are revealing. It comes as no surprise that we help the warm and competent in-group, both actively and passively. Besides helping and protecting the in-groups, we also associate and cooperate with them. It is also not surprising that we harm the extreme out-groups, both actively and passively. Both passive neglect of homeless people and active harm to them are sad but not surprising.

It is the ambivalent combinations that shine a new light on persistent societal tragedies. For example, the pitied out-groups—older or disabled people—receive both active help (assisting, protecting) and passive harm (neglecting, excluding). In fact, this is an apt description of putting someone away in an institution. Being institutionalized removes a person from normal social circles and the attention of other people; the person's physical health and safety are assured (assisting, helping, protecting), but in a way that makes it clear that he or she is not worth other people's time (a form of scorn).

Conversely, the envied groups—the rich, entrepreneurs, successful immigrants—receive passive help (associating) but also active harm (attacking, sabotaging). This volatile mix aptly describes mass violence under social breakdown, from rioting that destroys immigrants' shops to genocide that eliminates elites and entrepreneurial outsiders. This pattern describes the all-too-frequent and shocking transition from accommodation to destruction.

How to Promote a Positive Identity

Because we survive and thrive better in groups, as individuals we aim to be desirable group members in a process dubbed social selection.[85] Evolutionary processes should select for people adapted to be good group members, not just entirely self-serving individuals. One way to promote a positive identity—that is, to encourage acceptance by the group—is to behave in both warm and competent ways. Warmth conveys friendly, trustworthy intent, and competence conveys usefulness. Merely dominant behavior, the stereotypical alpha male behavior, may eliminate rivals, but it does not make the group treasure your membership. Groups need people filling a variety of roles to function well, and signaling a willingness to cooperate and share skills suggests adaption to the group.[86] Given the risks, most of us would prefer to belong to trusted, high-status groups—namely, the societal in-group and its allies.

Envied group members (for example, rich people) garner respect but dislike, so they must promote the warmth dimension, which is suspect in their case. In a Manhattan bar famous for its piano music, we once spotted former Beatle Paul McCartney, not only a Knight of the British Empire but one of the richest men in the United Kingdom. Before exiting between the pianist's sets, he made a point of having a private word with the piano player, evidently explaining why he had to leave. Bill Gates, one of the richest men in the United States, created his foundation to show his benign intent toward the world's unfortunate. Other wealthy individuals create charitable foundations that similarly improve their public image on the warmth dimension. Envied groups use similar strategies. Consider the community service requirements to enter elite colleges. In all these examples, competence is not in doubt, but benign intentions must be demonstrated.

Pitied group members (for example, older people) can assume that others will trust them, but they must fight for respect.[87] This dynamic used to drive my brilliant but elderly mother crazy when well-meaning pastoral students visited her retirement home and assumed in conversation with her that she had lost her intellectual edge. People with perfectly benign intentions unconsciously use high-pitched, demeaning baby talk when speaking to older adults and overaccommodate by speaking too loudly and too slowly to them.[88] Behind their backs, people distance themselves from older people.[89] Older workers are rated lower than younger workers with the same qualifications,[90] despite evidence that job performance does not decline with age.[91] Promoting a positive identity for pitied groups has to focus on the competence dimension.

The lowest of the low—poor people and immigrants all over the world—face identity challenges on both warmth and competence. With regard to immigrants, how the debate is framed makes all the difference. Are they coming to steal jobs from citizens or to take the jobs no one else wants? Will they pay taxes or exploit social services? These questions get to the heart of warmth and trustworthiness: just whose side are they on? Turning to competence, are they in fact all uneducated dropouts? Or are they selected, exceptionally ambitious, hard workers whose contributions will grow the economy? The most extreme out-groups face a double challenge to promote a positive identity.

Conclusion

For better or worse, groups impel us to compare, both inside the group—because all the members are people like us and we must determine our rank relative to them—and between groups, because status in society matters. When we worry about individual rank or social status, our uncertainty and anxiety coerce our comparisons, but can also tell us how to get beyond comparisons.

Chapter 7

Beyond Comparison: Transforming Envy and Scorn

FACULTY MEETINGS are famous for fights over the finer points of petty procedures. Academics like to quote an aphorism attributed to Henry Kissinger: University politics are so vicious because the stakes are so small. But not just the professoriate jockeys for position when placed in groups. Toddlers do it, dogs do it, chimps do it. All of us rank ourselves relative to others; we all make our well-being contingent on someone bigger, up the hierarchy. Faculty compare themselves to see how they rank relative to those above and below not only because the stakes are small but also because the criteria are ambiguous—unlike, say, in war, business, or horse races, where the winners and losers are clear. Members of the U.S. Congress constantly compare within and between parties. Perhaps this is not surprising, considering the importance of political advantage to the reelection prospects of representatives. Even presidents constantly track opinion polls. As long ago as the eve of the French Revolution, King Louis XVI of France was worried about being loved by the public.[1] But of course, he had to worry about keeping his head, a competition he lost. However rarefied the rank and whatever the stakes, everyone worries about position.

Status insecurity brings out the worst in people, individually and socially. Envy and scorn are anxiety syndromes on the sides of up and down. In this chapter, we will examine exactly when people are the most insecure, and then we will turn to the solutions: how do we get beyond comparison, if such a thing is possible?

Enviable and Scornful Individuals Are Unsettling

Nietzsche argued that inferiority promotes impotence: being bested makes a person feel helpless and hopeless.[2] Rather than take it out on ourselves, we find it far more soothing to blame someone else. Inferiority-based anger focuses on the fortunate precisely because facing our own shame is so intolerable.[3] And rightly so, for nothing is scarier than wounded pride: violence commonly erupts from threatened egoism, especially from an insecure egoist. Directing anger outward lets us avoid focusing on our own humiliation.[4] Comparisons thus lay the ground for violence because coming up short can be made the fault of someone else—or so it seems.

Small wonder, then, that both enviable and scornful individuals are unsettling. An enviable person makes everyone else feel inferior, but at least that agony is private. In contrast, a scornful person reveals our alleged inferiority, expressing our worthlessness. Both envying from below and being scorned from above trigger anger and humiliation. Knowing this, enviable people themselves may worry about their own potential for scorn and the mere fact that their position damages relationships. In either direction, enviable and scornful people provoke anxiety and insecurity.

Thus, comparison has costs in both directions, as Phillip Brickman and Ronnie Janoff-Bulman discuss so wisely.[5] The specific costs of inferiority include public indignity and private humiliation. People care when both their public face and their private self-esteem are threatened by coming out on the bottom. And those who feel for any reason vulnerable are likely to be the most unsettled by the threat of inferiority.

On the other hand, it is famously lonely at the top. The specific risks of superiority include public embarrassment at being singled out and the private ruination of peace of mind and personal relationships. Many enviable people worry about other people's reactions, namely, about the envy and resentment of other people. Privately, they may feel guilt or doubt about their position. The resentments of lower-status people may ruin their enjoyment of their position. Or lower-status people may bring down the elite, inadvertently by hard-luck contagion or purposely by demanding a share. Let's look at all these reciprocal insecurities in more detail.

The Face-to-Face Costs of Envy and Scorn

Envy and scorn are reciprocal: the envied are supposedly competent, whereas the scorned are not supposed to possess much ability. The envied are supposedly coldhearted, but some of the scorned may be nice, at least those whose low status is not their fault. Why are these differences considered costs if each side gets at least some credit—ability, on the one hand, and niceness, on the other? We saw in the last chapter that high- and low-status groups divvy up the images, with high status claiming competence and low status claiming warmth. Why is this a problem if both sides agree on the division of assets?

Assuming that elites are competent might seem a benign expectation, one fully in keeping with our collective faith in meritocracy, except for one thing: by linking status and competence, we too often make the reciprocal assumption that non-elites are stupid. And lower-status people rightly resent the implication of that expectation. A pair of experiments by Ann-Marie Russell shows this dynamic in operation when individuals confront a direct comparison.[6] In the first experiment, undergraduates arrived for a study of how people form quick impressions; they expected to learn online about a student from another school and then play a computer game together. They discovered that the other student had either two parents with professional jobs or a single mother in a low-income clerical job. They also received "subliminal" information about the person—actually just uninformative sentences flashed too quickly to read—but this gave them permission to judge the other person under the illusion of receiving information.[7]

Participants rated the other student both before and after the game. As meritocracy predicts, they did indeed expect the high-status person to be more competent and to have better GPA and SAT scores than the low-status person, who indeed was scorned as less competent based on nothing other than social-class information. The same pattern appeared in a second study, using a spontaneous, face-to-face game. Two students met in person to play an unscripted trivia challenge game, and they again believed that a randomly assigned "boss" was more competent and that the other player was less competent. These perceptions about relative competence were not rooted in reality. Actual performance in the game did not correlate with perceived performance. What is more, both students attributed competence to status even after the experimenter had announced their equivalent scores. In other words, even though they knew each other's scores, they used randomly assigned status to estimate competence, ignoring the available information (see figure 7.1).

As any higher-status person might fear, the high-status "bosses," being seen as competent, evoked more envy and jealousy than did the low-status targets, especially in competitive dyads. The competitive, low-status targets expressed significantly more envy and jealousy than did those with any other combination of status and competition conditions. Being subordinate in a zero-sum game is especially frustrating. And as Nietzsche would predict, inferiority makes people mad.[8]

The hydraulic warmth-competence trade-off helps explain the vigilance of the oppressed. We assume that high-status people are competent but not nice when we are comparing groups or individuals.[9] We all have a theory that smart people are cold, and that warm people are not too bright. It is unsettling to face an enviable (smart, high-status) person, because our default assumption is that this person is not on our side. So being one-down requires us to face not only our private envy, resentment, and humiliation but also the other person's probable scorn, neglect, and even boasting. Chapter 2 noted that people scorn those of low status, even to the point of dehumanizing them, as beneath contempt.[10] So low-status

Figure 7.1   How Status Confers Competence

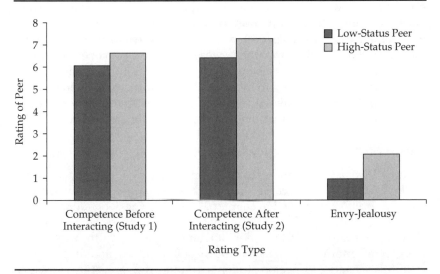

Source: Author's compilation based on data from Russell and Fiske (2008).
Note: Status confers competence, first as an expectation, then as an interpretation of an interaction, and finally as a spur to envy.

people are right to be vigilant because their theory that high-status people might scorn them proves to be true at least some of the time.

Low-status people have to be vigilant for another reason: from the position of the bottom looking up, status often correlates with power over resources, making their welfare contingent on the goodwill of those above them.[11] The superior's intentions matter a lot to the subordinate: if the boss is with you, great; the boss can help you get where you want to go. If the boss is not with you, you cannot predict help from that quarter, so you have to keep an eye on this person. Some of our lab's earliest experiments aimed to bottle this phenomenon, using an involving method. Undergraduates found themselves depending on another person for a valued prize that was awarded depending on their joint performance. In one scenario, they arrived to find a couple of dozen colorful windup toys (my favorites: a hopping hamburger with teeth and a back-flipping race car). They and their partner were supposed to use these toys to create educational games for elementary school children who were learning basic math concepts; for instance, they could illustrate subtraction by having one toy whizz away from the others.[12]

Before working together, they were given a chance to learn about their partner by reading post cards on which their peers had written their teaching evaluations. Stopwatches hidden in the experimenter's jacket pockets timed how long they looked at this information. When they had to work together—as compared with when they worked independently—they especially attended to the information we provided about their partner, but not to just any information. They homed in specifically on unexpected information, trying to make sense of it. When we asked them to think aloud into a tape recorder, they apparently were seeking a more coherent impression the more they had to depend on the other person. Our other studies show that they were trying to increase their sense of accuracy in order to gain control over their own outcomes.[13] Outcome dependency makes us smarter, or at least more attentive, making us aim for greater accuracy.

The Brain Makes Us Vigilant

Upward Vigilance Recently, Daniel Ames and I have begun to use a method that replaces the earlier stopwatches and tape recorders with brain scans (as briefly mentioned in chapter 2).[14] If outcome dependency makes us more socially intelligent, then the brain's social-cognition network should especially activate under outcome dependency in response to unexpected information, which is the most informative and diagnostic.

In this scenario, Princeton students volunteered for a study in which they would work with two Rutgers education majors, one at a time, as in the earlier stopwatch study, designing games that used the same windup toys (in storage since that time). With one of the experts, they could win a cash prize for the most creative educational games designed together. With the other expert, participants were eligible for another prize based on their own independent work. (In neither case did they compete with the experts; they were always either cooperating or working independently.) As these ground rules were explained, one of the experimenters covertly recorded how often the student glanced at each of the education experts. As expected, the participants paid more attention to the expert who could help them win the prize. This result confirmed our previous results in a new setting.

As in our earlier studies, one expert confidently described her qualifications for the task, whereas the other admitted that the task would not play to her strong suit. Half of the participants had to work with the skilled teacher but could work independently of the unskilled teacher, and the other half were faced with the reverse situation. (This counterbalancing allowed us to separate the effects of outcome dependency from the effects of the other person's expertise.) Regardless of the teacher's alleged skill level, half of the evaluations were positive and half were negative, so each series of teaching evaluations contained comments both consistent and inconsistent with each expert's self-appraisal. As is often true in real life, the comments were mixed.

Regardless of the experts' alleged skill level, the participants' neural responses to the expert who would determine their own outcomes became more sophisticated, as if forming an accurate impression mattered more when the outcome depended on another person. In the scanner, responses

Figure 7.2   Outcome-Dependent Attention Versus Independent Attention

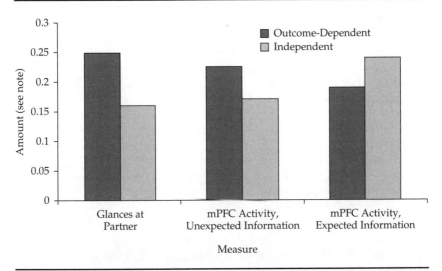

Source: Author's compilation based on data from Ames and Fiske (2010).
Note: Attention and thought go toward people who control our outcomes. Amount of glances, multiplied by ten, is average frequency (for example, 2.5 and 1.6, respectively); mPFC is percent signal change from baseline.

to this consequential expert uniquely distinguished surprising information, which was inconsistent with expectations, from uninformative information, which was consistent with expectations. As predicted, the medial prefrontal cortex (mPFC), that reliable center of the social cognition network, activated more to the surprising information, but only for the expert on whom their outcomes depended, not for the independent expert (see figure 7.2). Upward comparison—in this case, comparison that gauged the relative skill of an alleged expert—can engage the brain's social cognition networks adaptively.

What mattered here was not only that one person needed another person but that the first person still expected some reasonable degree of control. Our own earlier research indicated that people do not try hard to make sense of someone who holds all the cards when they think that they cannot possibly influence or predict that person's behavior.[15] All power is asymmetrical and imbalanced, so power by definition reduces the control of the underling. But it matters whether power is absolute or just unequal. The more imbalanced power is, the greater the frustration for the powerless. Remember Nietzsche's admonition about the impotence of the inferior, which leads to envious rage.

Our upward vigilance focuses on the people who control our outcomes but whom we may be able to influence. It took a French graduate student to tackle the balance-of-power problem with me. Originally, all of my

American students thought that the topic of overt power was too over the top (rude? taboo? paranoid?), but French culture understands the importance of realism. As chapter 1 noted, Eric Dépret and I set up undergraduates to participate in a study of distraction by roommates (a problem everywhere, but certainly at the University of Massachusetts–Amherst, where I was teaching then). Upon arriving, the student discovered that a group of other participants had supposedly arrived earlier, apparently depositing their backpacks and jackets before leaving to complete a preliminary briefing. Assigning the student to a single chair facing three others, the experimenter explained that the others were the "distracters." In the moderate power condition, they could only speak loudly to distract the participant, but in the evil, high-power condition, they could "also watch you, and each time they think you have been distracted, even slightly, they will punish you by making you start again from scratch; if they think you are very concentrated, they can also reward you by multiplying your final score by two." This high-power condition was designed to be particularly frustrating because a cash prize was at stake.

Naturally, given a chance to learn about the individual distracters, the participants typically spent a lot of time examining information about each distracter, especially anything surprising, as in other experiments with outcome-dependency. The more power the distracters held, the more carefully the students attended to this useful, diagnostic information. Dependency makes us vigilant.

But this baseline situation was easy compared with a situation we set up to mimic out-group conspiracies. All the participants were psychology majors, and some were made to think that they had been assigned to distracters who were a monolithic cabal of math majors (fiendishly clever distracters) or, alternatively, a monolithic cabal of art majors (fiendishly creative distracters). In response to both of these homogeneous factions, the psychology students simply gave up. Confronting a brick wall of math majors (or art majors), they did not bother to learn about them as individuals and reported instead how much more they preferred psych majors; those assigned to the more powerful distracters also reported being more unhappy, gloomier, and sadder. This psychology experiment created a scale model that vividly illustrated Nietzsche's impotence of the inferior.

These emotional and cognitive reactions fit the kinds of neural signatures described in chapter 2. When we confront someone who is higher status and perhaps powerful, our discrepancy detector (the anterior cingulate cortex, or ACC) and social-cognition analyzer (the medial prefrontal cortex, or mPFC) come on line. When the situation looks hopeless, all we can do is hunker down and hope that bad things happen to the powerful, as in neural signatures of schadenfreude.

Downward Inattention   On the other side, the emotional and cognitive reactions of people looking down from on high are consistent with scorn—

as in the studies of social class predicting merit or its lack. Characteristic reactions of higher-status people to down-and-out homeless people, as seen earlier, are the neural signatures of disgust (the insula) and dehumanization (less mPFC). But, even from underlings, praise captures their attention. The reward areas of the brains of high-status people reacting to others paying homage to them reflect the pleasure of positive regard.[16] The brain makes us vigilant to comparisons up and down.

Even if We Are Hardwired, We Can Overcome Envy and Scorn

Even though envy and scorn implicate the brain, it does not follow that the brain is hardwired in the sense of inevitably creating these reactions. Remember Mina Cikara's hedge fund manager stepping in dog poo? The brain's reward areas lit up, and people showed the impulse to smile (measured by facial electrodes), rating the incident (and others like it) as not so bad. They did not smile when the same "shit happens" to an older, homeless, or disabled person. Granted, these reactions were spontaneous, but that does not mean they were inevitable. Solutions focus on warmth.

Cikara showed that people can overcome their schadenfreude-glee by learning more about the other person. An investment banker who has been laid off but who keeps up appearances by commuting, with his briefcase, to Starbucks to search the want ads seems pathetic. If the same fallen master of the universe volunteers to advise and do pro bono bookkeeping for small business start-ups, he seems admirable. And of course, if instead he spends his severance package on cocaine, he is disgusting. The point is that even high-status, envious stereotypes can yield to individual information.

Low-status stereotypes can yield to individual information too. Chapter 6 described Ann-Marie Russell's dissertation showing that a hardworking low-income person gains admiration and support, whereas a lazy one provokes disgust. Evidence of a work ethic provides information that overcomes invidious comparisons.

Providing another eloquent case for overcoming envy and scorn, age stereotypes belong to one of the few categories whose boundary most of us hope to cross eventually, if not just yet. The default ageist prejudice is pity for older people; absent any knowledge to the contrary, we often apply this soft form of scorn. Pity is an ambivalent response: we acknowledge the generally benign intent of older people but consign them to incompetence: they are doddering but dear.[17] No one likes to be the object of pity, however benevolent the pity-prone may be feeling. Pity is a downward sort of reaction, one involving neglect and a certain prescriptive control (hence scorn). Younger people view older people as harmless only so long as the latter stay in their safe, low-status box.

Not surprisingly, older people may try to escape from this box, creating intergenerational tensions over social status. Michael North and I are devel-

Figure 7.3   The Age-Status Curve

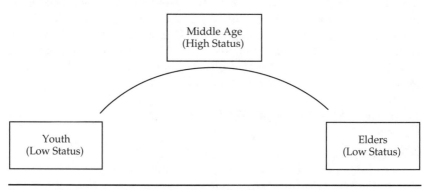

Source: Author's creation based on data from North and Fiske (2010).

oping a novel view of ageism that captures younger people's resentments toward their elders who get in the way of their own upward trajectory by not moving aside fast enough.[18] The age-status curve is an inverted-U, reflecting three age cohorts: younger people moving up as they develop, middle-aged people enjoying their prime, and older people on the decline. Older people can create three kinds of trouble at each point of this otherwise peaceful progression. In each case, the individual overcomes the stereotype to create more elaborated—and polarized—reactions, from the perspective of the younger people on the move. This curve fits our envy-scorn narrative because the young are looking at their rank relative to that of middle-aged and older people (figure 7.3).

First, at the peak of the age-status curve, older people (at least, those who are just past middle age) can refuse to get out of the way, holding on to enviable positions, power, and wealth past the point when they should have arranged for orderly succession. Consider older, stingy Max, who "has enough insurance and savings to comfortably handle his own expenses. But, despite his younger relatives' needs, he is reluctant to lend or share his money." Younger people resent him, relative to generous Max, who gives away his money; they like generous Max a lot. (A younger person doing the same thing excites neither resentment nor admiration.) The prescription for seniors' active succession grants a bonus to those who comply and imposes penalties on those who resist. Information can trump a stereotype when it exaggerates or contradicts it. All these processes depend on younger people comparing their situation to older people who share or who do not.

On the downward descent of the age-status curve, older people can get in the way more passively: through sheer inertia, they can consume shared societal resources. When older Max consumes expensive health care—

stubbornly choosing an expensive, elective medical procedure, regardless of the cost to family and caregivers—he evokes resentment in younger people, to whom he comes across as less warm, kind, competent, and capable, as well as less appealing to cooperate or associate with. When he acts with understanding of others' concerns and decides against the extraordinary medical procedure, reactions are more positive. (For younger health care consumers, the health care decision makes no difference because passive consumption of shared resources does not matter with them.) Once again, relevant information trumps a stereotype: younger people compare their share with the older people's share, but this time the resources are joint societal resources.

Finally, older people may try to escape the pitiful older-person stereotype by acting forever young. In this outrageous intrusion, they try to invade young people's ascending part of the age-status curve. An elderly youth-wannabe who crashes college parties or goes clubbing provokes contempt for this identity inversion, but an older person who sticks to retirement-home parties and community bingo is regarded with affection. Again, the relative position of different age cohorts inevitably creates comparisons. Still, the comparisons do not have inevitable effects. The stereotypic comparisons can budge, depending on what individuals actually do. In the case of old-age comparisons, issues of succession, identity, and consumption create dynamics that go beyond the pitiful default stereotype of elders, for better or for worse.

We can overcome envy up and scorn down when we gain information about each other. But cold hard facts are not enough.[19] Let's take a look at what Robert Abelson used to call hot cognition (versus cold cognition).

When to Expect Fallout from Comparison: It's the Insecurity, Stupid

We cannot help ourselves. We have to compare because we are wired that way, as chapter 2 argued. Our brains are alert to upward comparisons, with the discrepancy-monitoring anterior cingulate cortex and the person-analyzing medial prefrontal cortex coming on line to react rapidly. Our brains respond to downward comparisons by activating systems consistent with disgust and other emotional arousal (insula). And when we can feel superior to those below us, the brain's VS (ventral striatum) reward system lights up. Comparisons signal status via the envy and scorn emotions that alert us, and then our cognitive systems explain why we are feeling that way, up or down. Our behavior expresses those comparisons by revealing whether we feel larger than life or cut down to size. Still, being hardwired does not explain exactly why comparison happens—just partly how it happens. More reliable predictors of comparison fallout come from heeding other people's insecurities.

Everyone engages in comparison, but some do it more than others, as chapter 3 indicated. This gets us partway to why. People who are individually oriented to social comparison lack self-confidence. They are people-oriented but also self-aware, even self-conscious. In the extreme, they are neurotic and unhappy—in a word, insecure. But an insecure personality alone does not predispose a person to making comparisons: only when feeling unhappy and out of control is the insecure person especially likely to obsess about who is above and who is below.

Not all lack of confidence is about anxiety, of course; sometimes we are simply uncertain and need to know more in order to compete effectively. This may be the reason for men's greater tendency to compare, because male gender roles reward competitors. Women tend to prefer connection, which can be endangered by comparison, so they often avoid overt competition, except in gender-typed areas such as body image. Women do make themselves miserable by wishing for more perfect bodies and frequently lack confidence in the adequacy of their appearance. But, according to the research, men compare more generally. Whoever does it, all of us are definitely motivated to make comparisons by uncertainty about where we stand.

Ironically, comparison can create more uncertainty rather than relieve it; comparison may not always reassure. Even if brought on by circumstances, comparison malaise itself sounds like insecurity. Anytime we compare ourselves to someone else, we risk coming up short. Or we risk discovering that life is unfair. We have to value the potential for information over the potential for bad news. Liberals, for example, tolerate uncertainty and seek comparisons—as when they embrace the need to understand inequality because they want to reduce it. They are less likely than conservatives to believe that people get what they deserve. In contrast, defenders of the status quo value certainty; conservatives justify the hierarchy as inevitable and useful. Indeed, those who prefer certainty may avoid comparisons, preferring to assume the stable status quo. To the extent that those same people are those on top, they naturally prefer the hierarchy as it is or how they imagine it has always been.

Why do we make comparisons? The answer boils down to information, self-defense, and group identity. As chapter 4 showed, we make comparisons to seek information that will help us predict and control our life outcomes when we are motivated by insecurity (or, more kindly, uncertainty). How can we know where we stand unless we compare ourselves with similar others? Addressing this need is just logical and adaptive, but as a reason for making comparisons it does not go to the heart of the matter.

Comparisons defend us when we use downward comparisons to feel privileged—when we think, "There but for fortune," we are acknowledging our advantage. Even people in objectively awful situations almost always can find someone in a still more hideous situation to help themselves realize that things could be worse. As noted in chapter 5, we can also use inspiring upward comparison to improve ourselves—a form of self-defense in that we are using comparison to protect our sense of possibility and hope.

Finally, as social beings, our group identities matter to us. As discussed in chapter 6, we have been adapted to belong with others. Even if you are not doing so well yourself, your in-group certainty can create individual certainty. Collectivist cultures, for example, promote certainty through societal control and assurance. Groups in general reduce uncertainty by providing shared ideals. Between-group social comparison can be especially vicious and accounts for much of humans' inhumanity to other humans.

So we have a trinity of ways in which comparison—whether individually, face to face with another, or in groups—reduces uncertainty: by getting information we can use, protecting ourselves, and allowing us to join like-minded others. But what about the broader society?

In Society: It's the Inequality, Stupid

> Envy is of course closely connected with competition. We do not envy a good fortune which we conceive as quite hopelessly out of reach. In an age when the social hierarchy is fixed, the lowest classes do not envy the upper classes so long as the division between rich and poor is thought to be ordained by God. Beggars do not envy millionaires, though of course they will envy other beggars who are more successful. The instability of social status in the modern world and the equalitarian doctrines of democracy and socialism have greatly extended the range of envy. For the moment, this is an evil, but it is an evil which must be endured in order to arrive at a more just social system.
>
> —Bertrand Russell, *The Conquest of Happiness* (1930, 73)

Consider what modern society's necessary evil begets.

Populists have arisen throughout modern history, across continents, leaning left or right—for example, the Tea Party movement of the 2010s (right) and the Boston Tea Party of the 1770s (left). Any group can claim the populist title if it can promote a coherent image of "the people" and express the people's resentments against the elites.[20] As Ronald Formisano notes, "Clearly the populist style has been a central element of the American political tradition, and just as obviously style and rhetoric can be appropriated by just about anybody."[21] To stretch this point: in a rock-musical update of populism, *Bloody Bloody Andrew Jackson*, Jackson's followers sing, "Populism, yea, yea," asserting that because the elites do not care about them, they will use democracy to take a stand against the elites, who can "eat our dust."[22]

Uncertain and Out of Control

Populist movements arise at times of crisis, when national identity and the will of the people are up for grabs. Populism captures collective insecurity. When the people are feeling insecure about who exactly "we, the people" are, populisms tend to nominate one homogeneous camp that is intolerant of difference. Even populisms founded on egalitarian principles tend to be obsessed with who is and is not "one of us." "We are all alike and they are different" goes the logic; this is a strategy on a national scale that resembles social identity on a local scale.[23] Populist movements typically start locally, when regional politics feel out of control. External forces seem to threaten the local economy, autonomy, or rights, undermining security. The self-nominated people want to take back their self-defined domain. Given societal patterns of change, populism captures the imagination of people whose stable sense of how things work is under threat.[24]

Populism capitalizes (literally) on times when, as the Fox commentator and current populist Glenn Beck says, the PEOPLE FEEL that SOME-THING ISN'T RIGHT, even if they can't put it into words or figure out how to STOP IT.[25] People can feel out of control in large numbers under economic recession (directly experienced as unemployment risk), massive demographic change (feeling threatened by immigration), or cultural upheaval (disruption due to changing gender roles or religious pluralism). Populism arises when politics escapes the people's control; we believe we have the right to government by the people and the right to reclaim government when it seems alien.[26] *New York Times* columnist Frank Rich points out that some Americans realize that the economic game is unfair, controlled by a distant, nameless powerholder they can't identify.[27] In other words, things feel out of control, an unaccustomed feeling for a certain segment who are used to being the majority, the default: mainstream middle Americans.

The resulting rage brings to mind again Nietzsche's impotence of the inferior, but psychologists have long understood that frustration begets aggression.[28] When our goals are blocked—especially for illegitimate or arbitrary reasons—we become angry and aggressive.[29] When we feel uncertain about our fate because we feel that we cannot control what happens to us, we get mad as hell and won't take it anymore. At this writing, the Tea Party movement has demonstrated that kind of frustration and anger. As Frank Rich notes, our president and our representative democracy are being tested by citizens who may be enraged but fully sincere.[30]

Resenting Elites' Contempt

The rage of the frustrated comes from living in a world in which we are viewed with contempt by those elites who are against us. They want to treat us like dirt, but we are the competent, trustworthy ones. In the BIAS

Map space, this pits the pride groups (American, middle-class, Christian, "mainstream" identities) against the enviable groups (those rich business-people, politicians, or professionals). As Margaret Canovan explains, the populists complain that "we have been shut out of power by corrupt politicians and an unrepresentative elite who betray our interests, ignore our opinions, and treat us with contempt."[31] The envied groups hold power, which they do not use for the common good, and their scorn is particularly galling. Formisano agrees that populist movements (at least progressive ones) draw energy from

> resentment of those privileged economic interests that are able to manipulate capital, law, and politics to their profit. At the crudest level they protest that too few have too much; or they voice resentment against specific targets—the wealthy, corporations, professional politicians, professional elites or experts, social engineers, bureaucrats, or as a Kansas Populist once put it, "the aristocrats, plutocrats, and all the other rats."[32]

Since the early nineteenth century, populism has championed accountability to vanquish the political corruption of party bosses "as deceivers and manipulators with no regard for the public welfare or republican values, who trampled on public welfare for partisan and private ends, including lining the pockets of the party faithful."[33] Sound familiar?

Part of the resentment comes from the feeling that the powerful view the good, real people with contempt, with societal bystanders perhaps agreeing "that populists of whatever kind are sincere and stupid while traditional politicians are cynical and smart."[34] This view of the people with contempt and scorn also appears in Michael Kazin's account: identifying as populist has been "a handy way to signify that one was on the side of the people—those with more common sense than disposable income—and opposed to their elite enemies, whoever they might be."[35]

Thus, even those who by any objective measure are the elite want to claim to be populists, casting themselves as not too rich. Ever "since at least the early nineteenth century, . . . even candidates for office born on plantations have preferred to present themselves to the electorate as born in rude log cabins and have played upon their ties to and sympathies for the common man."[36] Andrew Jackson's annual address to Congress warned: "Experience proves that in proportion as agents to execute the will of the people are multiplied, there is danger of their wishes being frustrated."[37] Jackson preferred to be known as a soldier rather than as a plantation owner. Votes for him were votes for the people, against corruption in Washington. Likewise, Abraham Lincoln preferred to be cast as a rail-splitter rather than as a lawyer.[38] In this century, after his elitist father stumbled when he expressed surprise that cashiers used supermarket bar codes, George W. Bush cultivated the image of a common man so that voters would want to share a beer with the guy. Running against him, Al Gore appeared to the manor born, although both Gore and Bush were sons of the political establishment. When John Kerry ran against Bush in 2004, his wind-surfing and French-speaking made him seem too elitist. In the 2008 election season, John McCain tried to minimize his wife's wealth, while Hillary Clinton and Barack Obama both minimized their Ivy League degrees.

Whether politicians are cynical, realistic, or sincere, they understand that elitism risks the broader population's resentment of their presumed contempt and scorn. Democracy is crucial, of course. A populist sensibility indicates widespread, engaged political energy, and such energy is preferable to widespread passivity or neglect.[39] Disdain for the political capacity of ordinary people risks not only being voted out of office by the people expressing their will, but the core values of democracy itself. As Kazin notes: "At the core of populist tradition is an insight of great democratic and moral significance. No major problem can be seriously addressed, much less nudged along a path toward solution, unless . . . 'the productive and burden-bearing classes'—Americans of all races who work for a living, knit neighborhoods together, and cherish what the nation is supposed to stand for—participate in the task."[40]

Inequality Undermines Unity

How do citizens become divided from each other? The message of this book is that comparisons up and down the hierarchies divide us from each other. The bigger the span from bottom to top, the more potential for comparison, envy, and scorn. The United States now suffers from unprecedented inequality between the top and the bottom, with destructive effects on our unity.[41] As Richard Wilkinson and Kate Pickett show, income inequality undermines societies.[42] The social ills of inequality are not confined to the poor at the bottom but afflict the majority of the population—indeed, the entire society. In societies where income disparities become wider, the following changes occur, usually independently of the poverty level:

- Violence increases. In rich countries, homicides increase with inequality, not with poverty per se; this pattern can be seen across the fifty U.S. states. The rate of incarceration shows an even stronger relationship to inequality and, again, remains independent of sheer poverty.

- Health suffers under inequality, at least as much as from poverty. Life expectancy, infant mortality, and obesity are functions of sheer inequality in rich countries. Across the fifty states, these health indicators correlate separately with inequality and with average income as two independent effects.

- Community quality of life declines with inequality, separate from poverty. Places with more inequality have more teen births, lower educational performance, and more mental illness (along with more violence and ill health).

Although the psychology of these effects of inequality remains to be worked out, the evidence in this book that uncertainty and insecurity are hazardous to our collective health suggests that societies suffer as status competition dominates social affiliation.[43] Increased inequality may heighten status anxiety as people worry more about being evaluated under more intense competition. The main psychological variable available in cross-country and cross-state comparisons is trust, which does indeed decline massively with inequality. Average income has a separate effect on trust, but the effect of inequality is much bigger.

Consistent with the possible role of trust, where there is more inequality there is also less democracy.[44] Where the gap between the people and their leaders widens, people cannot expect their leaders to listen to them. The wider the gap, the greater the psychological distance and the harder to construct a joint political identity.

As in politics, so too in personal income mobility. The more inequality in a society, the less social mobility it can sustain.[45] Social mobility is generally defined as the correlation between parent and (adult) offspring income. Education accounts for much of the persistence of social status from parents to children. Education in turn depends on both cognitive skills and noncognitive skills (concentration, perseverance, ability to follow instructions, self-control) that grow through education.[46] Without social mobility, we can neither trust in opportunity nor trust that the system will respond to us.

In our comparisons across countries with more and less equality, we find a curious pattern.[47] More equal countries have a tighter, more straightforward theory of their societal groups. Groups are essentially either completely with us, trustworthy, and competent—citizens, the middle class, the middle-aged, members of the main religion—or against us. The outcasts— the poor, the unemployed, immigrants, nomads, refugees, the homeless, drug addicts—seem untrustworthy and useless, even a threat to the unified society. The narrative is that all of those who fully belong are equal and the outcasts are beyond the pale. Several European countries—Belgium, Greece, Ireland, Italy, Portugal, Spain, Switzerland (see figure 7.4), the United Kingdom, plus Australia and New Zealand—fit this pattern of high equality and essentially an us-versus-them structure. Historically, these have not been countries with high rates of receiving immigrants.

In the New World, in contrast to the more equal European countries, the United States, several Latin American countries (Bolivia, Chile, Costa Rica, Mexico, Peru), and other former colonies (Hong Kong, South Africa, Uganda) have a history of continuing to receive immigrants, even after the colonists arrived. These countries all suffer high rates of inequality but also

Figure 7.4   BIAS Map of Switzerland's Social Groups

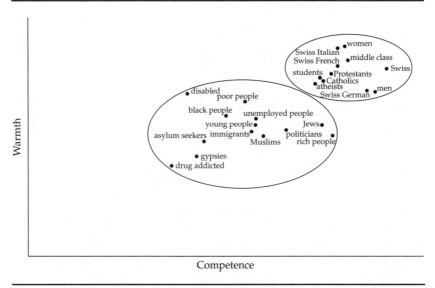

Source: Durante and Fiske (2010), reprinted with permission.
Note: In this highly equal society, note the mainstream groups in the top right and the various outcasts in the lower left. No groups are viewed with ambivalence.

endorse more complex maps of their social groups. Although their maps include the us-versus-them extremes, at least as many groups—and often more—are seen ambivalently (see the BIAS Map for Mexico in figure 7.5). In our terms, more groups are seen as high on warmth or competence, but not both. This ambivalence may reflect a greater need to placate with some redeeming features those groups that are neither at the top nor at the bottom. Ambivalence suggests a bigger role for uncertainty, originating in more diffuse status competition, even with low mobility.

Whatever the country, inequality pits groups against each other. Status competition without mobility makes people unhappy. Even primates know this, at least if they are low-status. Subordinate primates suffer the most in stable dominance hierarchies. They must attend upward and avoid the bigger guys; high stress hormone levels reflect their uncertainty and unease.[48]

Status anxiety makes for good stories because it is complicated and unpredictable. F. Scott Fitzgerald knew this:

"We're the damned middle class, that's what!" he complained to Kerry one day as he lay stretched out on the sofa, consuming a family of Fatimas [cigarettes] with contemplative precision.

Figure 7.5   BIAS Map of Mexico's Highly Unequal Social Groups

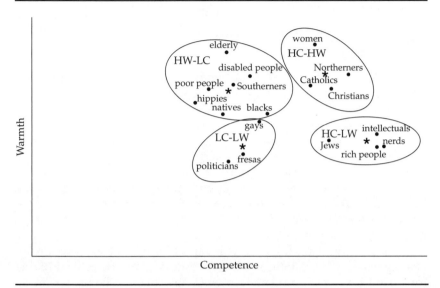

Source: Durante and Fiske (2010), reprinted with permission.
Note: Note the clusters in all four corners, as in U.S. society.

"Well, why not? We came to Princeton so we could feel that way toward the small colleges—have it on 'em, more self-confidence, dress better, cut a swathe—"

"Oh, it isn't that I mind the glittering caste system," admitted Amory. "I like having a bunch of hot cats on top, but gosh, Kerry, I've got to be one of them."[49]

How to Transform Envy and Scorn

Can we cure status anxiety? When I tell people that I am a psychologist, I am quick to add, "But not the kind who actually helps people. I do research." Usually they laugh, having assumed that a psychologist is necessarily a therapist. They also visibly relax when they realize that I do not read minds. But my intro is partly a lie. Research does help people, just indirectly, and I certainly hope that our field's research can help people. Still, I am certainly not a clinician, so it is with some trepidation that I offer this section of how-to advice. I am emboldened by two possibilities: that people, including me, can use these tips to improve their lives, and that research has provided some helpful hints on how to do that. Once again, let's work from the individual to relationships to groups, ending with society as a whole.

In each of these settings, the key to overcoming envy and scorn is making people feel more secure and valued.

As Individuals: Controlling Our Own Envy and Scorn

Scorn   People can suffer from scorning others, despite the apparent advantages of high status. Of course, people know about these advantages of status ("We came to Princeton so we could feel that way toward the small colleges—have it on 'em, more self-confidence, dress better, cut a swathe"). From primates to humans, status has its privileges, bestowing attention, access, credit, respect, and agenda-setting in the immediate situation.[50] And over the long term, status conveys some advantages, mainly access to resources, an obvious advantage to surviving and thriving. Status also divides the superior from the subordinate, creating a distance that may be desired, but in the process it also creates barriers to more shared and human experiences.

Over the long haul, high status is not uniformly a good experience. Having insecure high status is a health hazard, as noted earlier. Striving for financial success can damage family life, making family members unhappy, regardless of income level.[51] Even secure status carries costs: wealth may rob us of the ability to savor experiences and enjoy the moment.[52] Although people with high incomes are generally self-satisfied, in daily life they are more tense, less able to enjoy themselves, and not especially happier than anyone else.[53] Also, scorn is arguably a moral hazard of high status, whether in the form of thoughtless disregard for those who matter less, in the best case, or disgust, contempt, and dehumanization of others, in the worst case.

A more optimistic view is that we can control our feelings of scorn and contempt directed at the less fortunate. On the one hand, we do react to the stigmatized (the obese, people with piercings, transsexuals) with neural signatures of immediate disgust and alarm (the amygdala and insula activate). But on the other hand, we do have control systems that come on line immediately (the anterior cingulate cortex and lateral prefrontal cortex). The pattern suggests that the frontal cortex inhibits the subcortical, more reflexive responses.[54] We know immediately that we must not scorn the stigmatized or mock the afflicted. Our better natures can be evoked almost as automatically as our contempt.

Certain personalities, value systems, and emotions predispose us to empathy.[55] We can try to take the perspective of the stigmatized—someone with AIDS, a homeless person, a prisoner convicted of murder—and when we manage to empathize with such individuals, our attitude improves toward the out-group they represent.[56] In my lab, we imagine this process as one bringing the warmth dimension into a situation that is otherwise only about status. In Veronica Sevillano's study, participants who read a blog from an immigrant, describing all the ups and downs, generally felt little sympathy, with one exception. Those who not only were asked to take the immigrant's perspective but were by nature the kind of people who get immersed in stories viewed the immigrant as more warm and trustworthy than others did. Their empathy prevented them from feeling scorn for a group that is otherwise among the least valued.[57] As predicted, however, empathy improved only impressions of the immigrant's warmth and trust-worthiness, not impressions of competence and status. So without chang-ing relative status, we can turn contempt and disgust into sympathy and pity when we see the other person's perspective. This change does not improve the relative status of the stigmatized, but at least it puts people on the same team. Recognizing the humanity of even stigmatized others can make us feel more virtuous, valuable, and secure. When we catch ourselves at it, we prefer to think of ourselves as treating others as they deserve. But clearly, we can overcome our own tendency toward scorn when we take the trouble.

Envy   On the other side, envying upward is even more irksome. But we might as well try to control our feelings of envy because they can be cor-rosive. According to Peter Salovey and Judith Rodin, we use three strate-gies to cope with our everyday envy:

- Self-reliance: Commit to your own business. Don't give up. Control your resentment.
- Ignoring: Write it off. It's not that important.
- Self-bolstering: You have other good qualities.[58]

The first two of these intuitively sensible strategies focus on the cause of the envy, and they reportedly work well. The more emotion-focused coping strategy, self-bolstering, does reduce depression and anger, some of the emotional fallout from envy, so it works well in that way.

Besides these coping strategies, what do psychologists suggest? Julie Exline and Anne Zell propose several antidotes based on their analysis of the shame and secrecy that surround our feelings of envy. Drawing on the wildly successful techniques of cognitive behavioral therapy, they sug-gest that envy signals some unexamined assumptions that may be the root of the problem.[59] They would urge an envier to:

- Examine goals: Beliefs may be inaccurate (does a Corvette really make people happier?) or illogical (does a tidy desk really indicate produc-tivity?) or unsubstantiated (how do I know whether that winning prize makes up for being lonely?). Changing core beliefs allows more adaptive, useful ones to run your life.

- Face deficits: Acknowledge limitations, and strive to improve in realistic ways. Accept yourself; balance awareness of challenges with gratitude valuing what you do have.[60]

Even outside of therapeutic approaches, cognitive tricks can change your worldview. According to Mark Alicke and Ethan Zell, envy is all about social comparison, which is all relative. Compared to what? Compared with whom? They suggest the following:

- Shift time frames: No need to be stuck in the present. Instead of comparing with others, compare your own progress with your past and potential self. Have you not improved over time? Is the future promising?

- Question authority: Be subjective. Who says the other person is better? By what measure? Comparisons are always open to multiple interpretations.

- Channel anger: Maybe the comparison is unfair. If the enviable person has illegitimate success, then most of us feel angry. But anger is more mobilizing than envy, and resentment can be channeled into accomplishment.

- Control fate: If you have a chance to improve, then do it. Even if your rival's circumstances are better, diligence is on your side, because you can control effort, even if you can't control circumstances.[61]

Longing is envy's cousin. Benign envy wants to have what enviable others have, not to take it away from them. As one character put it in a novel by Henry James (William's psychologically astute brother): "My envy's not dangerous; it would not hurt a mouse. I don't want to destroy the people—I only want to *be* them."[62] Evidence for two types of envy comes from Niels van de Ven and his colleagues' research showing that benign envy is oriented toward moving oneself up rather than bringing the other down.[63] Even though benign envy is still frustrating and unpleasant, because the comparison is explicit, nevertheless it is energizing because it allows more control than malicious envy does. Another suggestion, then, based on this research, would be:

- Move up: Use benign envy to motivate yourself.

Liking transforms envy into inspiration and admiration. We feel admiration when the distance between ourselves and another person is large and we not only identify with that person as part of our own team or tribe but wish the best for him or her. Acknowledging that relative status and competence differ between ourselves and envied others, we can focus on shared tribal loyalties, cuing friendliness and trust. And if the distance is not too great, self-improvement may seem possible.[64] How do we act on such admiration?

- Congratulate: Complimenting another person sincerely acknowledges that the other is deserving, links our fates, and allows us to be inspired.

So we see that for those of us troubled by envious feelings, nearly a dozen coping strategies have emerged from common sense, clinical experience, and laboratory research.

As Dyads: Controlling Envy and Scorn in Relationships

Envy and scorn are two sides of a see-through mirror, like the one-way windows used in observation rooms. When the lights are lit on your side, all you see is yourself in the mirror, as an object of scorn or envy, all too aware of the costs. When the lights are off in your room but on in the other, you can see the other person but not your own reflection. Although the observer is shadowy, you can get a sense of the person's attention and attitude. For each side of the envy-scorn mirror-window, concentrating on self blinds you to anything but your own reflection. But concentrating on the other makes you forget yourself as a target of either envy or scorn and attend to the other person's feelings. In a relationship, this kind of responsiveness is a good thing.[65] Here are some ways to cultivate responsiveness, despite competition, in a close relationship.

Avoid Comparisons   Partners and friends are reluctant to compare openly because it risks damage on both sides, whoever comes out on top or on bottom.[66] The concerned superior wants to spare the partner the public indignity and private humiliation, and of course the inferior wants to avoid having those feelings. Conversely, the concerned inferior wants to spare the outperforming partner public envy and private guilt; again, of course, the superior wants to avoid having those feelings. Let's assume that both partners want to preserve the relationship and spare each other feeling one-up or one-down. (If they do not share that goal, then the relationship will soon degenerate into a state of each being in it alone, responsive only to self-interest. See prior section.) The simplest strategy deflects social comparisons in any potentially competitive domain. Spouses may minimize reports of their triumphs. Colleagues may discuss their toddlers to avoid discussing relative career accomplishments. High school classmates at a reunion may focus on the good old days to avoid awkward inequalities in the present.

Minimize Status Differences   In a discordant relationship, partners envy each other's good fortune or feel malicious joy (schadenfreude) at each other's bad fortune. Responsive partners may share harmonious goals—what Fritz Heider called a "sympathetic identification"—in which they experience each other's fortunes and misfortunes. True sympathy goes beyond mere emotional contagion.[67] To forge a harmonious relationship, the advantaged partner may downplay any privileges, disparaging or hiding them. This is the humble approach.[68] In close relationships, people worried about posing a threat to their partner may minimize any status differences by concealing their status, sabotaging themselves, self-deprecating, or promoting the partner, all efforts to close the gap.[69] In experimental games that simulate reciprocity in relationships, partners who come out ahead become hypercooperative and can alleviate the inequality by taking steps to reduce it.[70]

Explain Away Any Differences   In all relationships, origin stories (how we met) are cherished, but partners also value their shared mythology about relative expertise (who is good at what, and why). The partners carve up their expertise when each partner claims a valued domain.[71] One partner may be the scientist and the other the artist. This explains unequal accomplishment as grounded in distinctive talents. Sometimes partners can come to a mutual understanding by explaining any gap as fair.[72] For example, one partner may have made the effort to be a gourmet cook, whereas the other chose not to try; reporting the effort justifies the difference.[73] Expertise, talent, and motivation all are internal explanations.

Partners can also use external attributions to explain away difference. Explaining a success as a fluke minimizes any inherent differences, making the gap temporary.[74] Success stories that offer external, unstable, and uncontrollable factors (luck) make the teller seem modest and admirable.[75] In contrast, imputed arrogance comes from accounts that attribute success to internal, stable, uncontrollable, and desirable qualities, such as innate intelligence or beauty.

Reduce the Gap   The person on top can lift the partner up. This has to be handled with delicacy, but if the protégé admires the mentor, improvement is possible, and over time the gap can diminish. As we have seen, envy gives way to admiration when we feel that we have an opportunity to improve.[76] So for the one-down partner, the one-up partner's efforts can serve as an antidote to envy. And for the one-up partner, the appeal of the underdog increases if the one-down partner puts in the effort, thus deserving help and seeming more likable.[77]

Mind the Relationship   The key to concord is what Heider termed a "unit" relationship—one in which two people feel they belong together. Each includes the other in the self, as Arthur Aron, Elaine Aron, and their colleagues have so adroitly measured (figure 7.6).[78]

To encourage a unit relationship, emphasize the shared bond. For example, therapy works better when the therapist establishes co-membership early in the initial meeting.[79] That is, some kind of link to a mutual friend,

Figure 7.6   Overlap of Self and Other to Measure Varying Closeness

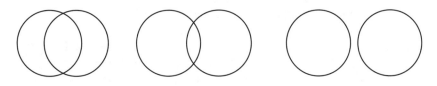

Source: Author's figure based on data from Aron et al. (1991).
Note: Participants choose the pair of circles that best represent their relationship.

a common identity, or a joint membership establishes safety and trust. In contrast, either envy or scorn signals a disconnect that needs repair.[80] Having a unit relationship ensures that comparison is not a zero-sum game because the partners' interests overlap.[81] Cuing a "we" connection makes us think of our similarities instead of our differences.[82] To promote this sense of being a unit, we may placate our partner by investing in the relationship.[83] If we are worried about being envied, we will appease by helping and advising our envious partner.[84]

In Groups: Teammates

At work, most of us operate in small face-to-face groups of three to six coworkers.[85] Given our drive to compete, according to the insights of evolutionary theorists[86] and all our earlier observations showing that comparison is human nature, managers might seem to have a problem on their hands. But the news is better than we might imagine. People do jockey for status, but the process is more constructive than "dog-eat-dog" versions of evolution might suggest, and the advice is clear-cut:

Show Commitment   Remember our refrain that we all need our groups to survive and thrive? To be safe, we compete for status and inclusion not just by beating others at the competence game but also by demonstrating our value to the group.[87] Cameron Anderson and Gavin Kilduff show that of course competence supports status, but so does commitment to the group; we must demonstrate our value to the group to earn both respect for our competence and trust in our cooperativeness as a good team player. We naturally earn status through apparent competence, but our actual skills may not be the only variable. Consistent with the tough evolutionary view, people with dominant personalities signal their alleged expertise by high rates of intervention: they are always quick to volunteer ideas and information. Still, other people dislike such bare-knuckled dominance. In a more emphatically social evolutionary way, we signal our commitment to the group by competitive altruism.[88] Generosity also garners influence. Selfless helping increases our value to the group, which rewards cooperators. Most of us know this: we understand our place in our group and even err on the side of modesty, being too humble, because we know that self-inflation leads to social rejection.[89]

Value Others   Our main antidotes to envy and scorn are making other people feel secure and valued, because these social comparison emotions arise from uncertainty. As Robert Vecchio shows, managers do well to heed the advice to praise and recognize their employees, to make them feel included and valued.[90] All of this soft diplomacy backfires if it is seen as manipulative, so sincerity and plausibility are key. Communality, a leadership skill stereotypically associated with women, works well regardless of the leader's gender, as Alice Eagly's meta-analyses demonstrate.[91]

Across Society: Class Warfare and Identity Politics

John Lennon's "Working Class Hero" (1970) protests being made to feel small, hated for being clever, and then being told that there is room at the top for the ruthless hypocrite. You do not have to be a flower child to notice social class tensions in society. This book has seen plenty of examples of status warfare. A visual image comes from our BIAS Map, described earlier.

Middle-class people are the admired, proud standard, the group seen as both competent (skilled, intelligent) and warm (trustworthy, friendly). At the other extreme, poor people are made to feel small and low-status; expected to be incompetent and untrustworthy, they are scorned downward as disgusting. Halfway between the middle class and the poor, blue-collar (working-class) people fall in the exact middle of the space, either because their image is polarized (the extremes average to the middle) or because people have truly mixed impressions of them. Rich people occupy the top of the status hierarchy; clever but untrustworthy, they are envied and resented.

Earn the Trust   Neither the rich nor the poor appear trustworthy—that is, as people like the rest of us. If rich people do become likable and trusted, they move to the in-group and its allies. Rich people who give away all their money and demand that their children earn their own money are American heroes.

Earn the Respect   The poor have to fight stereotypes from both the warmth and competence dimensions. If poor people overcome the untrustworthy stereotype by becoming likable and trusted, they move only to pity territory. If poor people are hardworking—in contrast to their lazy stereotype—they can earn respect for their competence. So the poor face double jeopardy and a dual challenge.

Other groups face the same dual dilemma. As the current debates suggest, immigrants are typically assumed to be Latinos and are despised in many areas. The terms of the debate determine its conclusion. If immigrants are associated with crime, lacking education, taking jobs away from citizens, and using social services, then they are untrustworthy and incompetent and they are not on our side. If, on the other hand, immigrants are understood to be just like previous generations of immigrants, coming from a variety of countries, with a lower crime rate than comparable citizens, ranging in education, taking jobs no one else wants, even creating new jobs and businesses, and underutilizing social services, then they are part of the American Dream.

Empathize   For societal groups, the lesson is the same as ever: make both sides feel secure and valued. People experience anxiety in intergroup encounters for fear of harm, ridicule, discomfort, or just the awkwardness of not knowing the ground rules. As Walter and Cookie Stephan show, both the past and the present of intergroup relations, stereotypes, and expectations, as well as personal experiences, generate anxiety.[92] Their research program includes encounters between white and black Americans, Latinos and Anglos, students and overseas hosts, immigrants and citizens, cancer or AIDS patients and healthy people. In most cases, realistic threats (competition for resources), symbolic threats (culture wars), intergroup anxiety, and negative stereotypes all contribute to biases about other people who seem to pose a threat. But the good news is that empathy mitigates anxiety. Once again, if we get beyond our own anxieties (insecurity, threat) to understand the situation of another person and sympathize with his or her difficulties, our own anxiety is reduced and our perceived differences are diminished.[93]

Cooperate   Under the right circumstances, intergroup contact reduces prejudices, including envy and scorn. Indeed, emotional reactions drive both the initial distance and the potential relaxation as we let down our guard.[94] Although acquired knowledge helps make the stranger familiar, it is the decreased anxiety and increased empathy that help us overcome our prejudices as we cooperate with out-group individuals in the service of shared goals. We do not have to become friends, but certain circumstances do allow friendship (equal-status cooperation toward shared goals, authority-approved). It is the friendship potential that reduces prejudice.

Even having contact by proxy opens our minds. If a friend has an out-group friend, that also reduces our intergroup anxiety because, in accepting our friend's friend, we develop new norms for accepting the other group as one of us, literally including the out-group in the self.[95] As we saw, social networks convey influence beyond the immediate relationship.

Conclusion

Maybe, in the end, we do not want to transform envy and scorn. Maybe, given what Exline and Zell call "cosmic unfairness," these comparison feelings are simply to be expected.[96] Not only are these feelings natural, but maybe they are even adaptive. Perhaps harmony works for the rich, but not for the poor.[97] Maybe envy—or the potential for envy—domesticates power, harnessing its excesses by threat of revolution.[98] People at the top and bottom alike strongly prefer a stable society and can justify all kinds of system inequalities, even if they are not beneficiaries.[99]

Acceptance of cosmic unfairness distresses some of us because inequality is not just about income—or at least its effects are not. It is about damage to well-being, to feelings of control, self-esteem, belonging, trusting, and understanding. For any of these fundamental needs, inequality catalyzes insecurity, which we know motivates comparison. When uncertainty looms, people need to get information, to protect themselves, and to identify with familiar groups. In turn, comparison can generate resentment and anger about unfairness if the inequality is illegitimate and out of keeping with our meritocracy. Comparison up underlies envy, and comparison down underlies scorn, dividing us from each other. We can only hope that the corrosion of comparison also mobilizes people for change.

Notes

Chapter 1

1. We originally called the two universal dimensions—status (competence) and friend-foe (warmth)—the Stereotype Content Model, which also predicts prejudiced emotions. Adding discriminatory behaviors creates the more aptly named BIAS (Behaviors from Intergroup Affect and Stereotypes) Map. The key papers are Cuddy, Fiske, and Glick (2007); Cuddy et al. (2009); and Fiske et al. (2002). For a short review, see Fiske, Cuddy, and Glick (2007); for a more exhaustive review, see Cuddy, Fiske, and Glick (2008).
2. When status and competence do not seem to coincide, a person may seem more dangerous, and these exceptions are interesting: how do people evaluate incompetent corporate executives or competent panhandlers? (Probably as a loose cannon in the former case and a skilled exploiter in the latter case.) These exceptions remain to be studied, but they would take us too far afield at present.
3. Keller (2005, ix).
4. General Social Survey (2001).
5. Gallup Organization (2002).
6. Russo (2007, 65).
7. Hodge (2008, 359).
8. See the authoritative review by the demographer Michael Hout (2008, 359). To be sure, when people are given another option (for example, "upper-middle"), "middle-class" is not chosen by a majority, but out of five choices, it does prevail as the most popular by an edge of about 20 percent over the last decade (Gallup polls April 11, 2002; January 12, 2003; April 9, 2003; April 7, 2005; April 13, 2006; May 7, 2006; June 25, 2008; June 25, 2008; September 7, 2008; and September 27, 2008); available at: http://institution. gallup.com.proxy.wexler.hunter.cuny.edu (accessed January 10, 2011).
9. Gallup Organization (1939).
10. Granted, there is another excuse for the "we are all middle-class" myth besides data from way back when. When pollsters do not put words in their mouths, people do spontaneously choose "middle-class," according to Hout, who actually asked questions in this open-ended way. He found that 90 percent of us agree that the United States consists of various social classes,

and 54 percent of that 90 percent volunteer that they are "middle-class." Hout then went an extra step and coaxed reluctant respondents to choose a social class. Among those forced to choose, almost equal numbers (about 40 percent each) identify as working- or middle-class. Still, if pollsters can so easily persuade people to label themselves "working-class" at rates about equal to "middle-class" identifications, then "middle-class" is not exactly a fixed identity. In a Pew Poll released as this book went to press, Americans responded to the five class labels without working class, as in the original 1939 Gallup Poll. In 2010, just 50 percent of us say we are middle class, though the overwhelming majority do claim to be middle class, if lower- and upper-middle class categories count as middle class ("Room for Debate: So You Think You're Middle Class?" *New York Times*, December 22, 2010. Available at: http://www.nytimes.com/roomfordebate/2010/12/22/what-does-middle-class-mean-today?hp [accessed December 23, 2010].)

11. *New York Times* (2005).
12. Scott and Leonhardt (2005).
13. See, for instance, Gallup Organization (1947).
14. Hartz (1952, 331).
15. Tocqueville (1840, 101). Translated from the original by Susan Fiske and Steven Grant.
16. Halle (1987); Rubin (1976); but see Vanneman and Cannon (1987).
17. Rockefeller Foundation, *Time* Magazine Campaign for American Workers, and Penn, Schoen, and Berland Associates (2008).
18. Pew Economic Mobility Project and Greenberg Quinlan Rosner Research and Public Opinion Strategies (2009).
19. Sawhill and McLanahan (2006).
20. DeNavas-Walt, Proctor, and Smith (2009).
21. Statistics from Central Intelligence Agency (CIA), "The World Factbook: Country Comparison: Distribution of Family Income—Gini Index," accessed July 12, 2010, from https://www.cia.gov/library/publications/the-world-factbook/rankorder/2172rank.html.
22. Smeeding (2005).
23. Beller and Hout (2006).
24. Kearney (2006).
25. Beller and Hout (2006).
26. Kluegel and Smith (1986).
27. Kluegel and Smith (1986).
28. Gallup Organization (2002 to 2009, various). Downloaded from Gallup Brain, available at: institution.gallup.com.proxy.wexler.hunter.cuny.edu (accessed September 2009).
29. Rockefeller Foundation, *Time* Magazine, Campaign for American Workers, and Penn, Schoen, and Berland Associates (2008).
30. Pew Economic Mobility Project and Greenberg Quinlan Rosner Research and Public Opinion Strategies (2009).
31. Opportunity Agenda (2007; available at: http://www.opportunityagenda.org/public_opinion [accessed September 2009]). Psychologists contrast situational explanations (circumstances are beyond one's own control) with

dispositional explanations (causes reside within oneself; some are controllable, such as effort, and some are not, such as sheer ability). Hence, psychologists see circumstances and effort as opposed explanations.

32. Cuddy et al. (2009).
33. Russell and Fiske (2009).
34. For a review, see Weiner (2006).
35. Chafel (1997); Cozzarelli, Wilkinson, and Tagler (2001).
36. Hochschild (1981).
37. Lamont (1992).
38. Associated Press (2005). Accessed at: surveys.ap.org/data/ipsos/national/2005 (accessed October 2009).
39. Kluegel and Smith (1986).
40. Gallup (2006).
41. Harris Interactive (2005).
42. Bobo (1991).
43. According to a simulation of people's preferences for an ideal society (Mitchell et al. 1993).
44. Unless one believes in the improbable scenario of more and more of the favored few working harder than ever before, while more and more slackers idle.
45. Later chapters expand on some people's persistent belief in a just world, which varies across individuals, and people's general propensity to justify the system in order to maintain stability.
46. Clinton is quoted, for example, in " 'Bitter' Is a Hard Pill for Obama to Swallow: He Stands By as Clinton Pounces," Perry Bacon and Shailagh Murray, *Washington Post*, April 12, 2008. Available at: http://www.washingtonpost.com/wp-dyn/content/article/2008/04/12/AR2008041202094.html (accessed October 10, 2009). Obama is quoted, for example, in "Obama: No Surprise that Hard-Pressed Pennsylvanians Turn Bitter," Mayhill Fowler, *Huffington Post*, April 11, 2008. Available at: http://www.huffingtonpost.com/mayhill-fowler/obama-no-surprise-that-ha_b_96188.html (accessed January 10, 2011).
47. Jeff Zeleny, "Obama Remarks Called 'Out of Touch'," *New York Times*, April 12, 2008, p. 15.
48. Jill Lawrence, "Obama Slams McCain's Inability to Tally Family-Owned Residences," *USA Today*, August 22, 2008, p. 6A.
49. As the *Independent*'s Rupert Cornwell reminded us in "The IoS Profile: John Kerry" (March 7, 2004).
50. As *Time*'s Margaret Carlson put it in "We Raised Him for It" (February 28, 2000).
51. Andrew Rosenthal, "Bush Encounters the Supermarket, Amazed," *New York Times*, February 5, 1992, p. A1.
52. David Brooks, "Clash of Titans," *New York Times*, March 6, 2004, p. 52.
53. NORC (2008).
54. Democracy Corps, Campaign for America's Future, and Greenberg Quinlan Rosner Research (2008).

55. CBS News/*New York Times* (2009).

56. Pew Global Attitudes Project (2009).

57. Pew Global Attitudes Project (2009).

58. Glick et al. (2006).

59. Brooks (2004).

60. Commentators have pointed out that power and status are not invariably correlated. For example, a lame-duck president or an emeritus professor has status but not power; a Department of Motor Vehicles (DMV) clerk or a Transportation Safety Administration (TSA) inspector has power but not status. These are interesting cases precisely because they uncouple status and power, but examining them here would take us too far off course.

61. Cheever (2004, 255–57).

62. Range et al. (2009).

63. Brosnan and de Waal (2003); Brosnan, Schiff, and de Waal (2004).

64. Smith and Kim (2008).

65. Envy is more specific than narcissistic rage, though they share the element of illegitimate threat to a deserving self.

66. Parrott (1991).

67. From Shakespeare student Lydia Emery (January 4, 2010 email): "There are also class issues involved. The audience learns in the first scene that Cassio has a lot of book-learning but no military experience, and he seems to be well off. Iago constructs the familiar story of the hardworking (middle-class?) soldier who gets passed over in favor of the privileged, inexperienced Ivy League type. 'The curse of service' is that 'preferment goes by letter and affection,/and not by old gradation' (I.1.34–36) (i.e., personal preference, not moving up through the ranks; it's who you know, not how hard you work, that refrain of the envious thinking the privileged are undeserving). Also, Cassio is scornful of lower rank/lower class: 'the lieutenant is to be saved before the ensign' (II.3.101–2). Moreover, Desdemona is just a means to shatter Othello himself. Iago is also taking away Othello's place in society (which Othello has laboriously cultivated given the prejudice against him) and self (by destroying Desdemona, Othello destroys himself)."

68. Parrott (1991).

69. See, for example, Glick et al. (2006).

70. "Les envieux mourrant, mais non jamais l'envie" (*Le Tartuffe; Or, The Hypocrite* [1667], V.3.14).

71. Parrott (1991, 27).

72. According to Niels van de Ven, Marcel Zeelenberg, and Rik Pieters (2009), who presumably understand "benijden" versus "afgunst."

73. Parrott (1991, 10).

74. Shaw (1921).

75. Doyle (1894/1986).

76. Herzog (2000, 237).

77. Adams (1805, 345–46, emphasis in original).

78. Darwin (1872/1987).

79. Ekman and Friesen (1986); Matsumoto and Ekman (2004, 536).

80. An alternative expression of scorn is showing one's moral superiority by scorning those whom society has anointed as superior. My bohemian friends report scorning "the suits." In Dostoyevsky's *Notes from Underground*, the narrator reports scorning his more successful officemates. Despite these reports, which ring true as individual experiences, those expressing scorn up the hierarchy are drawing on the assumption that scorn is normally directed downward, since they are challenging the conventional hierarchy by reversing the expected direction of scorn. The examples described in the main text overwhelmingly reflect unexamined scorn directed downward.

81. For a review, see Fiske (2010a).

82. Gruenfeld et al. (2008).

83. De Cremer and van Dijk (2005).

84. Galinsky et al. (2006).

85. For reviews, see Fiske (2010a); Magee and Galinsky (2008).

86. Goodwin et al. (2000).

87. Fiske (2010a).

88. Leyens et al. (2003).

89. Cuddy, Rock, and Norton (2007).

90. Fiske et al. (2002); Cuddy, Fiske, and Glick (2007). In figure 1.7, which shows the plot that looks more like a map, homeless people can be seen to be statistical outliers (three standard deviations from the center of the space).

91. For reviews, see Amodio and Frith (2006); Mitchell (2008).

92. Harris and Fiske (2006, 2007, 2009).

93. Cottrell and Neuberg (2005).

94. Cuddy, Fiske, and Glick (2007).

95. Haslam (2006); Loughnan and Haslam (2007); Haslam et al. (2008).

96. Thomas Pettigrew and Roel Meertens (1995) look at similar treatment of out-groups who were immigrants in Europe (for example, Turks in Germany, North Africans in France, and Pakistanis in Britain).

97. Smith et al. (2004).

98. Rosenberg, Ekman, and Blumenthal (1998).

99. Fredrickson (2001).

100. Jackson and Inglehart (1995).

101. As assessed by Vickie Mays, Susan Cochran, and Namdi Barnes (2007) in an overview of the most recent studies.

102. According to a review by Brenda Major and Laurie O'Brien (2005).

103. On people, see Schneiderman, Ironson, and Siegel (2005); on primates, see Sapolsky (2004).

104. Loughnan and Haslam (2007).

105. Fiske et al. (2002).

106. Dépret and Fiske (1999). This result did not depend on the power-holders being math majors (who might be stereotyped as cold); the effect was also replicated for a "conspiracy" of high-powered art majors (perhaps creative).

107. Cuddy, Fiske, and Glick (2007).

108. Cikara, Botvinick, and Fiske (2011); Cikara et al. (2010).
109. Kaiser Family Foundation, *Washington Post,* and Harvard University (2008).
110. Marlin Company and Zogby International (2008).
111. Uslaner and Brown (2005).
112. Chapter 4 returns to this issue to look at people's reactions to relative deprivation—that is, feeling shortchanged in relation to the most relevant comparison group.
113. Smith, Combs, and Thielke (2008, 296).
114. Dickerson and Kemeny (2004); McEwen (2000); Schneiderman, Ironson, and Siegel (2005).
115. Marmot (2003); Marmot et al. (1997).
116. According to an authoritative review by Linda Gallo and Karen Matthews (2003).
117. Russo (2007, 70, 13).
118. Mendes et al. (2001).
119. Smith et al. (2004).
120. Mullen (1985).
121. Smith et al. (2008).
122. Shelton, Richeson, and Vorauer (2006); Shnabel and Nadler (2008).
123. See Fiske (2010a) for a review of interpersonal stratification, from primates to individual human encounters to organizations to societal systems.
124. Oosterhof and Todorov (2008).
125. O'Mahen, Beach, and Tesser (2000).
126. Gruenfeld and Tiedens (2010).
127. Sidanius and Pratto (1999); for precedent, see Parsons (1964).
128. McGrath (2005, 193).
129. Adams (1805, 352–53).
130. Hill and Buss (2006, 2008); Smith, Combs, and Thielke (2008).
131. Schoeck (1969/1986, 26).
132. Fielding (1752/1988, 328).

Chapter 2

1. Fiske, Cuddy, and Glick (2007).
2. Wojciszke, Bazinska, and Jaworski (1998).
3. Hogg (2010).
4. Berger, Cohen, and Zelditch (1972); Ridgeway (1991, 1997).
5. Gruenfeld and Tiedens (2010).
6. Magee and Galinsky (2008); Jost and Kay (2010); Sidanius and Pratto (1999).
7. Psychological science most often interprets emotions as including some combination of conscious or unconscious experience, physiology, and action tendencies, among other signals. No single component is necessary or sufficient to label a human event an emotion. In what follows, I examine some clues from neuroscience, but this does not imply that we know the neural signa-

tures for any particular emotion. Like all the other components of emotions, these are just responses that tend to happen together and may converge to illuminate one level of analysis.

8. See, for example, Adolphs (2009); LeDoux (2000); Phelps (2006); Whalen (2007).

9. Fiske and Taylor (2008).

10. Harris and Fiske (2006). Note that these undergraduates also expressed pity toward the homeless and the drug addicts, but not as much as they expressed for the elderly and the disabled. Similarly, they admitted some disgust toward these pitied groups, but by far the most disgust toward the outcasts.

11. In this study, the amygdala activated higher than baseline to all pictures of people, but especially activated to the disgusting targets. In a later study, it also especially activated to envied targets (Harris, Cikara, and Fiske, 2008).

12. Rule et al. (2009).

13. To be fair, all of them were volunteers who had given informed consent, and none of them had an eating disorder. And of course, people compare their own bodies to others' all the time. (Think of the gym.) The authors are concerned with precisely this kind of potentially destructive social comparison. See Friederich et al. (2007).

14. Phelps et al. (2000); see also Hart et al. (2000).

15. Botvinick, Cohen, and Carter (2004). The ACC is a curved swath of cortex, and the focal area appears to be dorsal, that is, toward the top of the ACC curve.

16. Friederich et al. (2007).

17. Takahashi et al. (2009). Control comparisons included a superior but other-sex student or a mediocre other-sex student; participants envied neither of these irrelevant students.

18. Eisenberger, Lieberman, and Williams (2003); Sanfey et al. (2003).

19. Other summaries of this admittedly scant research agree with this assessment; see Joseph et al. (2008); Lieberman and Eisenberger (2009). Of course, the ACC is implicated in many processes, of which envy would be only one.

20. For reviews, see Amodio and Frith (2006); Mitchell (2008).

21. Friederich et al. (2007). The location of the mPFC activation is more dorsal (top), which is consistent with thinking about others, especially dissimilar others (Mitchell, Macrae, and Banaji 2006). Admittedly, self-thoughts also activate the mPFC, but usually in a more ventral (lower) region, according to Jason Mitchell, Mahzarin Banaji, and Neil Macrae (2005).

22. Harris, Cikara, and Fiske (2008).

23. Harris et al. (2007); van den Bos et al. (2007). Some parts of the mPFC activate to rewards in general, but social rewards especially light it up.

24. Ames and Fiske (2010).

25. Cottrell and Neuberg (2005).

26. Harris and Fiske (2006, 2009).

27. For meta-analyses of the insula's role in disgust, see Murphy, Nimmo-Smith, and Lawrence (2002); Phan et al. (2002). Note that the insula's broader role in arousal suggests that it is not specific to disgust. Rather, disgust reliably activates it.

28. Krendel et al. (2006).
29. Sambataro et al. (2006).
30. Fliessbach et al. (2007); Lieberman and Eisenberger (2009).
31. Izuma, Saito, and Sadato (2008).
32. Moll et al. (2007). Also arguably relevant might be studies showing VS activation when one is treated fairly; see, for example, Rilling et al. (2004); Tabibnia, Satpute, and Lieberman (2008).
33. See chapter 3, however, on cultural and individual differences.
34. Neural studies of schadenfreude tend to focus on peer competitors, especially those who play unfairly (see, for example, de Quervain et al. 2004; Singer et al. 2006). That kind of malicious pleasure does not necessarily target the envied, merely equal competitors, but it does activate the VS, just as the VS celebrates schadenfreude in bringing down the previously superior envied person.
35. Takahashi et al. (2009).
36. Keltner and Haidt (1999).
37. Bacon (1597/1985, 21).
38. The measure uses electrodes pasted onto the surface of the zygomaticus major; see Cikara and Fiske (2010).
39. van Dijk et al. (2006).
40. Feather and Naim (2005); Feather and Sherman (2002); Hareli and Weiner (2002); van Dijk et al. (2005).
41. Neuberg et al. (1994); Hebl and Mannix (2003).
42. Simon (1967).
43. Fiske, Cuddy, and Glick (2007); Oosterhof and Todorov (2008). People pick up disgust expressions even at subliminal presentation rates, according to Paula Niedenthal (1990).
44. Keltner and Haidt (1999).
45. Gaines et al. (2005); Smith et al. (2006); Webster et al. (2003).
46. Anderson and Berdahl (2002); Berdahl and Martorana (2006); Langner and Keltner (2008).
47. Mendes et al. (2001).
48. Tiedens (2001).
49. Knutson (1996).
50. Sinaceur and Tiedens (2006).
51. Fischer and Roseman (2007).
52. Tesser, Millar, and Moore (1988).
53. Smith, Seger, and Mackie (2007).
54. Keltner, Gruenfeld, and Anderson (2003); Langner and Keltner (2008).
55. Wojciszke and Struzynska-Kujalowicz (2007).
56. Mendes et al. (2001).
57. Tiedens (2001).
58. Knutson (1996).
59. Roseman, Wiest, and Swartz (1994).
60. Oosterhof and Todorov (2008); Zebrowitz and Montepare (2005).

61. Mohandas Gandhi quote from BrainyQuote.com, accessed July 18, 2010, from http://www.brainyquote.com/quotes/quotes/m/mohandasga103630.html.
62. Keltner and Haidt (1999).
63. Peters and Kashima (2007).
64. Smith, Seger, and Mackie (2007). See also Moons et al. (2009). Including the group in the self relates to including individual others (relationship partners) in the self; see, for example, Aron et al. (1991).
65. Cikara, Botvinick, and Fiske (2011). The relevant empathic pain network includes activations in the dorsal anterior cingulate cortex, the supplementary motor area, and the anterior insula, which correlates with self-reported pain.
66. Nietzsche (1887/1967, 37).
67. Leach and Spears (2008); Leach et al. (2008); Mikula, Scherer, and Athenstaedt (1998).
68. Branscombe, Schmitt, and Harvey (1999); Major, Quinton, and Schmader (2003); McCoy and Major (2003); Operario and Fiske (2001b); Sellers and Shelton (2003).
69. Jetten, Spears, and Manstead (1997); Wong, Eccles, and Sameroff (2003).
70. Branscombe and Wann (1994); Jetten et al. (2001); Major, Kaiser, and McCoy (2003); Major, Quinton, and Schmader (2003). Sometimes strong in-group identity makes prejudice more damaging to self-esteem because of overlap between self and in-group; see, for example, McCoy and Major (2003).
71. Coser (1960); Keltner et al. (2001).
72. Hogg (2007, 2010).
73. Rozin, Haidt, and Fincher (2009); Rozin et al. (1999).
74. Harris and Fiske (2009).
75. Peters, Kashima, and Clark (2009).
76. Heath, Bell, and Sternberg (2001).
77. Rozin et al. (1999).
78. Admittedly, contempt and disgust differ: contempt targets only people, whereas disgust can target people or objects. Emotion theorists distinguish the basic emotions (happy, sad, angry, disgusted) from the more social emotions (envy, jealousy, pride, pity). In contrast to the basic emotion of disgust, envy is a self-conscious emotion that results from thinking and motivates further thinking; see Niedenthal, Krauth-Gruber, and Ric (2006).
79. Silver and Sabini (1978).
80. Leach (2008); Smith (1991).
81. Exline and Lobel (1999, 2001); Parrott and Mosquera (2008).
82. See, for example, Fiske et al. (1998).
83. Festinger (1954a, 1954b).
84. Stapel and Blanton (2004).
85. Mussweiler, Rüter, and Epstude (2006).
86. As meta-analysis indicates; see Want (2009).
87. Blanton and Stapel (2008).
88. Chambers and Windschitl (2009).
89. Marsh and Hau (2003).

90. Tesser (1988).
91. Heider (1958).
92. Chambers and Windschitl (2009).
93. Blanton and Stapel (2008).
94. So too is the possible self. Considering "who I might become" restrains our urge to contrast ourselves with someone worse off or better off ("there but for fortune . . ."). Both the collective and possible selves assimilate, whereas the personal self contrasts.
95. Hogg (2007).
96. Hogg et al. (2007); Mullin and Hogg (1998).
97. Fathali Moghaddam (2005), in a more focused analysis of how people become terrorists, includes us-versus-them thinking, one form of categorical cognition that resolves uncertainty.
98. Lord et al. (2001).
99. Fiske (1993).
100. Dépret and Fiske (1999).
101. Cuddy et al. (2009).
102. Countless social scientists have made this point, but our data specify the status-equals-competence stereotypes; see, for example, Fiske et al. (2002); Lee and Fiske (2006).
103. Cuddy and Frantz (2009).
104. Bettencourt et al. (2001).
105. Alan Fiske (1992), author's brother.
106. Giessner and Schubert (2007); Jostmann, Lakens, and Schubert (2009); Schubert (2005); Schubert, Waldzus, and Giessner (2009).
107. Williams and Bargh (2008).
108. Chartrand and Bargh (1999).
109. Tiedens and Fragale (2003).
110. These cues illustrate turn-taking strategies. For more detail, see Starkey Duncan and Donald Fiske (1977), author's father. Specifically on looking while listening and not while talking, see Dovidio and Ellyson (1982).
111. Holtgraves (2010).
112. Dahl, Kazan, and Swicord (1996).
113. Guinote (2007); Magee (2009).
114. Dahl, Kazan, and Swicord (1996).
115. Tiedens and Fragale (2003).
116. Hall, Coats, and LeBeau (2005).
117. Kraus and Keltner (2009).
118. For an entertaining descriptive account, see Fussell (1983).
119. See Fiske (2010a) for a review.
120. Cuddy, Fiske, and Glick (2007); Fiske et al. (2002).
121. Eisenberger, Lieberman, and Williams (2003); Williams (2007).
122. Gonsalkorale and Williams (2007).
123. Weiner (1980).
124. National Coalition for the Homeless (2009).

125. Cikara et al. (2010).
126. Baumeister, Smart, and Boden (1996).
127. Cuddy, Fiske, and Glick (2007).
128. See, for example, Commins and Lockwood (1979); for a review of equity in close relationships, see Hatfield, Rapson, and Aumer-Ryan (2008).
129. de Quervain et al. (2004); Fehr and Fischbacher (2003).
130. Staub (1989).
131. David Brooks, "Clash of Titans," *New York Times,* March 6, 2004, p. A15.

Chapter 3

1. Gibbons and Buunk (1999).
2. Buunk and Gibbons (2006); Gibbons and Buunk (1999).
3. Fenigstein, Scheier, and Buss (1975).
4. Stapel and Tesser (2001).
5. Swap and Rubin (1983, 210).
6. Crocker and Knight (2005); Crocker and Wolfe (2001).
7. Buunk and Gibbons (2006).
8. Markus and Nurius (1986).
9. Alan Bond quote from Woopidoo! Quotations, accessed July, 19, 2010, from http://www.woopidoo.com/business_quotes/authors/alan-bond/index.htm.
10. Buunk and Brenninkmeijer (2001); van Yperen, Brenninkmeijer, and Buunk (2006).
11. Smith et al. (1999), printed with permission.
12. Of course, the correlations could go either way; see Smith and Kim (2007).
13. Smith et al. (1996).
14. McCullough, Emmons, and Tsang (2002); McCullough, Tsang, and Emmons (2004).
15. "Frienvy" definition from Urban Dictionary, accessed July 21, 2010, from http://www.urbandictionary.com/define.php?term=frienvy.
16. Thackeray (1879, 2); all antique oddities of spelling and capitalization are in the original.
17. Haidt, McCauley, and Rozin (1994).
18. Machiavelli (1965, 66)
19. Trapnell and Wiggins (1990).
20. Moeller, Robinson, and Zabelina (2008).
21. Robinson et al. (2008).
22. Assor, Aronoff, and Messé (1981, 1986); Battistich and Aronoff (1985).
23. Operario and Fiske (2001a).
24. General Social Survey (2006).
25. Lyubomirsky (2001).
26. Adams (1979/1996, 142, 236).
27. Lyubomirsky and Ross (1997).
28. Lyubomirsky, Tucker, and Kasri (2001).

29. See, for example, Taylor and Brown (1988).
30. Testa and Major (1990).
31. More research is needed, but the current literature hints at this plausible idea; see Smith and Kim (2007).
32. Proust (1913–27).
33. "Et peut-être, ce qu'il ressentait en ce moment de presque agréable, c'était autre chose aussi que l'apaisement d'un doute et d'une douleur: un plaisir de l'intelligence." Proust (1913–27, chapter 2 [no page numbers]), translated by the author, accessed July 21, 2010, from http://ebooks.adelaide.edu.au/p/proust/marcel/p96d/chapter2.html.
34. Greco and Roger (2001, 2003).
35. Hodson and Sorrentino (1999); Kruglanski and Webster (1996).
36. Roney and Sorrentino (1995a, 1995b).
37. Men and women are similar in that their self-esteem depends first on what other people think of them—so-called reflected appraisals (see text for items). Then they care about their own feelings of competence (assessed by how they value "getting a lot of work done," "solving a challenging problem," and "recognizing you've done a good job, even if no one else does"). Finally, both men and women care about social comparison (see text for items). Within this shared order of priorities, women are higher on the first and men are higher on the third—at least those men and women who are undergraduates (Schwalbe and Staples 1991).
38. Most gender differences are exaggerated, but the differences are large in meta-analyses across studies for physical aggression, assertiveness, and autocratic leadership style, and they are also reliable, if small, for competitive negotiation behavior (Hyde 2005; see also the review in Singleton and Vacca 2007).
39. Guimond et al. (2006).
40. Schwalbe and Staples (1991).
41. A reliable result across more than 150 studies; see Myers and Crowther (2009).
42. Wojciszke et al. (1998).
43. Gardner, Gabriel, and Hochschild (2002).
44. Kemmelmeier and Oyserman (2001a).
45. U.S. Department of Labor (2009).
46. Bylsma and Major (1992, 1994); Major and Forcey (1985); Major and Konar (1984); Major, McFarlin, and Gagnon (1984). On denial, see Crosby (1984).
47. O'Brien and Major (2009).
48. Stephens, Markus, and Townsend (2007).
49. Bobo (1991); Cozzarelli, Wilkinson, and Tagler (2001); Hunt (1996).
50. Pratto et al. (1994); Sidanius and Pratto (1999).
51. Guimond and Dambrun (2002).
52. Chiao et al. (2009).
53. Sibley and Duckitt (2008).

54. Haley and Sidanius (2005).
55. Christopher et al. (2008).
56. Duckitt (2006); Duckitt and Sibley (2009).
57. Kahn et al. (2009); Pratto, Sidanius, and Levin (2006).
58. Jost and Burgess (2000).
59. Sidanius and Pratto (1999).
60. Sidanius and Pratto (1999).
61. SDO correlates with right-wing authoritarianism (RWA, an indicator of social conservatism; see next section) at 0.32, but is stronger in countries with high ideological conflict (averaging 0.42 across samples in Italy, Germany, Belgium, Sweden, and New Zealand) versus low ideological conflict (averaging 0.20 in U.S. and Canadian samples); see Roccato and Ricolfi (2005).
62. Bartels (2008); McCarty, Poole, and Rosenthal (2006).
63. Bartels (2008, 295).
64. Christopher et al. (2008).
65. Cozzarelli, Wilkinson, and Tagler (2001); Zucker and Weiner (1993).
66. Sample items 1, 2, 3, 5, 7, 10, and 12 from the Right-Wing Authoritarianism Scale (Altemeyer 1998), reproduced by permission of the author; for the full scale, see www.theauthoritarians.com.
67. Altemeyer (1998). See a meta-analysis by Duckitt and Sibley (2009) of the personality correlates of RWA.
68. Christopher et al. (2008).
69. MacDonald (1972); Christopher and Schlenker (2005).
70. Alain de Botton, "A Kinder, Gentler Philosophy of Success" (67), filmed July 2009 for Ted Global, accessed February 3, 2010, from http://www.ted.com/talks/alain_de_botton_a_kinder_gentler_philosophy_of_success.html.
71. Sibley and Duckitt (2008).
72. Furnham (1997).
73. Janoff-Bulman (2009).
74. Thornhill and Fincher (2007).
75. Brooks (2004, 44).
76. Thornhill and Fincher (2007).
77. Hogg (2007).
78. Of course, people may have contradictory tendencies. Women tend to be more liberal than men on certain issues, so liberal women (for example, women who are aware of gender inequality) may make comparisons more than do conservative men (who are more comfortable with traditional gender hierarchies). Doubtless, a person's inclination depends on the primary relevant identity, the dimension of comparison, and the group or individual level of comparison. For example, a woman may recognize gender inequality at a group level but not at an individual level (Crosby 1984).
79. Markus and Kitayama (1991); Triandis (1995).
80. Oyserman, Coon, and Kemmelmeier (2002). Surprisingly, Latin American samples appear to be as individualist as the U.S. samples, but Oyserman

and her colleagues speculate that high-status student samples may underestimate the cultural differences.

81. Vandello and Cohen (1999).
82. Fiske and Yamamoto (2005).
83. Hornsey and Jetten (2005).
84. Shuper et al. (2004); Yamagishi, Cook, and Watabe (1998).
85. Allik and Realo (2004).
86. Stapel and Koomen (2001).
87. Lindholm (2008).
88. Freeman et al. (2009).
89. Nisbett and Cohen (1996).
90. Markus and Kitayama (1991).
91. Oyserman, Coon, and Kemmelmeier (2002).
92. Vandello and Cohen (1999). Probably because of its Mormon population, Utah is also a collectivist state.
93. Freeman et al. (2009).
94. Yamagishi, Cook, and Watabe (1998).
95. Brauer and Chaurand (2009).
96. Chiao et al. (2009).
97. Oyserman and Lee (2008).
98. Kemmelmeier and Oyserman (2001b).
99. Uchida et al. (2009).
100. For a collection of evil eye folklore, see Dundes (1981).
101. Dundes (1981, 192).
102. Lindholm (2008).
103. Fiske (2010a).
104. Gamache (1946, unnumbered advertising page, sequential p. 98). A search for Henri Gamache suggests that the name was a pseudonym and that Raymond Publishing no longer exists.
105. Caporael (1997).
106. Fiske (2010a).
107. Baumeister and Leary (1995).
108. Williams, Cheung, and Choi (2000).
109. Eisenberger et al. (2003).
110. Brown et al. (2003); Master et al. (2009).
111. DeWall et al. (2010).
112. Gardner, Pickett, and Knowles (2005).
113. Cacioppo and Patrick (2008).
114. Kiecolt-Glaser et al. (2002).
115. Lett et al. (2007).
116. House, Landis, and Umberson (1988).
117. Diener and Oishi (2005).
118. Molden et al. (2009).
119. Parrott and Mosquera (2008).

Chapter 4

1. Sedikides and Skowronski (1997).
2. Likewise, how do we know what to believe unless at least some relevant others share our views? ("Is this country generally going in the right direction?") Other people serve as a reality check on our beliefs ("I am glad I am not the only one who thinks that!") as well as our abilities ("Am I really good at this or not?").
3. Taylor and Brown (1988).
4. Laurin, Kay, and Moscovitch (2008).
5. Fiske (2010b).
6. Wood, Taylor, and Lichtman (1985).
7. Taylor, Lichtman, and Wood (1984).
8. As one of the field's founders, he is known for his theory of cognitive dissonance, which is not so relevant here. He lays out his social comparison theory in his lesser-known *Nebraska Symposium on Motivation* chapter (Festinger 1954a), which is more readable than his better-known *Human Relations* article (Festinger 1954b). For reviews of what followed, see Buunk and Gibbons (2007), Guimond (2006), Suls, Martin, and Wheeler (2000), and Suls and Wheeler (2000).
9. Suls, Martin, and Wheeler (2002).
10. Goethals and Darley (1977).
11. The proxy's performance is useful only if he or she exerts effort; see Suls, Martin, and Wheeler (2002).
12. Ames (2004).
13. Wert and Salovey (2004).
14. Baumeister, Zhang, and Vohs (2004); Dunbar (2004).
15. Ruscher, Cralley, and O'Farrell (2005).
16. Updike (1985, 48).
17. Goethals and Darley (1977).
18. Suls, Martin, and Wheeler (2000).
19. Wood (1989).
20. Mussweiler and Rüter (2003). For reviews of Mussweiler's work, see Mussweiler (2003) or Mussweiler, Rüter, and Epstude (2006).
21. Mussweiler, Rüter, and Epstude (2004). See also Stapel and Blanton (2004).
22. Mussweiler and Rüter (2003).
23. Gilbert, Giesler, and Morris (1995).
24. Fiske and Taylor (2008); Gladwell (2005).
25. Mussweiler (2003).
26. Häfner and Schubert (2009).
27. Blanton and Stapel (2008, study 3).
28. Blanton and Stapel (2008, studies 1a and 1b).
29. We not only judge ourselves by comparison with others but also automatically judge others by comparison with ourselves; see Dunning (2000).
30. Taylor and Lobel (1989).

31. Lockwood and Kunda (1997).
32. Chambers and Windschitl (2004).
33. Kruger et al. (2008).
34. Runciman (1966).
35. Donald Kinder and Cindy Kam (2009) provide an engaging account of a grim topic.
36. Stouffer et al. (1949).
37. The first mention of the term "relative deprivation" seems to be in Stouffer et al. (1949, 122–30).
38. Insko et al. (1990).
39. Pettigrew et al. (2008).
40. Wright and Tropp (2002).
41. Smith et al. (2010).
42. Smith and Ho (2002).
43. Wright and Tropp (2002).
44. Commonly attributed to Freud, but, according to the Freud Museum web-site (accessed October 12, 2010, from http://www.freud.org.uk/about/faq/), "this formula was cited by Erik Erikson but it is not to be found in Freud's works, although the sentiment is sometimes implied. During his long engagement Freud stated that his own ambition in life was to have Martha as his wife and to be able to work."
45. Marsh and Hau (2003).
46. Blanton et al. (1999).
47. Gibbons et al. (2000).
48. Huguet et al. (2001).
49. Huguet et al. (2009).
50. Trautwein et al. (2009).
51. Cheng and Lam (2007).
52. Dostoyevsky (1864/1994, 48).
53. Wheeler and Miyake (1992); Wood (1996).
54. For a comprehensive review, see Greenberg, Ashton-James, and Ashkanasy (2007).
55. Moore and Small (2007).
56. Vecchio (2000).
57. Vecchio (2005).
58. Vecchio (1997).
59. Bulwer (1836, 235–36).

Chapter 5

1. The key original references are Taylor and Lobel (1989) and Wood (1989). See Buunk and Gibbons (2007) for a recent review.
2. Klein (1997).
3. Moore and Klein (2008).

4. Sedikides and Gregg (2008). Although in some form fundamental to human nature, self-enhancement does differ across cultures; Westerners take a more obviously self-promoting view, and Easterners take a more modest self-sympathetic view (Markus and Kitayama 1991).

5. Pronin, Gilovich, and Ross (2004).

6. Ross and Wilson (2003); Wilson and Ross (2001). Again, this tendency varies by culture, the clearest example of "chumps to champs" thinking being provided by Westerners (Ross et al. 2005). Westerners sometimes revel in past glories, but only as long as they can continue to look good.

7. Sanitioso, Kunda, and Fong (1990).

8. Kunda (1990).

9. Taylor and Brown (1988).

10. Robins and Beer (2001).

11. On fantasy versus expectancy, see Oettingen and Mayer (2002); on the original "self-fulfilling prophecy," see Merton (1948).

12. Contemplating future events produces stronger emotions than contemplating past ones; see Caruso, Gilbert, and Wilson (2008). One exception may occur in older old age, when people stay cheerful in part by selecting the most positive current experiences and past memories to contemplate, thereby minimizing negative affect but using the limited future time horizon to live well in the present; see Carstensen and Charles (1998).

13. Redersdorff and Guimond (2006).

14. Weinstein (1980).

15. Gilbert and Wilson (2007); Wilson and Gilbert (2005).

16. Taylor (1991); Wilson and Gilbert (2008).

17. Gibbons and Gerrard (1995); Gibbons, Helweg-Larsen, and Gerrard (1995). A future orientation and imagining a possible self mimics these effects, according to Judith Ouellette and her colleagues (2005).

18. Sanitioso, Conway, and Brunot (2006).

19. Zell and Alicke (2009).

20. Gilbert et al. (2009).

21. Heider (1958).

22. Henagan and Bedeian (2009).

23. Exline and Lobel (1999).

24. Of course, despite the "unmanning" part, this thought experiment applies to women as well as to men. Powers (1972) appears in a wonderful meditation on the "pleasure and pain of social comparison" by Philip Brickman and Ronnie Janoff-Bulman (1977).

25. Exline and Lobel (1999) review dozens of studies that are relevant here.

26. Matina Horner (1972) described women's conflict between achievement and femininity, but later scholars interpreted that conflict as either the need of anyone, male or female, to compromise between goals (for instance, between achievement and friendship; see Hyland 1989) or the fear we all have of sex-role incongruence (Tresemer 1977). Most of us, however, do not value success regardless of its cost.

27. Examples are taken from Exline and Lobel (1999)—except for the Japanese salaryman, whose leeway under the influence I learned about from personal communication with colleagues.
28. Exline and Lobel (1999, table 1).
29. Smith (1991).
30. Salovey and Rothman (1991). In this scenario, malicious envy arises not just from the incursion into our own domain, but also from our subsequent sense of our own failure and low self-esteem; see Salovey and Rodin (1991).
31. James (1890/1983, 311).
32. Gibbons, Benbow, and Gerrard (1994); Johnson and Stapel (2007); Stapel and Johnson (2007). Our own performance expectations and the culture's stereotypes about our group can make us withdraw from achievement domains where we may expect to fail anyway. On personal expectations, see Aronson and Carlsmith (1962); on cultural stereotypes, see Steele (1997).
33. Alicke et al. (1997).
34. Lockwood and Kunda (1997).
35. Collins (2000).
36. Wills (1981). For an update, see Buunk and Gibbons (2007).
37. Gibbons et al. (2002).
38. Aspinwall and Taylor (1993); Gibbons (1986); Wayment and Taylor (1995).
39. Bauer, Wrosch, and Jobin (2008).
40. Roese (1994).
41. Downward comparison can involve actively seeking and derogating someone who is worse off. (Under major threat, people with high self-esteem do this the most; that is how they maintain their self-esteem.) Downward comparison can also involve passive encounters with people who are worse off. (People with low self-esteem are more often in this position.) In both cases, downward comparison makes people feel better, as they expect it will. For details, see Gibbons and Boney-McCoy (1991); Gibbons and Gerrard (1989); Gibbons et al. (2002). See also Wheeler and Miyake (1992).
42. Lockwood (2002).
43. Buunk et al. (1990); Michinov (2001).
44. Epstude and Mussweiler (2009).
45. Michinov and Bavent (2001).
46. Aspinwall and Taylor (1992).
47. Wayment and Taylor (1995).
48. Myers and Crowther (2009).
49. van den Berg et al. (2007).
50. Trampe, Stapel, and Siero (2007).
51. Hobza et al. (2007).
52. van den Berg and Thompson (2007).
53. Lew et al. (2007).
54. Taylor and Lobel (1989).
55. Kulik and Mahler (2000).

56. Taylor, Lichtman, and Wood (1984); Wood, Taylor, and Lichtman (1985). Taylor (1989) and Taylor and Brown (1988) both note the boundary between positive illusions and delusional extremes.

57. Helgeson and Taylor (1993); Taylor et al. (1991).

58. Taylor et al. (2000).

59. Segerstrom and Sephton (2010).

60. Affleck et al. (1987).

61. Tennen and Affleck (1990).

62. Affleck et al. (1987).

63. For a recent review, see Lechner, Tennen, and Affleck (2009).

64. Affleck and Tennen (1991). Of course, this outcome also depends on not having completely unreasonable expectations of control over events they cannot control.

65. Schulz and Decker (1985).

66. Janoff-Bulman (1992).

67. Original: Dans l'adversité de nos meilleurs amis nous trouvons toujours quelque chose ne nous déplaist pas.

68. An alternative version, also attributed to Vidal: "Whenever a friend succeeds a little something in me dies." Both quotes are all over the Internet. My original source was Powers (1972).

69. Singleton and Vacca (2007).

70. Heider (1958, 287).

71. Tesser (1988); see Beach and Tesser (1995).

72. Tesser, Campbell, and Smith (1984).

73. Tesser and Paulhus (1983).

74. Tesser and Smith (1980).

75. Pemberton and Sedikides (2001).

76. Tesser, Pilkington, and McIntosh (1989).

77. Tesser, Millar, and Moore (1988).

78. The classic study is Cialdini et al. (1976), but this study focuses on basking in a group's success; the next chapter describes it in more detail.

79. Pinkus et al. (2008).

80. Lockwood et al. (2004).

81. Tesser et al. (2000).

82. Beach et al. (1998); Mendolia, Beach, and Tesser (1996); Pilkington, Tesser, and Stephens (1991).

83. Exline and Lobel (2001).

84. Beach et al. (2001); O'Mahen, Beach, and Tesser (2000).

85. Karney and Frye (2002).

86. Frye and Karney (2002).

87. Frye and Karney (2002).

88. Endo, Heine, and Lehman (2000).

89. Buunk et al. (1991).

90. Buunk et al. (1990).

91. For an early meditation, see Heider (1958, ch. 11); for a more recent one, see Alicke and Zell (2008).
92. Fiske (2010a).
93. Lindholm (2008).
94. Schwinghammer, Stapel, and Blanton (2006).
95. Stapel and Johnson (2007).
96. Aron et al. (1991); Aron et al. (2004).
97. Bertolt Brecht lyrics from the 1954 Marc Blitzstein translation of *The Threepenny Opera* [*Die Dreigroschenoper*], with music by Kurt Weill, first performed in Berlin, 1928.
98. Maybe Carly Simon (1972) had the better strategy, going more public with her revenge and making money at it, with her hit, "You're So Vain (You Probably Think This Song Is About You)."
99. Jones and Pittman (1982).

Chapter 6

1. Eisenberger, Lieberman, and Williams (2003).
2. Brewer (1991).
3. Hatfield, Cacioppo, and Rapson (1994).
4. Chartrand and Bargh (1999).
5. Gump and Kulik (1997).
6. Cherulnik et al. (2001); McHugo et al. (1985).
7. To be sure, Americans conform less than people in some other cultures, and less now than we did in the 1950s, but conformity is still a hallmark of group life; see Bond and Smith (1996).
8. Crandall (1988).
9. Christakis and Fowler (2007); Smith and Christakis (2008).
10. Granovetter (1973).
11. Berkman et al. (2000).
12. Sacerdote (2001).
13. Leary et al. (1995).
14. Zadro, Williams, and Richardson (2004).
15. Baumeister and Leary (1995).
16. Leary (2007).
17. Spencer et al. (1998).
18. Fein and Spencer (1997); see also Sinclair and Kunda (1999, 2000). To be sure, people seem to enhance their own selves more than they enhance their group (at least individualist Westerners do). Also, under threat, people with high self-esteem protect themselves more (relative to those with low self-esteem) by derogating an out-group; see Crocker et al. (1987). For a review, see Sedikides and Gregg (2008).
19. Knowles et al. (2010).
20. Marilynn Brewer and Wendi Gardner (1996) invented the technique. Diederik Stapel and Willem Koomen (2001) conducted the research described here.

21. Gordijn and Stapel (2006). The assumption is that this must be unconscious behavior because people would not lower their test performance on purpose.

22. For some of the original authors, see Tajfel (1974) and Turner et al. (1987). For recent overviews of intergroup context and bias, see Yzerbyt and Demoulin (2010) and Dovidio and Gaertner (2010). For a brief introduction, see Fiske (2010b, chapters 11 and 12).

23. See, for example, Zagefka and Brown (2005). We are most likely to make this comparison when assessing our local status, which is often the most relevant to us, rather than when making some abstract judgment about people in general; see Miller, Turnbull, and McFarland (1988).

24. Zell and Alicke (2009).

25. Correll and Park (2005).

26. Cialdini et al. (1976).

27. Cialdini and De Nicholas (1989).

28. Crocker (1999).

29. Luhtanen and Crocker (1992).

30. Crocker and Luhtanen (1990).

31. Tennen, McKee, and Affleck (2000).

32. Finlay, Dinos, and Lyons (2001).

33. Mussweiler and Bodenhausen (2002).

34. Hall and Crisp (2008).

35. Moons et al. (2009); see also Cikara, Botvinick, and Fiske (2011), described later.

36. Smith, Seger, and Mackie (2007).

37. Campbell (1958).

38. Rothbart and Taylor (1992); Yzerbyt, Corneille, and Estrada (2001).

39. Hogg (2000).

40. Forsyth (2000).

41. Marx, Stapel, and Muller (2005).

42. Mussweiler, Gabriel, and Bodenhausen (2000).

43. Tajfel (1974, 70); see also Tajfel (1982) and Turner et al. (1987).

44. Buunk and Mussweiler (2001).

45. Wills (1981).

46. Dambrun, Guimond, and Taylor (2006); Garcia et al. (2006); Yzerbyt et al. (2006).

47. Bergsieker et al. (2010); Lee and Fiske (2006).

48. Bettencourt et al. (2001).

49. Brewer and Weber (1994); Lorenzi-Cioldi and Chatard (2006).

50. Scheepers et al. (2006).

51. Scheepers et al. (2006).

52. Ellemers, Spears, and Doosje (2002); Ellemers, Van Knippenberg, and Wilke (1990).

53. Verkuyten and Reijerse (2008). Granted, dual identity sometimes works; see Simon and Ruhs (2008).

54. Ellemers, Spears, and Doosje (1997); Ellemers et al. (1988); Ellemers, Van Knippenberg, and Wilke (1990).

55. Ellemers et al. (2004).
56. See, for example, Bettencourt et al. (2001); Brewer (1979); Mullen, Brown, and Smith (1992).
57. Verkuyten and Reijerse (2008).
58. Oldmeadow and Fiske (2010).
59. A second study used research capacity and community outreach, with similar results.
60. Tausch, Kenworthy, and Hewstone (2007).
61. On women, see Glick and Fiske (1996); on African Americans, see Pinel, Long, and Crimin (2008).
62. Making this argument for poor people are Jost and Banaji (1994), Kay and Jost (2003), and Kay, Jost, and Young (2005); Glick and Fiske (1996) make this argument for women.
63. Fiske, Cuddy, and Glick (2007); Fiske et al. (2002).
64. Judd et al. (2005); Kervyn et al. (2009); Yzerbyt, Kervyn, and Judd (2008).
65. Asch (1946); Thorndike (1920).
66. Cuddy, Fiske, and Glick (2007).
67. Northern Italian students occupy two in-groups—well-educated people and northerners—and for French-speaking Belgian students, the in-groups are the Wallonians and Catholics who populate that area; see Cuddy, Fiske, and Glick (2008). For West German students, the in-groups are West Germans and intellectuals; Eckes (2002). Other European samples, Australia, New Zealand, and Uganda (the one African sample) follow the same patterns; see Durante et al. (2010).
68. Durante et al. (2010).
69. East Asian data supply an anomaly compared with Western results for in-groups and reference groups. Reflecting a cultural norm endorsing modesty, three Asian samples demote their own societal reference groups and in-groups to a more moderate, middling position, deeming them to be both a little warm and a little competent—not the greatest, but not the worst; see Cuddy et al. (2009). However, a Malaysian sample looks more like the in-groups favored by Westerners; see Durante et al. (2010). In all other respects, the Asian samples resemble the Western ones.
70. Cuddy, Fiske, and Glick (2007); on immigrants, see Lee and Fiske (2006).
71. Durante et al. (2010). There are also some intriguing locally extreme out-groups: in Mexico, politicians and "fresas" (preppies); in Chile, "pokemones" (the latest local teen tribes); and in Australia, boy racers (hot-rodders), emos (overwrought teen narcissists), and goths (hostile punks).
72. Cuddy, Fiske, and Glick (2008). An interesting exception is Israel, where Jewish respondents identified 88 percent of Israeli groups ambivalently but Muslims identified no ambivalent groups: all were either completely positive or completely negative. This kind of polarized response appeared in another conflict zone as well, Northern Ireland, for both Protestant and Catholic samples; Durante et al. (2010). Perhaps acute conflict creates only good and bad people and leaves no room for ambivalence.
73. Cuddy, Fiske, and Glick (2008); Durante et al. (2010). Within several Northern Hemisphere countries, southerners appear warm and expressive; see Pennebaker, Rimé, and Blankenship (1996).

74. Faulkner (1936, 76). Reproduced with permission of Curtis Brown Group Ltd, London, on behalf of the Estate of William Faulkner. Copyright © 1936 The Estate of William Faulkner. From *Absalom, Absalom!* By William Faulkner. Copyright 1936 by William Faulkner. Copyright © 1964 by Estelle Faulkner and Jill Faulkner Summers. Used by permission of W. W. Norton & Company, Inc.

75. Cikara, Botvinick, and Fiske (2011).

76. Russell and Fiske (2008).

77. Harris, Cikara, and Fiske (2008). "Supra-human" implies above humans, whereas "super-human" implies more human.

78. Don Herzog (2000, 237) discusses two kinds of contempt: amiable (pity) and nasty (disgust). For present purposes, his two kinds of contempt capture our two kinds of scorn.

79. Russell and Fiske (2009).

80. Cuddy, Fiske, and Glick (2008).

81. Russell and Fiske (2008).

82. Cikara et al. (2010).

83. Cuddy, Fiske, and Glick (2007).

84. On the curvilinear finding, see Todorov, Baron, and Oosterhof (2008). On the approach-avoidance idea, and for a review, see Todorov et al. (2008).

85. Nesse (2010).

86. Caporael (1997).

87. Cuddy, Norton, and Fiske (2005).

88. Giles et al. (1994); Hummert et al. (1998); Nelson (2009); Williams and Giles (1998).

89. Martens et al. (2004).

90. Avolio and Barrett (1987).

91. Cleveland and Landy (1983); Liden, Stilwell, and Ferris (1996); McEvoy and Cascio (1989).

Chapter 7

1. Andress (2005); Hardman (1993); Tackett (2003). I am grateful to my daughter for suggesting this example and identifying these references.

2. Nietzsche (1887/1967).

3. Leach (2008).

4. Baumeister, Smart, and Boden (1996).

5. Brickman and Janoff-Bulman (1977).

6. Russell and Fiske (2008). Although the published data from the first study do not report the SAT-GPA results separately, they are significant and available from the author. Both studies also showed competition effects independent of status, manipulated by the rules of the online game, which was designed to encourage either cooperation (team game) or competition (winner takes all). In the first study, as predicted, participants also expected the competitor to be less nice. Then they played the game with their fictitious partner, who was preprogrammed to mimic their own responses, tit-for-tat,

creating a self-fulfilling prophecy. If participants expected the other person to be competitive and self-interested, they could bring about that pattern by playing that way themselves. They did indeed expect and experience the competitor to be less warm. In a follow-up study, participants also experienced an in-person human competitor to be less warm and friendly.

7. Yzerbyt et al. (1994).

8. Status polarizes a relationship, depending on the type of game. That is, status exaggerates both the curse of competition and the benefit of cooperation. The low-status cooperators rated their partner as especially cooperative, while low-status competitors viewed their partner's behavior as especially competitive. Perceived cooperativeness showed the reverse effect between high-status competitors and high-status cooperators, but did not differ by as wide a margin. Perhaps this exaggerated response in both directions occurs because inferior status makes people vigilant. Superior status, on the other hand, allows people to relax and make more moderate judgments.

9. Judd et al. (2005), Kervyn et al. (2009), and Yzerbyt, Kervyn, and Judd (2008), as noted in chapter 6, show this compensation effect for perceptions of groups. It has rarely appeared for individuals, but the comparative context is likely to bring it out.

10. Harris and Fiske (2006, 2009).

11. Fiske (2010a).

12. Erber and Fiske (1984).

13. Neuberg and Fiske (1987); Ruscher and Fiske (1990).

14. Ames and Fiske (2010).

15. Ruscher and Fiske (1990).

16. Izuma, Saito, and Sadato (2008).

17. Cuddy and Fiske (2002); Cuddy, Norton, and Fiske (2005).

18. North and Fiske (2010).

19. Ironically, establishing comparative equality carries some costs: it undermines people's pride and distinctiveness in their own identity compared with the other; see Brewer (1991) and Brickman and Janoff-Bulman (1977).

20. Lowndes (2008).

21. Formisano (2008, 2).

22. Michael Friedman, "Populism, Yea, Yea," in *Bloody Bloody Andrew Jackson*, book by Alex Timbers, music and lyrics by Michael Friedman. Premiered January 2008, Kirk Douglas Theatre, Los Angeles.

23. That is, social identity minimizes within-group differences and maximizes between-group differences (Yzerbyt and Demoulin 2010). Under siege, groups tend to view themselves as still more alike, even though on average people see their own group as more varied than a random out-group.

24. See, for example, Formisano (2008), Lowndes (2008), and, on a more psychological note, Sales (1973).

25. Beck (2009). Author's paraphrasing; emphasis added to demonstrate Beck's style of speech.

26. Canovan (1999).

27. Frank Rich, "Hollywood's Brilliant Coda to America's Dark Year," *New York Times,* December 13, 2009, p. 9.
28. Dollard et al. (1939).
29. Nicholas Pastore (1952) originally suggested this modification to the frustration-aggression hypothesis, but the emotion literature (see, for example, Roseman 1984) more generally classifies anger as an emotion elicited by negative outcomes that someone else intentionally caused for illegitimate reasons.
30. Frank Rich, "Even Glenn Beck Is Right Twice a Day," *New York Times,* September 20, 2009, p. 8.
31. Canovan (2002, 27; see also Canovan 1999).
32. Formisano (2008, 11).
33. Formisano (2008, 214).
34. Formisano (2008, 15).
35. Kazin (1998, 271).
36. Formisano (2008, 3).
37. Andrew Jackson, December 8, 1829, quoted in Brands (2005, 433).
38. Goodwin (2005).
39. Formisano (2008).
40. Kazin (1998, 283–84).
41. Note that inequality is distinct from poverty: inequality reflects the difference between top and bottom, distinct from the overall average. Indeed, the rising inequality in the United States comes from the exponential rise in the very top of the income distribution, not so much from wages at the bottom, which do not drop so much as they stagnate.
42. Wilkinson and Pickett (2009, 2010).
43. Wilkinson and Pickett (2009, 2010).
44. Acemoglu and Robinson (2007).
45. Blanden, Gregg, and Machin (2005).
46. Blanden, Gregg, and Macmillan (2007).
47. Durante et al. (2010).
48. Sapolsky (2004).
49. Fitzgerald (1920, 45). More recent generations continue to suffer at Ivy League schools; see Walter Kirn's 2009 memoir, *Lost in the Meritocracy: The Undereducation of an Overachiever.*
50. Fiske (2010a).
51. Nickerson et al. (2003).
52. Quoidbach et al. (2010).
53. Kahneman et al. (2006).
54. Krendl et al. (2006).
55. Mikulincer and Shaver (2010).
56. Batson et al. (1997); Batson et al. (2002).
57. Sevillano and Fiske (2010).
58. Salovey and Rodin (1988).
59. See, for example, Beck et al. (1979).

60. Exline and Zell (2008).
61. Alicke and Zell (2008).
62. James (1881/2001, 288).
63. van de Ven, Zeelenberg, and Pieters (2009).
64. Lockwood and Kunda (1997).
65. Clark and Lemay (2010).
66. Brickman and Janoff-Bulman (1977).
67. Heider (1958, chapter 11) formally analyzes these possibilities.
68. Parrott and Mosquera (2008).
69. Exline and Lobel (1999); Exline and Zell (2008).
70. Parks, Rumble, and Posey (2002).
71. Pilkington, Tesser, and Stephens (1991).
72. Parks, Rumble, and Posey (2002).
73. Parrott and Mosquera (2008).
74. Alicke and Zell (2008).
75. Hareli and Weiner (2000).
76. Alicke and Zell (2008); Lockwood and Kunda (1997).
77. Vandello, Goldschmied, and Richards (2007). Admittedly, I am extrapolating to dyadic relations from these data referring to perceptions of underdog teams.
78. Aron et al. (1991).
79. Erickson (2004).
80. Exline and Zell (2008).
81. Spinoza, quoted in Heider (1958, 197).
82. Mussweiler (2003).
83. Parrott and Mosquera (2008).
84. van de Ven, Zeelenberg, and Pieters (2010).
85. Levine and Moreland (1998).
86. Hill and Buss (2006).
87. Anderson and Kilduff (2009).
88. Hardy and Van Vugt (2006).
89. Anderson et al. (2006).
90. Vecchio (1997, 2000, 2005).
91. Eagly and Johnson (1990); Eagly, Karau, and Makhijani (1995); Eagly, Makhijani, and Klonsky (1992).
92. Stephan and Stephan (1985).
93. Stephan and Finlay (1999).
94. Pettigrew and Tropp (2006, 2008); Tropp and Pettigrew (2005).
95. Turner et al. (2008).
96. Exline and Zell (2008, 326).
97. Dixon et al. (2010). See also the relative deprivation literature reviewed in chapter 6.
98. For a classic, see Schoeck (1969/1986).
99. For a collection, see Jost, Kay, and Thorisdottir (2009).

References

Acemoglu, Daron, and James A. Robinson. 2007. "On the Economic Origins of Democracy." *Daedalus* 136(1): 160–62.

Adams, Douglas. 1996. *The Hitchhiker's Guide to the Galaxy*. New York: Random House. (Orig. pub. in 1979.)

Adams, John. 1805. *Discourses on Davila*. Boston, Mass.: Russell and Culter.

Adolphs, Ralph. 2009. "The Social Brain: Neural Basis of Social Knowledge." *Annual Review of Psychology* 60: 693–716.

Affleck, Glenn, and Howard Tennen. 1991. "Appraisal and Coping Predictors of Mother and Child Outcomes After Newborn Intensive Care." *Journal of Social and Clinical Psychology* 10(4): 424–47.

Affleck, Glenn, Howard Tennen, Sydney Croog, and Sol Levine. 1987. "Causal Attribution, Perceived Benefits, and Morbidity After a Heart Attack: An Eight-Year Study." *Journal of Consulting and Clinical Psychology* 55(1): 29–35.

Alicke, Mark D., Frank M. LoSchiavo, Jennifer Zerbst, and Shaobo Zhang. 1997. "The Person Who Outperforms Me Is a Genius: Maintaining Perceived Competence in Upward Social Comparison." *Journal of Personality and Social Psychology* 73(4): 781–89.

Alicke, Mark D., and Ethan Zell. 2008. "Social Comparison and Envy." In *Envy: Theory and Research*, edited by Richard H. Smith. New York: Oxford University Press.

Allik, Jüri, and Anu Realo. 2004. "Individualism-Collectivism and Social Capital." *Journal of Cross-Cultural Psychology* 35(1): 29–49.

Altemeyer, Bob. 1998. "The Other 'Authoritarian Personality.' " *Advances in Experimental Social Psychology* 30: 47–92.

Ames, Daniel R. 2004. "Strategies for Social Inference: A Similarity Contingency Model of Projection and Stereotyping in Attribute Prevalence Estimates." *Journal of Personality and Social Psychology* 87(5): 573–85.

Ames, Daniel L., and Susan T. Fiske. 2010. "Outcome Dependency Alters the Neural Substrates of Impression Formation." Unpublished manuscript under review.

Amodio, David M., and Chris D. Frith. 2006. "Meeting of Minds: The Medial Frontal Cortex and Social Cognition." *Nature Reviews Neuroscience* 7(4): 268–77.

Anderson, Cameron, and Jennifer L. Berdahl. 2002. "The Experience of Power: Examining the Effects of Power on Approach and Inhibition Tendencies." *Journal of Personality and Social Psychology* 83(6): 1362–77.

Anderson, Cameron, and Gavin J. Kilduff. 2009. "The Pursuit of Status in Social Groups." *Current Directions in Psychological Science* 18(5): 295–98.

Anderson, Cameron, Sanjay Srivastava, Jennifer S. Beer, Sandra E. Spataro, and Jennifer A. Chatman. 2006. "Knowing Your Place: Self-Perceptions of Status in Face-to-Face Groups." *Journal of Personality and Social Psychology* 91(6): 1094–1110.

Andress, David. 2005. *The Terror: The Merciless War for Freedom in Revolutionary France.* New York: Farrar, Straus, and Giroux.

Aron, Arthur, Elaine N. Aron, Michael Tudor, and Greg Nelson. 1991. "Close Relationships as Including Other in the Self." *Journal of Personality and Social Psychology* 60(2): 241–53.

Aron, Arthur, Tracy McLaughlin-Volpe, Debra Mashek, Gary Lewandowski, Stephen C. Wright, and Elaine N. Aron. 2004. "Including Others in the Self." *European Review of Social Psychology* 15: 101–32.

Aronson, Elliot, and J. Merrill Carlsmith. 1962. "Performance Expectancy as a Determinant of Actual Performance." *Journal of Abnormal and Social Psychology* 65(3): 178–82.

Asch, Solomon E. 1946. "Forming Impressions of Personality." *Journal of Abnormal and Social Psychology* 41(3): 258–90.

Aspinwall, Lisa G., and Shelley E. Taylor. 1992. "Modeling Cognitive Adaptation: A Longitudinal Investigation of the Impact of Individual Differences and Coping on College Adjustment and Performance." *Journal of Personality and Social Psychology* 63(6): 989–1003.

———. 1993. "Effects of Social Comparison Direction, Threat, and Self-Esteem on Affect, Self-Evaluation, and Expected Success." *Journal of Personality and Social Psychology* 64(5): 708–22.

Assor, Avi, Joel Aronoff, and Lawrence A. Messé. 1981. "Attribute Relevance as a Moderator of the Effects of Motivation on Impression Formation." *Journal of Personality and Social Psychology* 41(4): 789–96.

———. 1986. "An Experimental Test of Defensive Processes in Impression Formation." *Journal of Personality and Social Psychology* 50(3): 644–50.

Avolio, Bruce J., and Gerald V. Barrett. 1987. "Effects of Age Stereotyping in a Simulated Interview." *Psychology and Aging* 2(1): 56–63.

Bacon, Francis. 1985. "Of Envy." In *The Essays, or Councils, Civil and Moral.* New York: Penguin Putnam. (Orig. pub. in 1597.)

Balzac, Honoré de. 1975. *Les Paysans* [*The Peasants*]. Paris: Éditions Gallimard. (Orig. pub. in 1855.)

Bartels, Larry M. 2008. *Unequal Democracy: The Political Economy of the New Gilded Age.* New York: Russell Sage Foundation.

Batson, C. Daniel, Johee Chang, Ryan Orr, and Jennifer Rowland. 2002. "Empathy, Attitudes, and Action: Can Feeling for a Member of a Stigmatized Group Motivate One to Help the Group?" *Personality and Social Psychology Bulletin* 28(12): 1656–66.

Batson, C. Daniel, Marina P. Polycarpou, Eddie Harmon-Jones, Heidi J. Imhoff, Erin C. Mitchener, Lori L. Bednar, Tricia R. Klein, and Lori Highberger. 1997. "Empathy and Attitudes: Can Feeling for a Member of a Stigmatized Group Improve Feelings Toward the Group?" *Journal of Personality and Social Psychology* 72(1): 105–18.

Battistich, Victor A., and Joel Aronoff. 1985. "Perceiver, Target, and Situational Influences on Social Cognition: An Interactional Analysis." *Journal of Personality and Social Psychology* 49(3): 788–98.

Bauer, Isabelle, Carsten Wrosch, and Joelle Jobin. 2008. " 'I'm Better Off Than Most Other People': The Role of Social Comparisons for Coping with Regret in Young Adulthood and Old Age." *Psychology and Aging* 23(4): 800–811.

Baumeister, Roy F., and Mark R. Leary. 1995. "The Need to Belong: Desire for Interpersonal Attachments as a Fundamental Human Motivation." *Psychological Bulletin* 117(3): 497–529.

Baumeister, Roy F., Laura Smart, and Joseph M. Boden. 1996. "Relation of Threatened Egotism to Violence and Aggression: The Dark Side of High Self-Esteem." *Psychological Review* 103(1): 5–33.

Baumeister, Roy F., Liqing Zhang, and Kathleen D. Vohs. 2004. "Gossip as Cultural Learning." *Review of General Psychology* 8(2): 111–21.

Beach, Steven R. H., and Abraham Tesser. 1995. "Self-Esteem and the Extended Self-Evaluation Maintenance Model: The Self in Social Context." In *Efficacy, Agency, and Self-Esteem,* edited by Michael H. Kernis. New York: Plenum.

Beach, Steven R. H., Abraham Tesser, Frank D. Fincham, Deborah J. Jones, Debra Johnson, and Daniel J. Whitaker. 1998. "Pleasure and Pain in Doing Well, Together: An Investigation of Performance-Related Affect in Close Relationships." *Journal of Personality and Social Psychology* 74(4): 923–38.

Beach, Steven R. H., Daniel J. Whitaker, Deborah J. Jones, and Abraham Tesser. 2001. "When Does Performance Feedback Prompt Complementarity in Romantic Relationships?" *Personal Relationships* 8(3): 231–48.

Beck, Aaron T., A. John Rush, Brian F. Shaw, and Gary D. Emery. 1979. *Cognitive Therapy of Depression.* New York: Guilford Press.

Beck, Glenn. 2009. *Glenn Beck's Common Sense: The Case Against an Out-of-Control Government.* New York: Mercury Radio Arts.

Beller, Emily, and Michael Hout. 2006. "Intergenerational Social Mobility: The United States in Comparative Perspective." *The Future of Children* 16(2): 19–36.

Berdahl, Jennifer L., and Paul Martorana. 2006. "Effects of Power on Emotion and Expression During a Controversial Group Discussion." *European Journal of Social Psychology* 36(4): 497–509.

Berger, Joseph, Bernard P. Cohen, and Morris Zelditch. 1972. "Status Characteristics and Social Interaction." *American Sociological Review* 37(3): 241–55.

Bergsieker, Hilary B., Lisa M. Leslie, Vanessa S. Constantine, and Susan T. Fiske. 2010. "Stereotyping by Omission: Eliminate the Negative, Accentuate the Positive." Unpublished paper, Princeton University.

Berkman, Lisa F., Thomas Glass, Ian Brissette, and Teresa E. Seeman. 2000. "From Social Integration to Health: Durkheim in the New Millennium." *Social Science and Medicine* 51(6): 843–57.

Bettencourt, B. Ann, Kelly Charlton, Nancy Dorr, and Deborah L. Hume. 2001. "Status Differences and In-Group Bias: A Meta-Analytic Examination of the Effects of Status Stability, Status Legitimacy, and Group Permeability." *Psychological Bulletin* 127(4): 520–42.

Blanden, Jo, Paul Gregg, and Stephen Machin. 2005. "Intergenerational Mobility in Europe and North America." London: London School of Economics, Centre for Economic Performance.

Blanden, Jo, Paul Gregg, and Lindsey Macmillan. 2007. "Accounting for Intergenerational Income Persistence: Noncognitive Skills, Ability, and Education." *Economic Journal* 117(519): C43–60.

Blanton, Hart, Abraham P. Buunk, Frederick K. Gibbons, and Hans Kuyper. 1999. "When Better-Than-Others Compare Upward: Choice of Comparison and Comparative Evaluation as Independent Predictors of Academic Performance." *Journal of Personality and Social Psychology* 76(3): 420–30.

Blanton, Hart, and Diederik A. Stapel. 2008. "Unconscious and Spontaneous and . . . Complex: The Three Selves Model of Social Comparison Assimilation and Contrast." *Journal of Personality and Social Psychology* 94(6): 1018–32.

Bobo, Lawrence. 1991. "Social Responsibility, Individualism, and Redistributive Policies." *Sociological Forum* 6(1): 71–92.

Bond, Rod, and Peter B. Smith. 1996. "Culture and Conformity: A Meta-Analysis of Studies Using Asch's (1952b, 1956) Line Judgment Task." *Psychological Bulletin* 119(1): 111–37.

Botvinick, Matthew M., Jonathan D. Cohen, and Cameron S. Carter. 2004. "Conflict Monitoring and Anterior Cingulate Cortex: An Update." *Trends in Cognitive Sciences* 8(12): 539–46.

Brands, H. W. 2005. *Andrew Jackson: His Life and Times.* New York: Anchor Books.

Branscombe, Nyla R., Michael T. Schmitt, and Richard D. Harvey. 1999. "Perceiving Pervasive Discrimination Among African Americans: Implications for Group Identification and Well-Being." *Journal of Personality and Social Psychology* 77(1): 135–49.

Branscombe, Nyla R., and Daniel L. Wann. 1994. "Collective Self-Esteem Consequences of Out-Group Derogation When a Valued Social Identity Is on Trial." *European Journal of Social Psychology* 24(6): 641–57.

Brauer, Markus, and Nadine Chaurand. 2009. "Descriptive Norms, Prescriptive Norms, and Social Control: An Intercultural Comparison of People's Reactions to Uncivil Behaviors." *European Journal of Social Psychology* 39(3): 1–10.

Brewer, Marilynn B. 1979. "In-Group Bias in the Minimal Intergroup Situation: A Cognitive-Motivational Analysis." *Psychological Bulletin* 86(2): 307–24.

———. 1991. "The Social Self: On Being the Same and Different at the Same Time." *Personality and Social Psychology Bulletin* 17(5): 475–82.

Brewer, Marilynn B., and Wendi Gardner. 1996. "Who Is This 'We'? Levels of Collective Identity and Self Representations." *Journal of Personality and Social Psychology* 71(1): 83–93.

Brewer, Marilynn B., and Joseph G. Weber. 1994. "Self-Evaluation Effects of Interpersonal Versus Intergroup Social Comparison." *Journal of Personality and Social Psychology:* 66(2): 268–75.

Brickman, Philip, and Ronnie Janoff-Bulman. 1977. "Pleasure and Pain in Social Comparison." In *Social Comparison Processes: Theoretical and Empirical Perspectives,* edited by Jerry M. Suls and Richard L. Miller. Washington, D.C.: Hemisphere.

Brooks, David. 2004. *On Paradise Drive: How We Live Now (and Always Have) in the Future Tense.* New York: Simon & Schuster.

Brosnan, Sarah F., and Frans B. M. de Waal. 2003. "Monkeys Reject Unequal Pay." *Nature* 425(18): 297–99.

Brosnan, Sarah F., Hillary C. Schiff, and Frans B. M. de Waal. 2005. "Tolerance for Inequity May Increase with Social Closeness in Chimpanzees." *Proceedings of the Royal Society of London: Series B, Biological Sciences* 272(1560): 253–58.

Brown, Jennifer L., David Sheffield, Mark R. Leary, and Michael E. Robinson. 2003. "Social Support and Experimental Pain." *Psychosomatic Medicine* 65(2): 276–83.

Bulwer, Henry Lytton, Esq., M. P. 1836. *The Monarchy of the Middle Classes. France: Social, Literary, Political, second series*. Paris, France: A. and W. Galignani and Co.

Buunk, Abraham P., and Veerle Brenninkmeijer. 2001. "When Individuals Dislike Exposure to an Actively Coping Role Model: Mood Change as Related to Depression and Social Comparison Orientation." *European Journal of Social Psychology* 31(5): 537–48.

Buunk, Abraham P., Rebecca L. Collins, Shelley E. Taylor, Nico W. van Yperen, and Gayle A. Dakof. 1990. "The Affective Consequences of Social Comparison: Either Direction Has Its Ups and Downs." *Journal of Personality and Social Psychology* 59(6): 1238–49.

Buunk, Abraham P., and Frederick Gibbons. 2006. "Social Comparison Orientation: A New Perspective on Those Who Do and Those Who Don't Compare with Others." In *Social Comparison and Social Psychology: Understanding Cognition, Intergroup Relations, and Culture*, edited by Serge Guimond. New York: Cambridge University Press.

———. 2007. "Social Comparison: The End of a Theory and the Emergence of a Field." *Organizational Behavior and Human Decision Processes* 102(1): 3–21.

Buunk, Abraham P., and Thomas Mussweiler. 2001. "New Directions in Social Comparison Research." *European Journal of Social Psychology* 31(5): 467–75.

Buunk, Abraham P., Nico W. van Yperen, Shelley E. Taylor, and Rebecca L. Collins. 1991. "Social Comparison and the Drive Upward Revisited: Affiliation as a Response to Marital Stress." *European Journal of Social Psychology* 21(6): 529–46.

Bylsma, Wayne H., and Brenda Major. 1992. "Two Routes to Eliminating Gender Differences in Personal Entitlement: Social Comparisons and Performance Evaluations." *Psychology of Women Quarterly* 16(2): 193–200.

———. 1994. "Social Comparisons and Contentment: Exploring the Psychological Costs of the Gender Wage Gap." *Psychology of Women Quarterly* 18(2): 241–49.

Cacioppo, John T., and William Patrick. 2008. *Loneliness: Human Nature and the Need for Social Connection*. New York: Norton.

Campbell, Donald T. 1958. "Common Fate, Similarity, and Other Indices of the Status of Aggregates of Persons as Social Entities." *Behavioral Science* 3(1): 14–25.

Canovan, Margaret. 1999. "Trust the People! Populism and the Two Faces of Democracy." *Political Studies* 47(1): 2–16.

———. 2002. "Taking Politics to the People: Populism as the Ideology of Democracy." In *Democracies and the Populist Challenge*, edited by Yves Mény and Yves Surel. New York: Palgrave.

Caporael, Linda R. 1997. "The Evolution of Truly Social Cognition: The Core Configurations Model." *Personality and Social Psychology Review* 1(4): 276–98.

Carstensen, Laura L., and Susan Turk Charles. 1998. "Emotion in the Second Half of Life." *Current Directions in Psychological Science* 7(5): 144–49.

Caruso, Eugene M., Daniel T. Gilbert, and Timothy D. Wilson. 2008. "A Wrinkle in Time: Asymmetric Valuation of Past and Future Events." *Psychological Science* 19(8): 796–801.

CBS News/*New York Times*. 2009. Poll (April 1–5). iPOLL Databank, Roper Center for Public Opinion Research, University of Connecticut (accessed October 14, 2009).

Central Intelligence Agency (CIA). 2010. "The World Factbook: Country Comparison: Distribution of Family Income–Gini Index." Available at: https://www.cia.gov/library/publications/the-world-factbook/rankorder/2172rank.html (accessed July 12, 2010).

Chafel, Judith A. 1997. "Societal Images of Poverty: Child and Adult Beliefs." *Youth and Society* 28(4): 432–63.

Chambers, John R., and Paul D. Windschitl. 2004. "Biases in Social Comparative Judgments: The Role of Nonmotivated Factors in Above-Average and Comparative-Optimism Effects." *Psychological Bulletin* 130(5): 813–38.

———. 2009. "Evaluating One Performance Among Others: The Influence of Rank and Degree of Exposure to Comparison Referents." *Personality and Social Psychology Bulletin* 35(6): 776–92.

Chartrand, Tanya L., and John A. Bargh. 1999. "The Chameleon Effect: The Perception-Behavior Link and Social Interaction." *Journal of Personality and Social Psychology* 76(6): 893–910.

Cheever, John. 2000. *Stories of John Cheever.* London: Vintage Books.

Cheng, Rebecca W., and Shui-Fong Lam. 2007. "Self-Construal and Social Comparison Effects." *British Journal of Educational Psychology* 77(1): 197–211.

Cherulnik, Paul D., Kristina A. Donley, Tay Sha R. Wiewel, and Susan R. Miller. 2001. "Charisma Is Contagious: The Effect of Leaders' Charisma on Observers' Affect." *Journal of Applied Social Psychology* 31(10): 2149–59.

Chiao, Joan Y., Vani A. Mathur, Tokiko Harada, and Trixie Lipke. 2009. "Neural Basis of Preference for Human Social Hierarchy Versus Egalitarianism." *Annals of the New York Academy of Sciences* (special issue) 1167(1): 174–81.

Christakis, Nicholas A., and James H. Fowler. 2007. "The Spread of Obesity in a Large Social Network over Thirty-Two Years." *New England Journal of Medicine* 357(4): 370–79.

Christopher, Andrew N., Keith L. Zabel, Jason R. Jones, and Pam Marek. 2008. "Protestant Ethic Ideology: Its Multifaceted Relationships with Just World Beliefs, Social Dominance Orientation, and Right-Wing Authoritarianism." *Personality and Individual Differences* 45(6): 473–77.

Christopher, Andrew N., and Barry R. Schlenker. 2005. "The Protestant Work Ethic and Attributions of Responsibility: Applications of the Triangle Model." *Journal of Applied Social Psychology* 35(7): 1502–18.

Cialdini, Robert B., Richard J. Borden, Avril Thorne, Marcus Randall Walker, Stephen Freeman, and Lloyd Reynolds Sloan. 1976. "Basking in Reflected Glory: Three (Football) Field Studies." *Journal of Personality and Social Psychology* 34(3): 366–75.

Cialdini, Robert B., and Maralou E. De Nicholas. 1989. "Self-Presentation by Association." *Journal of Personality and Social Psychology* 57(4): 626–31.

Cikara, Mina, and Susan T. Fiske. 2010. "Stereotypes and Schadenfreude: Affective and Psychological Markers of Pleasure at Outgroups' Misfortunes." Unpublished manuscript.

Cikara, Mina, Matthew M. Botvinick, and Susan T. Fiske. 2011. "Us Versus Them: Social Identity Shapes Neural Responses to Intergroup Competition and Harm." *Psychological Sciences,* published first online January 26, 2011. Available at: http://pss.sagepub.com/content/early/2011/01/26/0956797610397667 (accessed February 28, 2011).

Cikara, Mina, Rachel A. Farnsworth, Lasana T. Harris, and Susan T. Fiske. 2010. "On the Wrong Side of the Trolley Track: Neural Correlates of Relative Social Valuation." *Social Cognitive and Affective Neuroscience* 5(4): 404–13.

Clark, Margaret S., and Edward P. Lemay, Jr. 2010. "Close Relationships." In *Handbook of Social Psychology,* vol. 2, 5th ed., edited by Susan T. Fiske, Daniel T. Gilbert, and Gardner Lindzey. Hoboken, N.J.: John Wiley and Sons.

Cleveland, Jeanette N., and Frank J. Landy. 1983. "The Effects of Person and Job Stereotypes on Two Personnel Decisions." *Journal of Applied Psychology* 68(4): 609–19.

Collins, Rebecca L. 2000. "Among the Better Ones: Upward Assimilation in Social Comparison." In *Handbook of Social Comparison: Theory and Research,* edited by Jerry Suls and Ladd Wheeler. Dordrecht, Netherlands: Academic/Plenum Publishers.

Commins, Barry, and John Lockwood. 1979. "The Effects of Status Differences, Favored Treatment, and Equity on Intergroup Comparisons." *European Journal of Social Psychology* 9(3): 281–89.

Correll, Joshua, and Bernadette Park. 2005. "A Model of the In-Group as a Social Resource." *Personality and Social Psychology Review* 9(4): 341–59.

Coser, Rose L. 1960. "Laughter Among Colleagues." *Psychiatry: Journal for the Study of Interpersonal Processes* 23(February): 81–89.

Cottrell, Catherine A., and Steven L. Neuberg. 2005. "Different Emotional Reactions to Different Groups: A Sociofunctional Threat-Based Approach to 'Prejudice.' " *Journal of Personality and Social Psychology* 88(5): 770–89.

Cozzarelli, Catherine, Anna V. Wilkinson, and Michael J. Tagler. 2001. "Attitudes Toward the Poor and Attributions for Poverty." *Journal of Social Issues* 57(2): 207–27.

Crandall, Christian S. 1988. "Social Contagion of Binge Eating." *Journal of Personality and Social Psychology* 55(4): 588–98.

Crocker, Jennifer. 1999. "Social Stigma and Self-Esteem: Situational Construction of Self-Worth." *Journal of Experimental Social Psychology* 35(1): 89–107.

Crocker, Jennifer, and Katherine M. Knight. 2005. "Contingencies of Self-Worth." *Current Directions in Psychological Science* 14(4): 200–203.

Crocker, Jennifer, and Riia Luhtanen. 1990. "Collective Self-Esteem and In-Group Bias." *Journal of Personality and Social Psychology* 58(1): 60–67.

Crocker, Jennifer, Leigh L. Thompson, Kathleen M. McGraw, and Cindy Ingerman. 1987. "Downward Comparison, Prejudice, and Evaluations of Others: Effects of Self-Esteem and Threat." *Journal of Personality and Social Psychology:* 52(5): 907–16.

Crocker, Jennifer, and Connie T. Wolfe. 2001. "Contingencies of Self-Worth." *Psychological Review* 108(3): 593–623.

Crosby, Faye. 1984. "The Denial of Personal Discrimination." *American Behavioral Scientist* 27(3): 371–86.

Cuddy, Amy J. C., and Susan T. Fiske. 2002. "Doddering, but Dear: Process, Content, and Function in Stereotyping of Older Persons." In *Ageism,* edited by Todd D. Nelson. Cambridge, Mass.: MIT Press.

Cuddy, Amy J. C., Susan T. Fiske, and Peter Glick. 2007. "The BIAS Map: Behaviors from Intergroup Affect and Stereotypes." *Journal of Personality and Social Psychology* 92(4): 631–48.

———. 2008. "Competence and Warmth as Universal Trait Dimensions of Interpersonal and Intergroup Perception: The Stereotype Content Model and the BIAS Map." In *Advances in Experimental Social Psychology*, vol. 40, edited by Mark P. Zanna. New York: Academic.

Cuddy, Amy J. C., Susan T. Fiske, Virginia S. Y. Kwan, Peter Glick, Stephanie Demoulin, Jacques-Philippe Leyens, Michael H. Bond, Jean-Claude Croizet, Naomi Ellemers, Ed Sleebos, Tin Tin Htun, Hyun-Jeong Kim, Greg Maio, Judi Perry, Kristina Petkova, Valery Todorov, Rosa Rodríguez-Bailón, Elena Morales, Miguel Moya, Marisol Palacios, Vanessa Smith, Rolando Perez, Jorge Vala, and Rene Ziegler. 2009. "Is the Stereotype Content Model Culture-Bound? A Cross-Cultural Comparison Reveals Systematic Similarities and Differences." *British Journal of Social Psychology* 48(1): 1–33.

Cuddy, Amy J. C., and Cynthia M. Frantz. 2009. Unpublished data on stay-at-home mothers.

Cuddy, Amy J. C., Michael I. Norton, and Susan T. Fiske. 2005. "This Old Stereotype: The Pervasiveness and Persistence of the Elderly Stereotype." *Journal of Social Issues* 61(2): 265–83.

Cuddy, Amy J. C., Mindi S. Rock, and Michael I. Norton. 2007. "Aid in the Aftermath of Hurricane Katrina: Inferences of Secondary Emotions and Intergroup Helping." *Group Processes and Intergroup Relations* 10(1): 107–18.

Dahl, Roald, Nicholas Kazan, and Robin Swicord. 1996. *Matilda* (the movie). Directed and produced by Danny DeVito.

Dambrun, Michael, Serge Guimond, and Donald M. Taylor. 2006. "The Counterintuitive Effect of Relative Gratification on Intergroup Attitudes: Ecological Validity, Moderators, and Mediators." In *Social Comparison and Social Psychology: Understanding Cognition, Intergroup Relations, and Culture*, edited by Serge Guimond. New York: Cambridge University Press.

Darwin, Charles. 1987. "Disdain—Contempt—Disgust—Guilt—Pride, Etc.—Helplessness—Patience—Affirmation and Negation." In *The Expressions of the Emotions in Man and Animals*, edited by Charles Darwin. London: John Murray. (Orig. pub. in 1872.)

de Botton, Alain. 2004. *Status Anxiety*. New York: Pantheon.

———. 2009. "A Kinder, Gentler Philosophy of Success." Ted Global 2009. Filmed July 2009. Available at: http://www.ted.com/talks/alain_de_botton_a_kinder_gentler_philosophy_of_success.htm (accessed February 3, 2010).

De Cremer, David, and Eric van Dijk. 2005. "When and Why Leaders Put Themselves First: Leader Behavior in Resource Allocations as a Function of Feeling Entitled." *European Journal of Social Psychology* 35(4): 553–63.

Democracy Corps, Campaign for America's Future, and Greenberg Quinlan Rosner Research. 2008. Survey (November 4–5). iPOLL Databank, Roper Center for Public Opinion Research, University of Connecticut (accessed September 23, 2009).

DeNavas-Walt, Carmen, Bernadette D. Proctor, and Jessica C. Smith. 2009. *Income, Poverty, and Health Insurance Coverage in the United States: 2008. Current Population Reports: Consumer Income*. Washington: U.S. Bureau of the Census.

Dépret, Eric F., and Susan T. Fiske. 1999. "Perceiving the Powerful: Intriguing Individuals Versus Threatening Groups." *Journal of Experimental Social Psychology* 35(5): 461–80.

de Quervain, Dominique J.-F., Urs Fischbacher, Valerie Treyer, Melanie Schellhammer, Ulrich Schnyder, Alfred Buck, and Ernst Fehr. 2004. "The Neural Basis of Altruistic Punishment." *Science* 305(5688): 1254–58.

DeWall, C. Nathan, Geoff MacDonald, Gregory D. Webster, Carrie L. Masten, Roy F. Baumeister, Caitlin Powell, David Combs, David R. Schurtz, Tyler F. Stillman, Dianne M. Tice, and Naomi I. Eisenberger. 2010. "Acetaminophen Reduces Social Pain: Behavioral and Neural Evidence." *Psychological Science* 21(7): 931–37.

Dickerson, Sally S., and Margaret E. Kemeny. 2004. "Acute Stressors and Cortisol Responses: A Theoretical Integration and Synthesis of Laboratory Research." *Psychological Bulletin* 130(3): 355–91.

Diener, Ed, and Shigehiro Oishi. 2005. "The Nonobvious Social Psychology of Happiness." *Psychological Inquiry* 16(4): 162–67.

Dixon, John, Linda R. Tropp, Kevin Durrheim, and Colin Tredoux. 2010. " 'Let Them Eat Harmony': Prejudice-Reduction Strategies and Attitudes of Historically Disadvantaged Groups." *Current Directions in Psychological Science* 19(2): 76–80.

Dollard, John E., Neal E. Miller, Leonard W. Doob, O. H. Mowrer, and Robert R. Sears. 1939. *Frustration and Aggression.* New Haven, Conn.: Yale University Press.

Dostoyevsky, Fyodor. 1994. *Notes from Underground.* New York: Vintage Books. (Orig. pub. in 1864.)

Dovidio, John F., and Steve L. Ellyson. 1982. "Decoding Visual Dominance Behavior: Attributions of Power Based on the Relative Percentages of Looking While Speaking and Looking While Listening." *Social Psychology Quarterly* 45(2): 106–13.

Dovidio, John F., and Samuel L. Gaertner. 2010. "Intergroup Bias." In *Handbook of Social Psychology,* vol. 2, edited by Susan T. Fiske, Daniel T. Gilbert, and Gardner Lindzey. New York: Wiley.

Doyle, Arthur Conan. 1986. "Silver Blaze." In *Sherlock Holmes: The Complete Novels and Stories,* vol. 1. New York: Bantam Classics. (Orig. pub. in 1894.)

Duckitt, John. 2006. "Differential Effects of Right-Wing Authoritarianism and Social Dominance Orientation on Out-Group Attitudes and Their Mediation by Threat from and Competitiveness to Out-Groups." *Personality and Social Psychology Bulletin* 32(5): 684–96.

Duckitt, John, and Chris G. Sibley. 2009. "A Dual-Process Motivational Model of Ideology, Politics, and Prejudice." *Psychological Inquiry* 20(2–3): 98–109.

Dunbar, Robin I. M. 2004. "Gossip in Evolutionary Perspective." *Review of General Psychology* 8(2): 100–110.

Duncan, Starkey, and Donald W. Fiske. 1977. *Face-to-Face Interaction: Research, Methods, and Theory.* Hillsdale, N.J.: Erlbaum.

Dundes, Alan, ed. 1981. *The Evil Eye: A Folklore Casebook.* New York: Garland Publishing.

Dunning, David. 2000. "Social Judgment as Implicit Social Comparison." In *Handbook of Social Comparison: Theory and Research,* edited by Jerry Suls and Ladd Wheeler. Dordrecht, Netherlands: Kluwer Academic Publishers.

Durante, Federica, Susan T. Fiske, Amy J. C. Cuddy, Nicolas Kervyn, Adebowale Akande, Fiona Kate Barlow, Gregory Bonn, Janine Bosak, Ed Cairns, Dora Capozza, René Centeno, Anjana Chandran, Xenia Chryssochoou, Juan Contreras, Stéphanie Demoulin, Claire Doherty, Roberto Gonzáles, Tilemachos Iatridis, Janet I. Lewis, Jacques-Philippe Leyens, Rui Lopes, Elena Morales, Miguel Moya, Maria Soledad Palacios, Ananthi Ramiah, Nadim N. Rouhana, Vanessa Smith

Castro, Rolando Perez, Rosa Rodríguez-Bailón, Chris G. Sibley, Chiara Storari, Romin W. Tafarodi, Gerald Tushabe, and Jorge Vala. 2010. "Around the World with Warmth-Competence Correlations." Unpublished data.

Eagly, Alice H., and Blair T. Johnson. 1990. "Gender and Leadership Style: A Meta-Analysis." *Psychological Bulletin* 108(2): 233–56.

Eagly, Alice H., Steven J. Karau, and Mona G. Makhijani. 1995. "Gender and the Effectiveness of Leaders: A Meta-Analysis." *Psychological Bulletin* 117(1): 125–45.

Eagly, Alice H., Mona G. Makhijani, and Bruce G. Klonsky. 1992. "Gender and the Evaluation of Leaders: A Meta-Analysis." *Psychological Bulletin* 111(1): 3–22.

Eckes, Thomas. 2002. "Paternalistic and Envious Gender Stereotypes: Testing Predictions from the Stereotype Content Model." *Sex Roles* 47(3–4): 99–114.

Eisenberger, Naomi I., Matthew D. Lieberman, and Kipling D. Williams. 2003. "Does Rejection Hurt? An fMRI Study of Social Exclusion." *Science* 302(5643): 290–92.

Ekman, Paul, and Wallace V. Friesen. 1986. "A New Pan-Cultural Facial Expression of Emotion." *Motivation and Emotion* 10(2): 159–68.

Ellemers, Naomi, Russell Spears, and Bertjan Doosje. 1997. "Sticking Together or Falling Apart: In-Group Identification as a Psychological Determinant of Group Commitment Versus Individual Mobility." *Journal of Personality and Social Psychology* 72(3): 617–26.

———. 2002. "Self and Social Identity." *Annual Review of Psychology* 53: 161–86.

Ellemers, Naomi, Henriette van den Heuvel, Dick de Gilder, Anne Maass, and Alessandra Bonvini. 2004. "The Underrepresentation of Women in Science: Differential Commitment or the Queen Bee Syndrome?" *British Journal of Social Psychology* 43(3): 315–38.

Ellemers, Naomi, Ad van Knippenberg, Nanne de Vries, and Henk Wilke. 1988. "Social Identification and Permeability of Group Boundaries." *European Journal of Social Psychology* 18(6): 497–513.

Ellemers, Naomi, Ad van Knippenberg, and Henk A. Wilke. 1990. "The Influence of Permeability of Group Boundaries and Stability of Group Status on Strategies of Individual Mobility and Social Change." *British Journal of Social Psychology* 29(3): 233–46.

Endo, Yumi, Steven J. Heine, and Darrin R. Lehman. 2000. "Culture and Positive Illusions in Close Relationships: How My Relationships Are Better Than Yours." *Personality and Social Psychology Bulletin* 26(12): 1571–86.

Epstude, Kai, and Thomas Mussweiler. 2009. "What You Feel Is How You Compare: How Comparisons Influence the Social Induction of Affect." *Emotion* 9(1): 1–14.

Erber, Ralph, and Susan T. Fiske. 1984. "Outcome Dependency and Attention to Inconsistent Information." *Journal of Personality and Social Psychology* 47(4): 709–26.

Erickson, Frederick. 2004. *Talk and Social Theory: Ecologies of Speaking and Listening in Everyday Life*. Cambridge: Polity Press.

Exline, Julie J., and Marci Lobel. 1999. "The Perils of Outperformance: Sensitivity About Being the Target of a Threatening Upward Comparison." *Psychological Bulletin* 125(3): 307–37.

———. 2001. "Private Gain, Social Strain: Do Relationship Factors Shape Responses to Outperformance?" *European Journal of Social Psychology* 31(5): 593–607.

Exline, Julie J., and Anne L. Zell. 2008. "Antidotes to Envy: A Conceptual Framework." In *Envy: Theory and Research*, edited by Richard H. Smith. New York: Oxford University Press.

Faulkner, William. 1936. *Absalom, Absalom!* New York: Random House.

Feather, N. T., and Katherine Naim. 2005. "Resentment, Envy, Schadenfreude, and Sympathy: Effects of Own and Others' Deserved or Undeserved Status." *Australian Journal of Psychology* 57(2): 87–102.

Feather, N. T., and Rebecca Sherman. 2002. "Envy, Resentment, Schadenfreude, and Sympathy: Reactions to Deserved and Undeserved Achievement and Subsequent Failure." *Personality and Social Psychology Bulletin* 28(7): 953–61.

Fehr, Erich, and Urs Fischbacher. 2003. "The Nature of Human Altruism." *Nature* 425(6960): 785–91.

Fein, Steven, and Steven J. Spencer. 1997. "Prejudice as Self-Image Maintenance: Affirming the Self Through Derogating Others." *Journal of Personality and Social Psychology* 73(1): 31–44.

Fenigstein, Allan, Michael F. Scheier, and Arnold H. Buss. 1975. "Public and Private Self-Consciousness: Assessment and Theory." *Journal of Consulting and Clinical Psychology* 43(4): 522–27.

Festinger, Leon. 1954a. "Motivations Leading to Social Behavior." In *Nebraska Symposium on Motivation*, edited by Marshall R. Jones. Lincoln: University of Nebraska Press.

———. 1954b. "A Theory of Social Comparison Processes." *Human Relations* 7(1954): 117–40.

Fielding, Henry. 1988. *The Covent-Garden Journal and a Plan of the Universal Register Office*, edited by Bertrand A. Goldgar. Middletown, Conn.: Wesleyan University Press. (Orig. pub. in 1752.)

Finlay, W. M. L., S. Dinos, and E. Lyons. 2001. "Stigma and Multiple Social Comparisons in People with Schizophrenia." *European Journal of Social Psychology* 31(5): 579–92.

Fischer, Agneta H., and Ira J. Roseman. 2007. "Beat Them or Ban Them: The Characteristics and Social Functions of Anger and Contempt." *Journal of Personality and Social Psychology* 93(1): 103–15.

Fiske, Alan P. 1992. "The Four Elementary Forms of Sociality: Framework for a Unified Theory of Social Relations." *Psychological Review* 99(4): 689–723.

Fiske, Alan Page, Shinobu Kitayama, Hazel Rose Markus, and Richard E. Nisbett. 1998. "The Cultural Matrix of Social Psychology." In *The Handbook of Social Psychology*, vol. 2, 4th ed., edited by Daniel T. Gilbert, Susan T. Fiske, and Gardner Lindzey. New York: McGraw-Hill.

Fiske, Susan T. 1993. "Controlling Other People: The Impact of Power on Stereotyping." *American Psychologist* 48(6): 621–28.

———. 2010a. "Interpersonal Stratification: Status, Power, and Subordination." In *Handbook of Social Psychology*, 5th ed., edited by Susan T. Fiske, Daniel T. Gilbert, and Gardner Lindzey. New York: Wiley.

———. 2010b. *Social Beings: Core Motives in Social Psychology*. 2d ed. New York: Wiley.

Fiske, Susan T., Amy J. C. Cuddy, and Peter Glick. 2007. "Universal Dimensions of Social Perception: Warmth and Competence." *Trends in Cognitive Science* 11(2): 77–83.

Fiske, Susan T., Amy J. C. Cuddy, Peter Glick, and Jun Xu. 2002. "A Model of (Often Mixed) Stereotype Content: Competence and Warmth Respectively Follow from Perceived Status and Competition." *Journal of Personality and Social Psychology* 82(6): 878–902.

Fiske, Susan T., and Shelley E. Taylor. 2008. *Social Cognition: From Brains to Culture*. New York: McGraw-Hill.

Fiske, Susan T., and Mariko Yamamoto. 2005. "Coping with Rejection: Core Social Motives Across Cultures." In *The Social Outcast: Ostracism, Social Exclusion, Rejection, and Bullying,* edited by Kipling D. Williams, Joseph P. Forgas, and William von Hippel. Sydney Symposium of Social Psychology Series. New York: Psychology Press.

Fitzgerald, F. Scott. 1920. *This Side of Paradise.* New York: Scribner.

Fliessbach, Klaus, Bernd Weber, Peter Trautner, Thomas Dohmen, Uwe Sunde, Christian E. Elger, and Armin Falk. 2007. "Social Comparison Affects Reward-Related Brain Activity in the Human Ventral Striatum." *Science* 318(5854): 1305–8.

Formisano, Ronald P. 2008. *For the People: American Populist Movements from the Revolution to the 1850s.* Chapel Hill: University of North Carolina Press.

Forsyth, Donelson R. 2000. "Social Comparison and Influence in Groups." In *Handbook of Social Comparison: Theory and Research,* edited by Jerry Suls and Ladd Wheeler. Dordrecht, Netherlands: Kluwer Academic/Plenum Publishers.

Fredrickson, Barbara L. 2001. "The Role of Positive Emotions in Positive Psychology: The Broaden-and-Build Theory of Positive Emotions." *American Psychologist* 56(3): 218–26.

Freeman, Jonathan B., Nicholas O. Rule, Reginald B. Adams Jr., and Nalini Ambady. 2009. "Culture Shapes a Mesolimbic Response to Signals of Dominance and Subordination That Associates with Behavior." *NeuroImage* 47(1): 353–59.

Friederich, Hans-Christoph, Rudolf Uher, Samantha Brooks, Vincent Giampietro, Mick Brammer, Steve C. R. Williams, Wolfgang Herzog, Janet Treasure, and Iain C. Campbell. 2007. "I'm Not as Slim as That Girl: Neural Bases of Body Shape Self-Comparison to Media Images." *NeuroImage* 37(2): 674–81.

Frye, Nancy E., and Benjamin R. Karney. 2002. "Being Better or Getting Better? Social and Temporal Comparisons as Coping Mechanisms in Close Relationships." *Personality and Social Psychology Bulletin* 28(9): 1287–99.

Furnham, Adrian. 1997. "The Relationship Between Work and Economic Values." *Journal of Economic Psychology* 18(1): 1–14.

Fussell, Paul. 1983. *Class: A Guide Through the American Status System.* New York: Touchstone.

Gaines, Leslie M., Jamieson Duvall, J. Matthew Webster, and Richard H. Smith. 2005. "Feeling Good After Praise for a Successful Performance: The Importance of Social Comparison Information." *Self and Identity* 4(4): 373–89.

Galinsky, Adam D., Joe C. Magee, M. Ena Inesi, and Deborah H. Gruenfeld. 2006. "Power and Perspectives Not Taken." *Psychological Science* 17(12): 1068–74.

Gallo, Linda C., and Karen A. Matthews. 2003. "Understanding the Association Between Socioeconomic Status and Physical Health: Do Negative Emotions Play a Role?" *Psychological Bulletin* 129(1): 10–51.

Gallup Organization. 1939. Poll 150 (March 2).

———. 1947. Poll 393 (March 26).

———. 2002. "Who Do We Trust? iPOLL Databank, Roper Center for Public Opinion Research, University of Connecticut (accessed September 23, 2009).

———. 2006. Survey (November 27–29). iPOLL Databank, Roper Center for Public Opinion Research, University of Connecticut (accessed October 14, 2009).

Gamache, Henri. 1946. *Terrors of the Evil Eye Exposed.* Dallas, Tex.: Raymond Publishing.

Garcia, Donna M., Nyla R. Branscombe, Serge Desmarais, and Stephanie S. Gee. 2006. "Attitudes Toward Redistributive Social Policies: The Effects of Social Comparisons and Policy Experience." In *Social Comparison and Social Psychology: Understanding Cognition, Intergroup Relations, and Culture,* edited by Serge Guimond. New York: Cambridge University Press.

Gardner, Wendi L., Shira Gabriel, and Laura Hochschild. 2002. "When You and I Are 'We,' You Are Not Threatening: The Role of Self-Expansion in Social Comparison." *Journal of Personality and Social Psychology* 82(2): 239–51.

Gardner, Wendi L., Cynthia L. Pickett, and Megan Knowles. 2005. "Social Snacking and Shielding: Using Symbols, Selves, and Surrogates in the Service of Belonging Needs." In *The Social Outcast: Ostracism, Social Exclusion, Rejection, and Bullying,* edited by Kipling D. Williams, Joseph P. Forgas, and William von Hippel. Sydney Symposium of Social Psychology Series. New York: Psychology Press.

General Social Survey (GSS). 2001. iPOLL Databank, Roper Center for Public Opinion Research, University of Connecticut (accessed September 23, 2009).
———. 2006. (March). iPOLL Databank, Roper Center for Public Opinion Research, University of Connecticut (accessed September 23, 2009).

Gibbons, Frederick X. 1986. "Social Comparison and Depression: Company's Effect on Misery." *Journal of Personality and Social Psychology* 51(1): 140–48.

Gibbons, Frederick X., Camilla Persson Benbow, and Meg Gerrard. 1994. "From Top Dog to Bottom Half: Social Comparison Strategies in Response to Poor Performance." *Journal of Personality and Social Psychology* 67(4): 638–52.

Gibbons, Frederick X., Hart Blanton, Meg Gerrard, Abraham P. Buunk, and Tami Eggleston. 2000. "Does Social Comparison Make a Difference? Optimism as a Moderator of the Relation Between Comparison Level and Academic Performance." *Personality and Social Psychology Bulletin* 26(5): 637–48.

Gibbons, Frederick X., and Sue Boney-McCoy. 1991. "Self-Esteem, Similarity, and Reactions to Active Versus Passive Downward Comparison." *Journal of Personality and Social Psychology* 60(3): 414–24.

Gibbons, Frederick X., and Abraham P. Buunk. 1999. "Individual Differences in Social Comparison: Development of a Scale of Social Comparison Orientation." *Journal of Personality and Social Psychology* 76(1): 129–42.

Gibbons, Frederick X., and Meg Gerrard. 1989. "Effects of Upward and Downward Social Comparison on Mood States." *Journal of Social and Clinical Psychology* 8(1): 14–31.
———. 1995. "Predicting Young Adults' Health Risk Behavior." *Journal of Personality and Social Psychology* 69(3): 505–17.

Gibbons, Frederick X., Marie Helweg-Larsen, and Meg Gerrard. 1995. "Prevalence Estimates and Adolescent Risk Behavior: Cross-Cultural Differences in Social Influence." *Journal of Applied Psychology* 80(1): 107–21.

Gibbons, Frederick X., David J. Lane, Meg Gerrard, Monica Reis-Bergan, Carrie L. Lautrup, Nancy A. Pexa, and Hart Blanton. 2002. "Comparison-Level Preferences After Performance: Is Downward Comparison Theory Still Useful?" *Journal of Personality and Social Psychology* 83(4): 865–80.

Giessner, Steffen R., and Thomas W. Schubert. 2007. "High in the Hierarchy: How Vertical Location and Judgments of Leaders' Power Are Interrelated." *Organizational Behavior and Human Decision Processes* 104(1): 30–44.

Gilbert, Daniel T., R. B. Giesler, and Kathryn A. Morris. 1995. "When Comparisons Arise." *Journal of Personality and Social Psychology* 69(2): 227–36.

Gilbert, Daniel T., Matthew A. Killingsworth, Rebecca N. Eyre, and Timothy D. Wilson. 2009. "The Surprising Power of Neighborly Advice." *Science* 323(5921): 1617–19.

Gilbert, Daniel T., and Timothy D. Wilson. 2007. "Prospection: Experiencing the Future." *Science* 317(5843): 1351–54.

Giles, Howard, Susan Fox, Jake Harwood, and Angie Williams. 1994. "Talking Age and Aging Talk: Communicating Through the Life Span." In *Interpersonal Communication in Older Adulthood: Interdisciplinary Theory and Research,* Sage Focus Editions, vol. 173, edited by Mary Lee Hummert, John M. Wiemann, and Jon F. Nussbaum. Thousand Oaks, Calif.: Sage Publications.

Gladwell, Malcolm. 2005. *Blink: The Power of Thinking Without Thinking.* New York: Little, Brown.

Glick, Peter, and Susan T. Fiske. 1996. "The Ambivalent Sexism Inventory: Differentiating Hostile and Benevolent Sexism." *Journal of Personality and Social Psychology* 70(3): 491–512.

Glick, Peter, Susan T. Fiske, Dominic Abrams, Benoit Dardenne, Maria Cristina Ferreira, Roberto Gonzalez, Christopher Hachfeld, Li-Li Huang, Paul Hutchison, Hyun-Jeong Kim, Anna Maria Manganelli, Barbara Masser, Angelica Mucchi-Faina, Shinya Okiebisu, J. C. X. Pek, Nadim Rouhana, Jose L. Saiz, Nuray Sakalli-Ugurlu, Chiara Volpato, Mariko Yamamoto, and Vincent Yzerbyt. 2006. "Anti-American Sentiment and America's Perceived Intent to Dominate: An Eleven-Nation Study." *Basic and Applied Social Psychology* (special issue) 28(4): 363–73.

Goethals, George R., and John Darley. 1977. "Social Comparison Theory: An Attributional Approach." In *Social Comparison Processes: Theoretical and Empirical Perspectives,* edited by Jerry Suls and Richard L. Miller. Washington, D.C.: Hemisphere.

Gonsalkorale, Karen, and Kipling D. Williams. 2007. "The KKK Won't Let Me Play: Ostracism Even by a Despised Out-Group Hurts." *European Journal of Social Psychology* 37(6): 1176–86.

Goodwin, Doris Kearns. 2005. *Team of Rivals: The Political Genius of Abraham Lincoln.* New York: Simon and Schuster.

Goodwin, Stephanie A., Alexandra Gubin, Susan T. Fiske, and Vincent Yzerbyt. 2000. "Power Can Bias Impression Formation: Stereotyping Subordinates by Default and by Design." *Group Processes and Intergroup Relations* 3(3): 227–56.

Gordijn, Ernestine H., and Diederik A. Stapel. 2006. "Behavioral Effects of Automatic Interpersonal Versus Intergroup Social Comparison." *British Journal of Social Psychology* 45(4): 717–29.

Granovetter, Mark S. 1973. "The Strength of Weak Ties." *American Journal of Sociology* 78(6): 1360–80.

Greco, Veronica, and Derek Roger. 2001. "Coping with Uncertainty: The Construction and Validation of a New Measure." *Personality and Individual Differences* 31(4): 519–34.

———. 2003. "Uncertainty, Stress, and Health." *Personality and Individual Differences* 34(6): 1057–68.

Greenberg, Jerald, Claire E. Ashton-James, and Neal M. Ashkanasy. 2007. "Social Comparison Processes in Organizations." *Organizational Behavior and Human Decision Processes* 102(1): 22–41.

Gruenfeld, Deborah H., M. Ena Inesi, Joe C. Magee, and Adam D. Galinsky. 2008. "Power and the Objectification of Social Targets." *Journal of Personality and Social Psychology* 95(1): 111–27.

Gruenfeld, Deborah H., and Larissa Z. Tiedens. 2010. "Organizational Preferences and Their Consequences." In *Handbook of Social Psychology*, 5th ed., edited by Susan T. Fiske, Daniel T. Gilbert, and Gardner Lindzey. New York: Wiley.

Guimond, Serge, ed. 2006. *Social Comparison and Social Psychology: Understanding Cognition, Intergroup Relations, and Culture.* New York: Cambridge University Press.

Guimond, Serge, Armand Chatard, Delphine Martinot, Richard J. Crisp, and Sandrine Redersdorff. 2006. "Social Comparison, Self-Stereotyping, and Gender Differences in Self-Construals." *Journal of Personality and Social Psychology* 90(2): 221–42.

Guimond, Serge, and Michaël Dambrun. 2002. "When Prosperity Breeds Intergroup Hostility: The Effects of Relative Deprivation and Relative Gratification on Prejudice." *Personality and Social Psychology Bulletin* 28(7): 900–912.

Guinote, Ana. 2007. "Power and Goal Pursuit." *Personality and Social Psychology Bulletin* 33(8): 1076–87.

Gump, Brooks B., and James A. Kulik. 1997. "Stress, Affiliation, and Emotional Contagion." *Journal of Personality and Social Psychology* 72(2): 305–19.

Häfner, Michael, and Thomas W. Schubert. 2009. "Feel the Difference! The Influence of Ease Experiences on the Direction of Social Comparisons." *Journal of Experimental Social Psychology* 45(1): 291–94.

Haidt, Jonathan, Clark McCauley, and Paul Rozin. 1994. "Individual Differences in Sensitivity to Disgust: A Scale Sampling Seven Domains of Disgust Elicitors." *Personality and Individual Differences* 16(5): 701–13.

Haley, Hillary, and Jim Sidanius. 2005. "Person-Organization Congruence and the Maintenance of Group-Based Social Hierarchy: A Social Dominance Perspective." *Group Processes and Intergroup Relations* 8(2): 187–203.

Hall, Judith A., Erik J. Coats, and Lavonia Smith LeBeau. 2005. "Nonverbal Behavior and the Vertical Dimension of Social Relations: A Meta-Analysis." *Psychological Bulletin* 131(6): 898–924.

Hall, Natalie R., and Richard J. Crisp. 2008. "Assimilation and Contrast to Group Primes: The Moderating Role of In-Group Identification." *Journal of Experimental Social Psychology* 44(2): 344–53.

Halle, David. 1987. *America's Working Man.* Chicago: University of Chicago Press.

Hardman, John. 1993. *Louis XVI.* New Haven, Conn.: Yale University Press.

Hardy, Charlie L., and Mark Van Vugt. 2006. "Nice Guys Finish First: The Competitive Altruism Hypothesis." *Personality and Social Psychology Bulletin* 32(10): 1402–13.

Hareli, Shlomo, and Bernard Weiner. 2000. "Accounts for Success as Determinants of Perceived Arrogance and Modesty." *Motivation and Emotion* 24(3): 215–36.

———. 2002. "Dislike and Envy as Antecedents of Pleasure at Another's Misfortune." *Motivation and Emotion* 26(4): 257–57.

Harris Interactive. 2005. Harris Poll no. 24, May 3, 2000. Summary available at: http://harrisinteractive.com/vault/Harris-Interactive-Poll-Research-THE-PUBLIC-TENDS-TO-BLAME-THE-POOR-THE-UNEMPLOYED-2000-05.pdf (accessed February 27, 2011).

Harris, Lasana T., Mina Cikara, and Susan T. Fiske. 2008. "Envy as Predicted by the Stereotype Content Model: A Volatile Ambivalence." In *Envy: Theory and Research*, edited by Richard H. Smith. New York: Oxford University Press.

Harris, Lasana T., and Susan T. Fiske. 2006. "Dehumanizing the Lowest of the Low: Neuro-Imaging Responses to Extreme Out-Groups." *Psychological Science* 17(10): 847–53.

———. 2007. "Social Groups That Elicit Disgust Are Differentially Processed in mPFC." *Social Cognitive and Affective Neuroscience* 2(1): 45–51.

———. 2009. "Dehumanized Perception: The Social Neuroscience of Thinking (or Not Thinking) About Disgusting People." In *European Review of Social Psychology*, vol. 20, edited by Miles Hewstone and Wolfgang Stroebe. London: Wiley.

Harris, Lasana T., Samuel M. McClure, Wouter van den Bos, Jonathan D. Cohen, and Susan T. Fiske. 2007. "Regions of MPFC Differentially Tuned to Social and Non-Social Affective Evaluation." *Cognitive and Behavioral Neuroscience* 7(4): 309–16.

Hart, Allen J., Paul J. Whalen, Lisa M. Shin, Sean C. McInerney, Håkan Fischer, and Scott L. Rauch. 2000. "Differential Response in the Human Amygdala to Racial Out-Group Versus In-Group Face Stimuli." *NeuroReport: For Rapid Communication of Neuroscience Research* 11(11): 2351–55.

Hartz, Louis. 1952. "American Political Thought and the American Revolution." *American Political Science Review* 46(2): 321–42.

Haslam, Nick. 2006. "Dehumanization: An Integrative Review." *Personality and Social Psychology Review* 10(3): 252–64.

Haslam, Nick, Kashima Yoshihisa, Stephen Loughnan, Junqi Shi, and Caterina Suitner. 2008. "Subhuman, Inhuman, and Superhuman: Contrasting Humans with Nonhumans in Three Cultures." *Social Cognition* 26(2): 248–58.

Hatfield, Elaine, John T. Cacioppo, and Richard L. Rapson. 1994. *Emotional Contagion*. New York: Cambridge University Press.

Hatfield, Elaine, Richard L. Rapson, and Katherine Aumer-Ryan. 2008. "Social Justice in Love Relationships: Recent Developments." *Social Justice Research* 21(4): 413–31.

Heath, Chip, Chris Bell, and Emily Sternberg. 2001. "Emotional Selection in Memes: The Case of Urban Legends." *Journal of Personality and Social Psychology* 81(6): 1028–41.

Hebl, Michelle R., and Laura M. Mannix. 2003. "The Weight of Obesity in Evaluating Others: A Mere Proximity Effect." *Personality and Social Psychology Bulletin* 29(1): 28–38.

Heider, Fritz. 1958. *Psychology of Interpersonal Relations*. New York: Wiley.

Helgeson, Vicki S., and Shelley E. Taylor. 1993. "Social Comparisons and Adjustment Among Cardiac Patients." *Journal of Applied Social Psychology* 23(15): 1171–95.

Henagan, Stephanie C., and Arthur G. Bedeian. 2009. "The Perils of Success in the Workplace: Comparison Target Responses to Coworkers' Upward Comparison Threat." *Journal of Applied Social Psychology* 39(10): 2438–68.

Herzog, Don. 2000. *Poisoning the Mind of the Lower Orders.* Princeton, N.J.: Princeton University Press.

Hill, Sarah E., and David M. Buss. 2006. "Envy and Positional Bias in the Evolutionary Psychology of Management." *Managerial and Decision Economics* 27(2–3): 131–43.

———. 2008. "The Mere Presence of Opposite-Sex Others on Judgments of Sexual and Romantic Desirability: Opposite Effects for Men and Women." *Personality and Social Psychology Bulletin* 34(5): 635–47.

Hobza, Cody L., Karen E. Walker, Oksana Yakushko, and James L. Peugh. 2007. "What About Men? Social Comparison and the Effects of Media Images on Body and Self-Esteem." *Psychology of Men and Masculinity* 8(3): 161–72.

Hochschild, Jennifer L. 1981. *What's Fair: American Beliefs About Distributive Justice.* Cambridge, Mass.: Harvard University Press.

Hodge, Roger. 2008. "Class Notes." In *Social Class: How Does It Work?* edited by Annette Lareau and Dalton Conley. New York: Russell Sage Foundation.

Hodson, Gordon, and Richard M. Sorrentino. 1999. "Uncertainty Orientation and the Big Five Personality Structure." *Journal of Research in Personality* 33(2): 253–61.

Hogg, Michael A. 2000. "Social Identity and Social Comparison." In *Handbook of Social Comparison: Theory and Research,* edited by Jerry Suls and Ladd Wheeler. Dordrecht, Netherlands: Kluwer Academic/Plenum Publishers.

———. 2007. "Uncertainty-Identity Theory." In *Advances in Experimental Social Psychology,* vol. 39, edited by Mark P. Zanna. San Diego: Elsevier Academic Press.

———. 2010. "Influence and Leadership." In *Handbook of Social Psychology,* 5th ed., edited by Susan T. Fiske, Daniel T. Gilbert, and Gardner Lindzey. New York: Wiley.

Hogg, Michael A., David K. Sherman, Joel Dierselhuis, Angela T. Maitner, and Graham Moffitt. 2007. "Uncertainty, Entitativity, and Group Identification." *Journal of Experimental Social Psychology* 43(1): 135–42.

Holtgraves, Thomas. 2010. "Social Psychology and Language: Words, Utterances, and Conversations." In *Handbook of Social Psychology,* 5th ed., edited by Susan T. Fiske, Daniel T. Gilbert, and Gardner Lindzey. New York: Wiley.

Horner, Matina S. 1972. "Toward an Understanding of Achievement-Related Conflicts in Women." *Journal of Social Issues* 28(2): 157–75.

Hornsey, Matthew J., and Jolanda Jetten. 2005. "Loyalty Without Conformity: Tailoring Self-Perception as a Means of Balancing Belonging and Differentiation." *Self and Identity* 4(1): 81–95.

House, James S., Karl R. Landis, and Debra Umberson. 1988. "Social Relationships and Health." *Science* 241(4865): 540–45.

Hout, Michael. 2008. "How Class Works: Objective and Subjective Aspects of Class Since the 1970s." In *Social Class: How Does It Work?* edited by Annette Lareau and Dalton Conley. New York: Russell Sage Foundation.

Huguet, Pascal, Florence Dumas, Herbert Marsh, Isabelle Régner, Ladd Wheeler, Jerry Suls, Marjorie Seaton, and John Nezlek. 2009. "Clarifying the Role of Social Comparison in the Big-Fish–Little-Pond Effect (BFLPE): An Integrative Study." *Journal of Personality and Social Psychology* 97(1): 156–70.

Huguet, Pascal, Florence Dumas, Jean M. Monteil, and Nicolas Genestoux. 2001. "Social Comparison Choices in the Classroom: Further Evidence for Students' Upward Comparison Tendency and Its Beneficial Impact on Performance." *European Journal of Social Psychology* 31(5): 557–78.

Hummert, Mary Lee, Jaye L. Shaner, Teri A. Garstka, and Clark Henry. 1998. "Communication with Older Adults: The Influence of Age Stereotypes, Context, and Communicator Age." *Human Communication Research* 25(1): 124–51.

Hunt, Matthew O. 1996. "The Individual, Society, or Both? A Comparison of Black, Latino, and White Beliefs About the Causes of Poverty." *Social Forces* 75(1): 293–322.

Hyde, Janet Shibley. 2005. "The Gender Similarities Hypothesis." *American Psychologist* 60(6): 581–92.

Hyland, Michael E. 1989. "There Is No Motive to Avoid Success: The Compromise Explanation for Success-Avoiding Behavior." *Journal of Personality* 57(3): 665–93.

Insko, Chester A., John Schopler, Rick H. Hoyle, Gregory J. Dardis, and Kenneth A. Graetz. 1990. "Individual-Group Discontinuity as a Function of Fear and Greed." *Journal of Personality and Social Psychology* 58(1): 68–79.

Izuma, Keise, Daisuke N. Saito, and Norihiro Sadato. 2008. "Processing of Social and Monetary Rewards in the Human Striatum." *Neuron* 58(2): 284–94.

Jackson, James S., and Marita R. Inglehart. 1995. "Reverberation Theory: Stress and Racism in Hierarchically Structured Communities." In *Extreme Stress and Communities: Impact and Intervention* (NATO ASI series), edited by Stevan E. Hobfoll and Marten W. deVries. New York: Kluwer Academic/Plenum Publishers.

James, Henry. 2001. *Portrait of a Lady.* New York: Modern Library. (Orig. pub. in 1881.)

James, William. 1983. *The Principles of Psychology.* Cambridge, Mass.: Harvard University Press. (Orig. pub. in 1890.)

Janoff-Bulman, Ronnie. 1992. *Shattered Assumptions: Towards a New Psychology of Trauma.* New York: Free Press.

———. 2009. "To Provide or Protect: Motivational Bases of Political Liberalism and Conservatism." *Psychological Inquiry* 20(2–3): 120–28.

Jetten, Jolanda, Nyla R. Branscombe, Michael T. Schmitt, and Russell Spears. 2001. "Rebels with a Cause: Group Identification as a Response to Perceived Discrimination from the Mainstream." *Personality and Social Psychology Bulletin* 27(9): 1204–13.

Jetten, Jolanda, Russell Spears, and Antony S. R. Manstead. 1997. "Distinctiveness Threat and Prototypicality: Combined Effects on Intergroup Discrimination and Collective Self-Esteem." *European Journal of Social Psychology* 27(6): 635–57.

Johnson, Camille S., and Diederik A. Stapel. 2007. "No Pain, No Gain: The Conditions Under Which Upward Comparisons Lead to Better Performance." *Journal of Personality and Social Psychology* 92(6): 1051–67.

Jones, Edward E., and Thane S. Pittman. 1982. "Toward a General Theory of Strategic Self-Presentation." In *Psychological Perspectives on the Self*, edited by Jerry Suls. Hillsdale, N.J.: Erlbaum.

Joseph, Jane E., Caitlin A. J. Powell, Nathan F. Johnson, and Gayannée Kedia. 2008. "The Functional Neuroanatomy of Envy." In *Envy: Theory and Research*, edited by Richard H. Smith. New York: Oxford University Press.

Jost, John T., and Mahzarin R. Banaji. 1994. "The Role of Stereotyping in System-Justification and the Production of False Consciousness." *British Journal of Social Psychology* 33(1): 1–27.

Jost, John T., and Diana Burgess. 2000. "Attitudinal Ambivalence and the Conflict Between Group and System Justification Motives in Low-Status Groups." *Personality and Social Psychology Bulletin* 26(3): 293–305.

Jost, John T., and Aaron C. Kay. 2010. "Social Justice: History, Theory, and Research." In *Handbook of Social Psychology*, 5th ed., edited by Susan T. Fiske, Daniel T. Gilbert, and Gardner Lindzey. New York: Wiley.

Jost, John T., Aaron C. Kay, and Hulda Thorisdottir, eds. 2009. *Social and Psychological Bases of Ideology and System Justification.* New York: Oxford University Press.

Jostmann, Nils B., Daniël Lakens, and Thomas W. Schubert. 2009. "Weight as an Embodiment of Importance." *Psychological Science* 20(9): 1169–74.

Judd, Charles M., Laurie James-Hawkins, Vincent Yzerbyt, and Yoshihisa Kashima. 2005. "Fundamental Dimensions of Social Judgment: Understanding the Relations Between Judgments of Competence and Warmth." *Journal of Personality and Social Psychology* 89(6): 899–913.

Kaiser Family Foundation, *Washington Post*, and Harvard University. 2008. Survey (June 18–July 7). iPOLL Databank, Roper Center for Public Opinion Research, University of Connecticut (accessed October 14, 2009).

Kahn, Kimberly, Arnold K. Ho, Jim Sidanius, and Felicia Pratto. 2009. "The Space Between Us and Them: Perceptions of Status Differences Group." *Processes and Intergroup Relations* 12(5): 591–604.

Kahneman, Daniel, Alan B. Krueger, David Schkade, Norbert Schwarz, and Arthur A. Stone. 2006. "Would You Be Happier if You Were Richer? A Focusing Illusion." *Science* 312(5782): 1908–10.

Karney, Benjamin R., and Nancy E. Frye. 2002. " 'But We've Been Getting Better Lately': Comparing Prospective and Retrospective Views of Relationship Development." *Journal of Personality and Social Psychology* 82(2): 222–38.

Kay, Aaron C., and John T. Jost. 2003. "Complementary Justice: Effects of 'Poor but Happy' and 'Poor but Honest' Stereotype Exemplars on System Justification and Implicit Activation of the Justice Motive." *Journal of Personality and Social Psychology* 85(5): 823–37.

Kay, Aaron C., John T. Jost, and Sean Young. 2005. "Victim Derogation and Victim Enhancement as Alternate Routes to System Justification." *Psychological Science* 16(3): 240–46.

Kazin, Michael. 1998. *The Populist Persuasion: An American History.* Ithaca, N.Y.: Cornell University Press.

Kearney, Melissa S. 2006. "Intergenerational Mobility for Women and Minorities in the United States." *The Future of Children* 16(2): 37–53.

Keller, Bill. 2005. Introduction to *Class Matters*, edited by Correspondents of the *New York Times*. New York: Times Books.

Keltner, Dacher, Lisa Capps, Ann M. Kring, Randall C. Young, and Erin A. Heereys. 2001. "Just Teasing: A Conceptual Analysis and Empirical Review." *Psychological Bulletin* 127(2): 229–48.

Keltner, Dacher, and Jonathan Haidt. 1999. "Social Functions of Emotions at Four Levels of Analysis." *Cognition and Emotion* 13(5): 505–21.

Keltner, Dacher, Deborah H. Gruenfeld, and Cameron Anderson. 2003. "Power, Approach, and Inhibition." *Psychological Review* 110(2): 265–84.

Kemmelmeier, Markus, and Daphna Oyserman. 2001a. "Gendered Influence of Downward Social Comparisons on Current and Possible Selves." *Journal of Social Issues* 57(1): 129–48.

———. 2001b. "The Ups and Downs of Thinking About a Successful Other: Self-Construals and the Consequences of Social Comparisons." *European Journal of Social Psychology* 31(3): 311–20.

Kervyn, Nicolas, Vincent Y. Yzerbyt, Charles M. Judd, and Ana Nunes. 2009. "A Question of Compensation: The Social Life of the Fundamental Dimensions of Social Perception." *Journal of Personality and Social Psychology* 96(4): 828–42.

Kiecolt-Glaser, Janice K., Lynanne McGuire, Theodore F. Robles, and Ronald Glaser. 2002. "Psychoneuroimmunology: Psychological Influences on Immune Function and Health." *Journal of Consulting and Clinical Psychology* 70(3): 537–47.

Kinder, Donald R., and Cindy D. Kam. 2009. *Us Against Them: Ethnocentric Foundations of American Opinion.* Chicago: University of Chicago Press.

Kirn, Walter. 2009. *Lost in the Meritocracy: The Undereducation of an Overachiever.* New York: Doubleday.

Klein, William M. 1997. "Objective Standards Are Not Enough: Affective, Self-Evaluative, and Behavioral Responses to Social Comparison Information." *Journal of Personality and Social Psychology* 72(4): 763–74.

Kluegel, James R., and Eliot R. Smith. 1986. *Beliefs About Inequality: Americans' Views of What Is and What Ought to Be.* Edison, N.J.: Aldine Transaction.

Knowles, Megan L., Gale M. Lucas, Daniel C. Molden, Wendi L. Gardner, and Kristy K. Dean. 2010. "There's No Substitute for Belonging: Self-Affirmation Following Social and Nonsocial Threats." *Personality and Social Psychology Bulletin* 36(2): 173–86.

Knutson, Brian. 1996. "Facial Expressions of Emotion Influence Interpersonal Trait Inferences." *Journal of Nonverbal Behavior* 20(3): 165–82.

Kraus, Michael W., and Dacher Keltner. 2009. "Signs of Socioeconomic Status: A Thin-Slicing Approach." *Psychological Science* 20(1): 99–106.

Krendl, Anne C., C. Neil Macrae, William M. Kelley, Jonathan A. Fugelsang, and Todd F. Heatherton. 2006. "The Good, the Bad, and the Ugly: An fMRI Investigation of the Functional Anatomic Correlates of Stigma." *Social Neuroscience* 1(1): 5–15.

Kruger, Justin, Paul D. Windschitl, Jeremy Burrus, Florian Fessel, and John R. Chambers. 2008. "The Rational Side of Egocentrism in Social Comparisons." *Journal of Experimental Social Psychology* 44(2): 220–32.

Kruglanski, Arie W., and Donna M. Webster. 1996. "Motivated Closing of the Mind: 'Seizing' and 'Freezing.' " *Psychological Review* 103(2): 263–83.

Kulik, James A., and Heike I. M. Mahler. 2000. "Social Comparison, Affiliation, and Emotional Contagion Under Threat." In *Handbook of Social Comparison: Theory and Research*, edited by Jerry Suls and Ladd Wheeler. Dordrecht, Netherlands: Kluwer Academic/Plenum Publishers.

Kunda, Ziva. 1990. "The Case for Motivated Reasoning." *Psychological Bulletin* 108(3): 480–98.

Lamont, Michèle. 1992. *Money, Morals, and Manners: The Culture of French and American Upper-Middle Class.* Chicago: University of Chicago Press.

Langner, Carrie A., and Dacher Keltner. 2008. "Social Power and Emotional Experience: Actor and Partner Effects Within Dyadic Interactions." *Journal of Experimental Social Psychology* 44(3): 848–56.

La Rochefoucauld, François, Duc de. 1665. *Réflexions*. Paris: Garnier.

Laurin, Kristin, Aaron C. Kay, and David A. Moscovitch. 2008. "On the Belief in God: Towards an Understanding of the Emotional Substrates of Compensatory Control." *Journal of Experimental Social Psychology* 44(6): 1559–62.

Leach, Colin W. 2008. "Envy, Inferiority, and Injustice: Three Bases of Anger About Inequality." In *Envy: Theory and Research*, edited by Richard H. Smith. New York: Oxford University Press.

Leach, Colin W., and Russell Spears. 2008. "A Vengefulness of the Impotent: The Pain of In-Group Inferiority and Schadenfreude Toward Successful Out-Groups." *Journal of Personality and Social Psychology* 95(6): 1383–96.

Leach, Colin W., Martijn van Zomeren, Sven Zebel, Michael L. W. Vliek, Sjoerd F. Pennekamp, Bertjan Doosje, Jaap W. Ouwerkerk, and Russell Spears. 2008. "Group-Level Self-Definition and Self-Investment: A Hierarchical (Multi-component) Model of In-Group Identification." *Journal of Personality and Social Psychology* 95(1): 144–65.

Leary, Mark R. 2007. "Motivational and Emotional Aspects of the Self." *Annual Review of Psychology* 58: 317–44.

Leary, Mark R., Ellen S. Tambor, Sonja K. Terdal, and Deborah L. Downs. 1995. "Self-Esteem as an Interpersonal Monitor: The Sociometer Hypothesis." *Journal of Personality and Social Psychology* 68(3): 518–30.

Lechner, Suzanne C., Howard Tennen, and Glenn Affleck. 2009. "Benefit-Finding and Growth." In *Oxford Handbook of Positive Psychology*, 2d ed., edited by Shane J. Lopez and C. R. Snyder. New York: Oxford University Press.

LeDoux, Joseph E. 2000. "Emotion Circuits in the Brain." *Annual Review of Neuroscience* 23(1): 155–84.

Lee, Tiane L., and Susan T. Fiske. 2006. "Not an Out-Group, but Not Yet an In-Group: Immigrants in the Stereotype Content Model." *International Journal of Intercultural Relations* 30(6): 751–68.

Lett, Heather S., James A. Blumenthal, Michael A. Babyak, Diane J. Catellier, Robert M. Carney, Lisa F. Berkman, Matthew M. Burg, Pamela Mitchell, Allan S. Jaffe, and Neil Schneiderman. 2007. "Social Support and Prognosis in Patients at Increased Psychosocial Risk Recovering from Myocardial Infarction." *Health Psychology* 26(4): 418–27.

Levine, John M., and Richard L. Moreland. 1998. "Small Groups." In *The Handbook of Social Psychology*, vol. 2, 4th ed., edited by Daniel T. Gilbert, Susan T. Fiske, and Gardner Lindzey. New York: McGraw-Hill.

Lew, Ann-Marie, Traci Mann, Hector Myers, Shelley Taylor, and Julienne Bower. 2007. "Thin-Ideal Media and Women's Body Dissatisfaction: Prevention Using Downward Social Comparisons on Non-Appearance Dimensions." *Sex Roles* 57(7–8): 543–56.

Leyens, Jacques-Philippe, Brezo Cortes, Stéphanie Demoulin, John F. Dovidio, Susan T. Fiske, Ruth Gaunt, Maria-Paola Paladino, Armando Rodriguez-Perez, Ramon Rodriguez-Torres, and Jeroen Vaes. 2003. "Emotional Prejudice, Essentialism, and Nationalism: The 2002 Tajfel Lecture." *European Journal of Social Psychology* 33(6): 703–17.

Liden, Robert C., Dean Stilwell, and Gerald R. Ferris. 1996. "The Effects of Supervisor and Subordinate Age on Objective Performance and Subjective Performance Ratings." *Human Relations* 49(3): 327–47.

Lieberman, Matthew D., and Naomi I. Eisenberger. 2009. "Pains and Pleasures of Social Life." *Science* 323(5916): 890–91.

Lindholm, Charles. 2008. "Culture and Envy." In *Envy: Theory and Research,* edited by Richard H. Smith. New York: Oxford University Press.

Lockwood, Penelope. 2002. "Could It Happen to You? Predicting the Impact of Downward Comparisons on the Self." *Journal of Personality and Social Psychology* 82(3): 343–58.

Lockwood, Penelope, Dan Dolderman, Pamela Sadler, and Elinora Gerchak. 2004. "Feeling Better About Doing Worse: Social Comparisons Within Romantic Relationships." *Journal of Personality and Social Psychology* 87(1): 80–95.

Lockwood, Penelope, and Ziva Kunda. 1997. "Superstars and Me: Predicting the Impact of Role Models on the Self." *Journal of Personality and Social Psychology* 73(1): 91–103.

Lord, Robert G., Douglas J. Brown, Jennifer L. Harvey, and Rosalie J. Hall. 2001. "Contextual Constraints on Prototype Generation and Their Multilevel Consequences for Leadership Perceptions." *Leadership Quarterly* 12(3): 311–38.

Lorenzi-Cioldi, Fabio, and Armand Chatard. 2006. "The Cultural Norm of Individualism and Group Status: Implications for Social Comparisons." In *Social Comparison and Social Psychology: Understanding Cognition, Intergroup Relations, and Culture,* edited by Serge Guimond. New York: Cambridge University Press.

Loughnan, Stephen, and Nick Haslam. 2007. "Animals and Androids: Implicit Associations Between Social Categories and Nonhumans." *Psychological Science* 18(2): 116–21.

Lowndes, Joseph E. 2008. *From the New Deal to the New Right: Race and the Southern Origins of Modern Conservatism.* New Haven, Conn.: Yale University Press.

Luhtanen, Riia, and Jennifer Crocker. 1992. "A Collective Self-Esteem Scale: Self-Evaluation of One's Social Identity." *Personality and Social Psychology Bulletin* 18(3): 302–18.

Lyubomirsky, Sonja. 2001. "Why Are Some People Happier Than Others? The Role of Cognitive and Motivational Processes in Well-Being." *American Psychologist* 56(3): 239–49.

Lyubomirsky, Sonja, and Lee Ross. 1997. "Hedonic Consequences of Social Comparison: A Contrast of Happy and Unhappy People." *Journal of Personality and Social Psychology* 73(6): 1141–57.

Lyubomirsky, Sonja, Kari L. Tucker, and Fazilet Kasri. 2001. "Responses to Hedonically Conflicting Social Comparisons: Comparing Happy and Unhappy People." *European Journal of Social Psychology* 31(5): 511–35.

MacDonald, A. P. 1972. "More on the Protestant Ethic." *Journal of Consulting and Clinical Psychology* 39(1): 116–22.

Machiavelli, Niccolò. 1965. *The Chief Works and Others,* 3 vols., translated by A. Gilbert. Durham, N.C.: Duke University Press.

Magee, Joe C. 2009. "Seeing Power in Action: The Roles of Deliberation, Implementation, and Action in Inferences of Power." *Journal of Experimental Social Psychology* 45(1): 1–14.

Magee, Joe C., and Adam D. Galinsky. 2008. "Social Hierarchy: The Self-Reinforcing Nature of Power and Status." *Academy of Management Annals* 2(1): 351–98.

Major, Brenda, and Blythe Forcey. 1985. "Social Comparisons and Pay Evaluations: Preferences for Same-Sex and Same-Job Wage Comparisons." *Journal of Experimental Social Psychology* 21(4): 393–405.

Major, Brenda, Cheryl R. Kaiser, and Shannon K. McCoy. 2003. "It's Not My Fault: When and Why Attributions to Prejudice Protect Self-Esteem." *Personality and Social Psychology Bulletin* 29(6): 772–81.

Major, Brenda, and Ellen Konar. 1984. "An Investigation of Sex Differences in Pay Expectations and Their Possible Causes." *Academy of Management Journal* 27(4): 777–92.

Major, Brenda, Dean B. McFarlin, and Diana Gagnon. 1984. "Overworked and Underpaid: On the Nature of Gender Differences in Personal Entitlement." *Journal of Personality and Social Psychology* 47(6): 1399–1412.

Major, Brenda, and Laurie T. O'Brien. 2005. "The Social Psychology of Stigma." *Annual Review of Psychology* 56(2005): 393–421.

Major, Brenda, Wendy J. Quinton, and Toni Schmader. 2003. "Attributions to Discrimination and Self-Esteem: Impact of Group Identification and Situational Ambiguity." *Journal of Experimental Social Psychology* 39(3): 220–31.

Markus, Hazel R., and Shinobu Kitayama. 1991. "Culture and the Self: Implications for Cognition, Emotion, and Motivation." *Psychological Review* 98(2): 224–53.

Markus, Hazel, and Paula Nurius. 1986. "Possible Selves." *American Psychologist* 41(9): 954–69.

Marlin Company and Zogby International. 2008. Survey (May 12–14). iPOLL Databank, Roper Center for Public Opinion Research, University of Connecticut (accessed October 14, 2009).

Marmot, Michael G. 2003. "Social Resources and Health." In *Expanding the Boundaries of Health and Social Science: Case Studies in Interdisciplinary Innovation,* edited by Frank Kessel, Patricia L. Rosenfield, and Norman B. Anderson. New York: Oxford University Press.

Marmot, Michael G., H. Bosma, H. Hemingway, E. J. Brunner, and S. Stansfield. 1997. "Contribution of Job Control and Other Risk Factors to Social Variations in Coronary Heart Disease Incidence." *Lancet* 350(9073): 235–39.

Marsh, Herbert W., and Kit-Tai Hau. 2003. "Big-Fish–Little-Pond Effect on Academic Self-Concept: A Cross-Cultural (Twenty-Six-Country) Test of the Negative Effects of Academically Selective Schools." *American Psychologist* 58(5): 364–76.

Martens, Andy, Jeff Greenberg, Jeff Schimel, and Mark J. Landau. 2004. "Ageism and Death: Effects of Mortality Salience and Perceived Similarity to Elders on Reactions to Elderly People." *Personality and Social Psychology Bulletin* 30(12): 1524–36.

Marx, David M., Diederik A. Stapel, and Dominique Muller. 2005. "We Can Do It: The Interplay of Construal Orientation and Social Comparisons Under Threat." *Journal of Personality and Social Psychology* 88(3): 432–46.

Master, Sarah L., Naomi I. Eisenberger, Shelley E. Taylor, Bruce D. Naliboff, David Shirinyan, and Matthew D. Lieberman. 2009. "A Picture's Worth: Partner Photographs Reduce Experimentally Induced Pain." *Psychological Science* 20(11): 1316–18.

Matsumoto, David, and Paul Ekman. 2004. "The Relationship among Expressions, Labels, and Descriptions of Contempt." *Journal of Personality and Social Psychology* 87(4): 529–40.

Mays, Vickie M., Susan D. Cochran, and Namdi W. Barnes. 2007. "Race, Race-Based Discrimination, and Health Outcomes Among African Americans." *Annual Review of Psychology* 58(January): 201–25.

McCarty, Nolan, Keith T. Poole, and Howard Rosenthal. 2006. *Polarized America: The Dance of Ideology and Unequal Riches.* Cambridge, Mass.: MIT Press.

McCoy, Shannon K., and Brenda Major. 2003. "Group Identification Moderates Emotional Responses to Perceived Prejudice." *Personality and Social Psychology Bulletin* 29(8): 1005–17.

McCullough, Michael E., Robert A. Emmons, and Jo-Ann Tsang. 2002. "The Grateful Disposition: A Conceptual and Empirical Topography." *Journal of Personality and Social Psychology* 82(1): 112–27.

McCullough, Michael E., Jo-Ann Tsang, and Robert A. Emmons. 2004. "Gratitude in Intermediate Affective Terrain: Links of Grateful Moods to Individual Differences and Daily Emotional Experience." *Journal of Personality and Social Psychology* 86(2): 295–309.

McEvoy, Glenn M., and Wayne F. Cascio. 1989. "Cumulative Evidence of the Relationship Between Employee Age and Job Performance." *Journal of Applied Psychology* 74(1): 11–17.

McEwen, Bruce S. 2000. "The Neurobiology of Stress: From Serendipity to Clinical Relevance." *Brain Research* 886(1–2): 172–89.

McGrath, Charles. 2005. "In Fiction, a Long History of Fixation on the Social Gap." In *Class Matters,* edited by Correspondents of the *New York Times.* New York: Times Books.

McHugo, Gregory J., John T. Lanzetta, Denis G. Sullivan, Roger D. Masters, and Basil G. Englis. 1985. "Emotional Reactions to a Political Leader's Expressive Displays." *Journal of Personality and Social Psychology* 49(6): 1513–29.

Mendes, Wendy Berry, Jim Blascovich, Brenda Major, and Mark Seery. 2001. "Challenge and Threat Responses During Downward and Upward Social Comparisons." *European Journal of Social Psychology* 31(5): 477–97.

Mendolia, Marilyn, Steven R. H. Beach, and Abraham Tesser. 1996. "The Relationship Between Marital Interaction Behaviors and Affective Reactions to One's Own and One's Spouse's Self-Evaluation Needs." *Personal Relationships* 3(3): 279–92.

Merton, Robert K. 1948. "The Self-Fulfilling Prophecy." *Antioch Review* 8(2): 193–210.

Michinov, Nicolas 2001. "When Downward Comparison Produces Negative Affect: The Sense of Control as a Moderator." *Social Behavior and Personality* 29(5): 427–44.

Michinov, Nicolas, and Louis Bavent. 2001. "Upward Persistence and Downward Desistence: Some Reactions to Social-Comparison Deprivation After a Threat." *European Psychologist* 6(2): 112–22.

Mikula, Gerold, Klaus R. Scherer, and Ursula Athenstaedt. 1998. "The Role of Injustice in the Elicitation of Differential Emotional Reactions." *Personality and Social Psychology Bulletin* 24(7): 769–83.

Mikulincer, Mario, and Philip R. Shaver. 2010. *Prosocial Motives, Emotions, and Behavior: The Better Angels of Our Nature.* Washington, D.C.: American Psychological Association.

Miller, Dale T., William Turnbull, and Cathy McFarland. 1988. "Particularistic and Universalistic Evaluation in the Social Comparison Process." *Journal of Personality and Social Psychology* 55(6): 908–17.

Mitchell, Jason P. 2008. "Contributions of Functional Neuroimaging to the Study of Social Cognition." *Current Directions in Psychological Science* 17(2): 142–46.

Mitchell, Gregory, Philip E. Tetlock, Barbara A. Mellers, and Lisa D. Ordóñez. 1993. "Judgments of Social Justice: Compromises between Equality and Efficiency." *Journal of Personality and Social Psychology* 65(4): 629–39.

Mitchell, Jason P., Mahzarin R. Banaji, and C. Neil Macrae. 2005. "The Link Between Social Cognition and Self-Referential Thought in the Medial Prefrontal Cortex." *Journal of Cognitive Neuroscience* 17(8): 1306–15.

Mitchell, Jason P., C. Neil Macrae, and Mahzarin R. Banaji. 2006. "Dissociable Medial Prefrontal Contributions to Judgments of Similar and Dissimilar Others." *Neuron* 50(4): 655–63.

Moeller, Sara K., Michael D. Robinson, and Darya L. Zabelina. 2008. "Personality Dominance and Preferential Use of the Vertical Dimension of Space: Evidence from Spatial Attention Paradigms." *Psychological Science* 19(4): 355–61.

Moghaddam, Fathali M. 2005. "The Staircase to Terrorism: A Psychological Exploration." *American Psychologist* 60(2): 161–69.

Molden, Daniel C., Gale M. Lucas, Wendi L. Gardner, Kristy Dean, and Megan L. Knowles. 2009. "Motivations for Prevention or Promotion Following Social Exclusion: Being Rejected Versus Being Ignored." *Journal of Personality and Social Psychology* 96(2): 415–31.

Moll, Jorge, Richardo de Oliveira-Souza, Griselda J. Garrido, Ivanei E. Bramati, Egas M. Caparelli-Daquer, Mirella L. M. F. Paiva, Roland Zahn, and Jordan Grafman. 2007. "The Self as a Moral Agent: Linking the Neural Bases of Social Agency and Moral Sensitivity." *Social Neuroscience* 2(3–4): 336–52.

Moons, Wesley G., Diana J. Leonard, Diane M. Mackie, and Eliot R. Smith. 2009. "I Feel Our Pain: Antecedents and Consequences of Emotional Self-Stereotyping." *Journal of Experimental Social Psychology* 45(4): 760–69.

Moore, Don A., and William M. P. Klein. 2008. "Use of Absolute and Comparative Performance Feedback in Absolute and Comparative Judgments and Decisions." *Organizational Behavior and Human Decision Processes* 107(1): 60–74.

Moore, Don A., and Deborah A. Small. 2007. "Error and Bias in Comparative Judgment: On Being Both Better and Worse Than We Think We Are." *Journal of Personality and Social Psychology* 92(6): 972–89.

Mullen, Brian. 1985. "Strength and Immediacy of Sources: A Meta-Analytic Evaluation of the Forgotten Elements of Social Impact Theory." *Journal of Personality and Social Psychology* 48(6): 1458–66.

Mullen, Brian, Rupert Brown, and Colleen Smith. 1992. "In-Group Bias as a Function of Salience, Relevance, and Status: An Integration." *European Journal of Social Psychology* 22(2): 103–22.

Mullin, Barbara-Ann, and Michael A. Hogg. 1998. "Dimensions of Subjective Uncertainty in Social Identification and Minimal Intergroup Discrimination." *British Journal of Social Psychology* 37(3): 345–65.

Murphy, Fionnula C., Ian Nimmo-Smith, and Andrew D. Lawrence. 2002. "Functional Neuroanatomy of Emotions: A Meta-Analysis." *Cognitive, Affective, and Behavioral Neuroscience* 3(3): 207–33.

Mussweiler, Thomas. 2003. "Comparison Processes in Social Judgment: Mechanisms and Consequences." *Psychological Review* 110(3): 472–89.

Mussweiler, Thomas, and Galen V. Bodenhausen. 2002. "I Know You Are, but What Am I? Self-Evaluative Consequences of Judging In-Group and Out-Group Members." *Journal of Personality and Social Psychology* 82(1): 19–32.

Mussweiler, Thomas, Shira Gabriel, and Galen V. Bodenhausen. 2000. "Shifting Social Identities as a Strategy for Deflecting Threatening Social Comparisons." *Journal of Personality and Social Psychology* 79(3): 398–409.

Mussweiler, Thomas, and Katja Rüter. 2003. "What Friends Are For! The Use of Routine Standards in Social Comparison." *Journal of Personality and Social Psychology* 85(3): 467–81.

Mussweiler, Thomas, Katja Rüter, and Kai Epstude. 2004. "The Man Who Wasn't There: Subliminal Social Comparison Standards Influence Self-Evaluation." *Journal of Experimental Social Psychology* 40(5): 689–96.

———. 2006. "The Why, Who, and How of Social Comparison: A Social-Cognition Perspective." In *Social Comparison and Social Psychology: Understanding Cognition, Intergroup Relations, and Culture,* edited by Serge Guimond. New York: Cambridge University Press.

Myers, Taryn A., and Janis H. Crowther. 2009. "Social Comparison as a Predictor of Body Dissatisfaction: A Meta-Analytic Review." *Journal of Abnormal Psychology* 118(4): 683–98.

National Coalition for the Homeless. 2009. *Hate, Violence, and Death on Main Street USA: A Report on Hate Crimes and Violence Against People Experiencing Homelessness, 2008.* Washington, D.C.: National Coalition for the Homeless.

National Opinion Research Center (NORC). University of Chicago. 2006. Survey (March 10–August 7). iPOLL Databank, Roper Center for Public Opinion Research, University of Connecticut (accessed October 14, 2009).

———. 2008. Survey (April 17–September 13). iPOLL Databank, Roper Center for Public Opinion Research, University of Connecticut (accessed October 14, 2009).

Nelson, Todd D. 2009. "Ageism." In *Handbook of Prejudice, Stereotyping, and Discrimination,* edited by Todd D. Nelson. New York: Psychology Press.

Nesse, Randolph M. 2010. "Social Selection and the Origins of Culture." In *Evolution, Culture, and the Human Mind,* edited by Mark Schaller, Ara Norenzayan, Steven J. Heine, Toshio Yamagishi, and Tatsuya Kameda. New York: Psychology Press.

Neuberg, Steven L., and Susan T. Fiske. 1987. "Motivational Influences on Impression Formation: Outcome Dependency, Accuracy-Driven Attention, and Individuating Processes." *Journal of Personality and Social Psychology* 53(3): 431–44.

Neuberg, Steven L., Dylan M. Smith, Jonna C. Hoffman, and Frank J. Russell. 1994. "When We Observe Stigmatized and 'Normal' Individuals Interacting: Stigma by Association." *Personality and Social Psychology Bulletin* 20(2): 196–209.

New York Times. 2005. *Class Matters,* edited by Correspondents of the *New York Times.* New York: Times Books.

Nickerson, Carol, Norbert Schwarz, Ed Diener, and Daniel Kahneman. 2003. "Zeroing in on the Dark Side of the American Dream: A Closer Look at the Negative Consequences of the Goal for Financial Success." *Psychological Science* 14(6): 531–36.

Niedenthal, Paula M. 1990. "Implicit Perception of Affective Information." *Journal of Experimental Social Psychology* 26(6): 505–27.

Niedenthal, Paula M., Silvia Krauth-Gruber, and François Ric. 2006. *The Psychology of Emotion: Interpersonal, Experiential, and Cognitive Approaches.* New York: Psychology Press.

Nietzsche, Friedrich W. 1967. *On the Genealogy of Morals and Ecce Homo.* Translated by Walter Kaufmann and R. J. Hollingdale. New York: Random House. (Orig. pub. in 1887.)

Nisbett, Richard E., and Dov Cohen. 1996. *Culture of Honor: The Psychology of Violence in the South.* Boulder, Colo.: Westview Press.

North, Michael S., and Susan T. Fiske. 2010. "Succession, Identity, and Consumption: Dimensions of Control in Age-Based Prejudice." Poster presented at the annual meeting of the Society for Personality and Social Psychology. Las Vegas (January 27–30).

O'Brien, Laurie T., and Brenda Major. 2009. "Group Status and Feelings of Personal Entitlement: The Roles of Social Comparison and System-Justifying Beliefs." In *Social and Psychological Bases of Ideology and System Justification,* edited by John T. Jost, Aaron C. Kay, and Hulda Thorisdottir. New York: Oxford University Press.

Oettingen, Gabriele, and Doris Mayer. 2002. "The Motivating Function of Thinking About the Future: Expectations Versus Fantasies." *Journal of Personality and Social Psychology* 83(5): 1198–1212.

Oldmeadow, Julian A., and Susan T. Fiske. 2010. "Social Status and the Pursuit of Positive Social Identity: Systematic Domains of Intergroup Differentiation and Discrimination for High- and Low-Status Groups." *Group Processes and Intergroup Relations* 13(4): 425–44.

O'Mahen, Heather A., Steven R. H. Beach, and Abraham Tesser. 2000. "Relationship Ecology and Negative Communication in Romantic Relationships: A Self-Evaluation Maintenance Perspective." *Personality and Social Psychology Bulletin* 26(11): 1343–52.

Oosterhof, Nikolaas N., and Alexander Todorov. 2008. "The Functional Basis of Face Evaluation." *Proceedings of the National Academy of Sciences* 105(32): 11087–92.

Operario, Don, and Susan T. Fiske. 2001a. "Effects of Trait Dominance on Power-Holders' Judgments of Subordinates." *Social Cognition* 19(2): 161–80.

———. 2001b. "Ethnic Identity Moderates Perceptions of Prejudice: Judgments of Personal Versus Group Discrimination and Subtle Versus Blatant Bias." *Personality and Social Psychology Bulletin* 27(5): 550–61.

Opportunity Agenda. 2007. Available at: http://www.opportunityagenda.org/public_opinion (accessed September 2009).

Ouellette, Judith A., Robert Hessling, Frederick X. Gibbons, Monica Reis-Bergan, and Meg Gerrard. 2005. "Using Images to Increase Exercise Behavior: Prototypes Versus Possible Selves." *Personality and Social Psychology Bulletin* 31(5): 610–20.

Oyserman, Daphna, Heather M. Coon, and Markus Kemmelmeier. 2002. "Rethinking Individualism and Collectivism: Evaluation of Theoretical Assumptions and Meta-Analyses." *Psychological Bulletin* 128(1): 3–72.

Oyserman, Daphna, and Spike W. S. Lee. 2008. "Does Culture Influence What and How We Think? Effects of Priming Individualism and Collectivism." *Psychological Bulletin* 134(2): 311–42.

Parks, Craig D., Ann C. Rumble, and Donelle C. Posey. 2002. "The Effects of Envy on Reciprocation in a Social Dilemma." *Personality and Social Psychology Bulletin* 28(4): 509–20.

Parrott, W. Gerrod. 1991. "The Emotional Experience of Envy and Jealousy." In *The Psychology of Jealousy and Envy*, edited by Peter Salovey. New York: Guilford Press.

Parrott, W. Gerrod, and Patricia M. Rodriguez Mosquera. 2008. "On the Pleasures and Displeasures of Being Envied." In *Envy: Theory and Research*, edited by Richard H. Smith. New York: Oxford University Press.

Parsons, Talcott. 1964. "Evolutionary Universals in Society." *American Sociological Review* 29(3): 339–57.

Pastore, Nicholas. 1952. "The Role of Arbitrariness in the Frustration-Aggression Hypothesis." *Journal of Abnormal and Social Psychology* 47(3): 728–31.

Pemberton, Michael, and Constantine Sedikides. 2001. "When Do Individuals Help Close Others Improve? The Role of Information Diagnosticity." *Journal of Personality and Social Psychology* 81(2): 234–46.

Pennebaker, James W., Bernard Rimé, and Virginia E. Blankenship. 1996. "Stereotypes of Emotional Expressiveness of Northerners and Southerners: A Cross-Cultural Test of Montesquieu's Hypotheses." *Journal of Personality and Social Psychology* 70(2): 372–80.

Peters, Kim, and Yoshihisa Kashima. 2007. "From Social Talk to Social Action: Shaping the Social Triad with Emotion Sharing." *Journal of Personality and Social Psychology* 93(5): 780–97.

Peters, Kim, Yoshihisa Kashima, and Anna Clark. 2009. "Talking About Others: Emotionality and the Dissemination of Social Information." *European Journal of Social Psychology* 39(2): 207–22.

Pettigrew, Thomas F., Oliver Christ, Ulrich Wagner, Roel W. Meertens, Rolf van Dick, and Andreas Zick. 2008. "Relative Deprivation and Intergroup Prejudice." *Journal of Social Issues* 64(2): 385–401.

Pettigrew, Thomas F., and Roel W. Meertens. 1995. "Subtle and Blatant Prejudice in Western Europe." *European Journal of Social Psychology* 25(1): 57–75.

Pettigrew, Thomas F., and Linda R. Tropp. 2006. "A Meta-Analytic Test of Intergroup Contact Theory." *Journal of Personality and Social Psychology* 90(5): 751–83.

———. 2008. "How Does Intergroup Contact Reduce Prejudice? Meta-Analytic Tests of Three Mediators." *European Journal of Social Psychology* 38(6): 922–34.

Pew Global Attitudes Project. Pew Research Center. 2009. "Most Muslim Publics Not So Easily Moved: Confidence in Obama Lifts U.S. Image Around the World" (press release). July 23.

Pew Economic Mobility Project and Greenberg Quinlan Rosner Research and Public Opinion Strategies. 2009. Survey (January 27–February 8). iPOLL Databank, Roper Center for Public Opinion Research, University of Connecticut (accessed September 23, 2009).

Pew Research Center for the People and the Press and Princeton Survey Research Associates International. 2009. Survey (March 31–April 21). iPOLL Databank, Roper Center for Public Opinion Research, University of Connecticut (accessed October 14, 2009).

Phan, K. Luan, Tor Wager, Stephan F. Taylor, and Israel Liberzon. 2002. "Functional Neuroanatomy of Emotion: A Meta-Analysis of Emotion Activation Studies in PET and fMRI." *Neuroimage* 16(2): 331–48.

Phelps, Elizabeth A. 2006. "Emotion and Cognition: Insights from Studies of the Human Amygdala." *Annual Review of Psychology* 57: 27–53.

Phelps, Elizabeth A., Kevin J. O'Connor, William A. Cunningham, E. Sumie Funayama, J. Christopher Gatenby, John C. Gore, and Mahzarin R. Banaji. 2000. "Performance on Indirect Measures of Race Evaluation Predicts Amygdala Activation." *Journal of Cognitive Neuroscience* 12(5): 729–38.

Pilkington, Constance J., Abraham Tesser, and Deborah Stephens. 1991. "Complementarity in Romantic Relationships: A Self-Evaluation Maintenance Perspective." *Journal of Social and Personal Relationships* 8(4): 481–504.

Pinel, Elizabeth C., Anson F. Long, and Leslie A. Crimin. 2008. "We're Warmer (They're More Competent): I-Sharing and African-Americans' Perceptions of the In-Group and Out-Group." *European Journal of Social Psychology* 38(7): 1184–92.

Pinkus, Rebecca T., Penelope Lockwood, Ulrich Schimmack, and Marc A. Fournier. 2008. "For Better and for Worse: Everyday Social Comparisons Between Romantic Partners." *Journal of Personality and Social Psychology* 95(5): 1180–1201.

Powers, Thomas. 1972. "Can Friendship Survive Success?" *Ms.* (January): 16–18.

Pratto, Felicia, Jim Sidanius, and Shana Levin. 2006. "Social Dominance Theory and the Dynamics of Intergroup Relations: Taking Stock and Looking Forward." *European Review of Social Psychology* 17(8): 271–320.

Pratto, Felicia, Jim Sidanius, Lisa M. Stallworth, and Bertram F. Malle. 1994. "Social Dominance Orientation: A Personality Variable Predicting Social and Political Attitudes." *Journal of Personality and Social Psychology* 67(40): 741–63.

Pronin, Emily, Thomas Gilovich, and Lee Ross. 2004. "Objectivity in the Eye of the Beholder: Divergent Perceptions of Bias in Self Versus Others." *Psychological Review* 111(3): 781–99.

Proust, Marcel. 1913–27. *À la Recherche du temps perdu: Du côté de chez Swann [In Search of Lost Time: Swann's Way].* Paris: Grasset.

Quoidbach, Jordi, Elizabeth W. Dunn, K. V. Petrides, and Moïra Mikolajczak. 2010. "Money Giveth, Money Taketh Away: The Dual Effect of Wealth on Happiness." *Psychological Science* 21(6): 759–63.

Range, Friederike, Lisa Horn, Zsófia Viranyi, and Ludwig Huber. 2009. "The Absence of Reward Induces Inequity Aversion in Dogs." *Proceedings of the National Academy of Sciences* 106(1): 340–45.

Redersdorff, Sandrine, and Serge Guimond. 2006. "Comparing Oneself over Time: The Temporal Dimension in Social Comparison." In *Social Comparison and Social Psychology: Understanding Cognition, Intergroup Relations, and Culture,* edited by Serge Guimond. New York: Cambridge University Press.

Ridgeway, Cecilia L. 1991. "The Social Construction of Status Value: Gender and Other Nominal Characteristics." *Social Forces* 70(2): 367–86.

———. 1997. "Interaction and the Conservation of Gender Inequality: Considering Employment." *American Sociological Review* 62(2): 218–35.

Rilling, James K., Alan G. Sanfey, Jessica A. Aronson, Leigh E. Nystrom, and Jonathan D. Cohen. 2004. "Opposing BOLD Responses to Reciprocated and Unreciprocated Altruism in Putative Reward Pathways." *NeuroReport: For Rapid Communication of Neuroscience Research* 15(16): 2539–43.

Robins, Richard W., and Jennifer S. Beer. 2001. "Positive Illusions About the Self: Short-Term Benefits and Long-Term Costs." *Journal of Personality and Social Psychology* 80(2): 340–52.

Robinson, Michael D., Darya L. Zabelina, Scott Ode, and Sara K. Moeller. 2008. "The Vertical Nature of Dominance-Submission: Individual Differences in Vertical Attention." *Journal of Research in Personality* 42(4): 933–48.

Roccato, Michele, and Luca Ricolfi. 2005. "On the Correlation Between Right-Wing Authoritarianism and Social Dominance Orientation." *Basic and Applied Social Psychology* 27(3): 187–200.

Rockefeller Foundation, *Time* Magazine Campaign for American Workers, and Penn, Schoen, and Berland Associates. 2008. Survey (June 19–29). iPOLL Databank, Roper Center for Public Opinion Research, University of Connecticut (accessed September 23, 2009).

Roese, Neal J. 1994. "The Functional Basis of Counterfactual Thinking." *Journal of Personality and Social Psychology* 66(5): 805–18.

Roney, Christopher J. R., and Richard M. Sorrentino. 1995a. "Self-Evaluation Motives and Uncertainty Orientation: Asking the 'Who' Question." *Personality and Social Psychology Bulletin* 21(12): 1319–29.

———. 1995b. "Uncertainty Orientation, the Self, and Others: Individual Differences in Values and Social Comparison." *Canadian Journal of Behavioural Science/Revue Canadienne des Sciences du Comportement* 27(2): 157–70.

Roseman, Ira J. 1984. "Cognitive Determinants of Emotion: A Structural Theory." *Review of Personality and Social Psychology* 5: 11–36.

Roseman, Ira J., Cynthia Wiest, and Tamara S. Swartz. 1994. "Phenomenology, Behaviors, and Goals Differentiate Discrete Emotions." *Journal of Personality and Social Psychology* 67(2): 206–21.

Rosenberg, Erika L., Paul Ekman, and James A. Blumenthal. 1998. "Facial Expression and the Affective Component of Cynical Hostility in Male Coronary Heart Disease Patients." *Health Psychology* 17(4): 376–80.

Ross, Michael, Steven J. Heine, Anne E. Wilson, and Shinkichi Sugimori. 2005. "Cross-Cultural Discrepancies in Self-Appraisals." *Personality and Social Psychology Bulletin* 31(9): 1175–88.

Ross, Michael, and Anne E. Wilson. 2003. "Autobiographical Memory and Conceptions of Self: Getting Better All the Time." *Current Directions in Psychological Science* 12(2): 66–69.

Rothbart, Myron, and Marjorie Taylor. 1992. "Category Labels and Social Reality: Do We View Social Categories as Natural Kinds?" In *Language, Interaction, and Social Cognition,* edited by Gün R. Semin and Klaus Fiedler. Thousand Oaks, Calif.: Sage Publications.

Rozin, Paul, Jonathan Haidt, and Katrina Fincher. 2009. "From Oral to Moral." *Science* 323(5918): 1179–80.

Rozin, Paul, Laura Lowery, Sumio Imada, and Jonathan Haidt. 1999. "The CAD Triad Hypothesis: A Mapping Between Three Moral Emotions (Contempt, Anger, Disgust) and Three Moral Codes (Community, Autonomy, Divinity)." *Journal of Personality and Social Psychology* 76(4): 574–86.

Rubin, Lillian Breslow. 1976. *Worlds of Pain: Life in the Working-Class Family.* New York: Basic Books.

Rule, Nicholas O., Joseph M. Moran, Jonathan B. Freeman, John D. E. Gabrieli, Susan Whitfield-Gabrieli, and Nalini Ambady. 2009. "Amygdala Responses Reflect the Accuracy of First Impressions." Paper presented to the annual meeting of the Social and Affective Neuroscience Society. New York (October 10).

Runciman, Walter Garrison. 1966. *Relative Deprivation*. London: Routledge & Kegan Paul.

Ruscher, Janet B., Elizabeth L. Cralley, and Kimberly J. O'Farrell. 2005. "How Newly Acquainted Dyads Develop Shared Stereotypic Impressions Through Conversation." *Group Processes and Intergroup Relations* 8(3): 259–70.

Ruscher, Janet B., and Susan T. Fiske. 1990. "Interpersonal Competition Can Cause Individuating Processes." *Journal of Personality and Social Psychology* 58(5): 832–43.

Russell, Ann Marie, and Susan T. Fiske. 2008. "It's All Relative: Social Position and Interpersonal Perception." *European Journal of Social Psychology* 38(7): 1193–1201.

———. 2009. "From Sweet Charity to Moral Indignation: Polarized Reactions to the Socially Disadvantaged." Poster presented at the annual meeting of the Society for Personality and Social Psychology.

Russell, Bertrand. 1930. *The Conquest of Happiness*. New York: Norton.

Russo, Richard. 2007. *Bridge of Sighs*. New York: Vintage.

Sacerdote, Bruce. 2001. "Peer Effects with Random Assignment: Results for Dartmouth Roommates." *Quarterly Journal of Economics* 116(2): 681–704.

Sales, Stephen M. 1973. "Threat as a Factor in Authoritarianism: An Analysis of Archival Data." *Journal of Personality and Social Psychology* 28(1): 44–57.

Salovey, Peter, and Judith Rodin. 1988. "Coping with Envy and Jealousy." *Journal of Social and Clinical Psychology* 7(1): 15–33.

———. 1991. "Provoking Jealousy and Envy: Domain Relevance and Self-Esteem Threat." *Journal of Social and Clinical Psychology* 10(4): 395–413.

Salovey, Peter, and Alexander J. Rothman. 1991. "Envy and Jealousy: Self and Society." In *The Psychology of Jealousy and Envy,* edited by Peter Salovey. New York: Guilford Press.

Sambataro, Fabio, Savino Dimalta, Annabella Di Giorgio, Paolo Taurisano, Giuseppe Blasi, Tommaso Scarabino, Guiseppe Giannatempo, Marcello Nardini, and Alessandro Bertolino. 2006. "Preferential Responses in Amygdala and Insula During Presentation of Facial Contempt and Disgust." *European Journal of Neuroscience* 24(8): 2355–62.

Sanfey, Alan G., James K. Rilling, Jessica A. Aronson, Leigh E. Nystrom, and Jonathan D. Cohen. 2003. "The Neural Basis of Economic Decision-Making in the Ultimatum Game." *Science* 300(56260): 1755–58.

Sanitioso, Rasyid B., Martin A. Conway, and Sophie Brunot. 2006. "Autobiographical Memory, the Self, and Comparison Processes." In *Social Comparison and Social Psychology: Understanding Cognition, Intergroup Relations, and Culture,* edited by Serge Guimond. New York: Cambridge University Press.

Sanitioso, Rasyid B., Ziva Kunda, and Geoffrey T. Fong. 1990. "Motivated Recruitment of Autobiographical Memories." *Journal of Personality and Social Psychology* 59(2): 229–41.

Sapolsky, Robert M. 2004. "Social Status and Health in Humans and Other Animals." *Annual Review of Anthropology* 33(October): 393–418.

Sawhill, Isabel, and Sara McLanahan. 2006. "Introducing the Issue: Opportunity in America." *The Future of Children* 16(2): 3–16.

Scheepers, Daan, Russell Spears, Bertjan Doosje, and Antony S. R. Manstead. 2006. "The Social Functions of In-Group Bias: Creating, Confirming, or Changing Social Reality." *European Review of Social Psychology* 17: 359–96.

Schneiderman, Neil, Gail Ironson, and Scott D. Siegel. 2005. "Stress and Health: Psychological, Behavioral, and Biological Determinants." *Annual Review of Clinical Psychology* 1(1): 607–28.

Schoeck, Henry. 1986. *Envy: A Theory of Social Behavior.* Translated by M. Glenny and B. Ross. Indianapolis: Liberty Fund. (Orig. pub. in 1969.)

Schubert, Thomas W. 2005. "Your Highness: Vertical Positions as Perceptual Symbols of Power." *Journal of Personality and Social Psychology* 89(1): 1–21.

Schubert, Thomas W., Sven Waldzus, and Steffen R. Giessner. 2009. "Control over the Association of Power and Size." *Social Cognition* 27(1): 1–19.

Schulz, Richard, and Susan Decker. 1985. "Long-Term Adjustment to Physical Disability: The Role of Social Support, Perceived Control, and Self-Blame." *Journal of Personality and Social Psychology* 48(5): 1162–72.

Schwalbe, Michael L., and Clifford L. Staples. 1991. "Gender Differences in Sources of Self-Esteem." *Social Psychology Quarterly* 54(2): 158–68.

Schwinghammer, Saskia A., Diederik A. Stapel, and Hart Blanton. 2006. "Different Selves Have Different Effects: Self-Activation and Defensive Social Comparison." *Personality and Social Psychology Bulletin* 32(1): 27–39.

Scott, Janny, and David Leonhardt. 2005. "Shadowy Lines That Still Divide." In *Class Matters,* edited by Correspondents of the *New York Times.* New York: Times Books.

Sedikides, Constantine, and Aiden P. Gregg. 2008. "Self-Enhancement: Food for Thought." *Perspectives on Psychological Science* 3(2): 102–16.

Sedikides, Constantine, and John J. Skowronski. 1997. "The Symbolic Self in Evolutionary Context." *Personality and Social Psychology Review* 1(1): 80–102.

Segerstrom, Suzanne C., and Sandra E. Sephton. 2010. "Optimistic Expectancies and Cell-Mediated Immunity: The Role of Positive Affect." *Psychological Science* 21(3): 448–55.

Sellers, Robert M., and Nicole J. Shelton. 2003. "The Role of Racial Identity in Perceived Racial Discrimination." *Journal of Personality and Social Psychology* 84(5): 1079–1192.

Sevillano Triguero, Veronica, and Susan T. Fiske. 2010. "Empathy Warms Up Stereotype Content but Ignores Perceived Incompetence." Poster presented at the annual meetings of the Society of Personality and Social Psychology (January 30).

Shaw, George Bernard. 1921. *Back to Methuselah.* New York: Brentano.

Shelton, J. Nicole, Jennifer A. Richeson, and Jacquie D. Vorauer. 2006. "Threatened Identities and Interethnic Interactions." *European Review of Social Psychology* 17: 321–58.

Shnabel, Nurit, and Arie Nadler. 2008. "A Needs-Based Model of Reconciliation: Satisfying the Differential Emotional Needs of Victim and Perpetrator as a Key to Promoting Reconciliation." *Journal of Personality and Social Psychology* 94(1): 116–32.

Shuper, Paul A., Richard M. Sorrentino, Yasunao Otsubo, Gordon Hodson, and A. Marie Walker. 2004. "A Theory of Uncertainty Orientation: Implications for the Study of Individual Differences Within and Across Cultures." *Journal of Cross-Cultural Psychology* 35(4): 460–80.

Sibley, Chris G., and John Duckitt. 2008. "Personality and Prejudice: A Meta-Analysis and Theoretical Review." *Personality and Social Psychology Review* 12(3): 248–79.

Sidanius, Jim, and Felicia Pratto. 1999. *Social Dominance: An Intergroup Theory of Social Hierarchy and Oppression.* New York: Cambridge University Press.

Silver, Maury, and John P. Sabini. 1978. "The Perception of Envy." *Social Psychology* 41(2): 105–11.

Simon, Bernd, and Daniela Ruhs. 2008. "Identity and Politicization Among Turkish Migrants in Germany: The Role of Dual Identification." *Journal of Personality and Social Psychology* 95(6): 1354–66.

Simon, Carly. 1972. "You're So Vain (You Probably Think This Song Is About You)." Published by C'est Music.

Simon, Herbert A. 1967. "Motivational and Emotional Controls of Cognition." *Psychological Review* 74(1): 29–39.

Sinaceur, Marwan, and Larissa Z. Tiedens. 2006. "Get Mad and Get More Than Even: When and Why Anger Expression Is Effective in Negotiations." *Journal of Experimental Social Psychology* 42(30): 314–22.

Sinclair, Lisa, and Ziva Kunda. 1999. "Reactions to a Black Professional: Motivated Inhibition and Activation of Conflicting Stereotypes." *Journal of Personality and Social Psychology* 77(5): 885–904.

———. 2000. "Motivated Stereotyping of Women: She's Fine if She Praised Me but Incompetent if She Criticized Me." *Personality and Social Psychology Bulletin* 26(11): 1329–42.

Singer, Tania, Ben Seymour, John P. O'Doherty, Klass E. Stephan, Raymond J. Dolan, and Chris D. Frith. 2006. "Empathic Neural Responses Are Modulated by the Perceived Fairness of Others." *Nature* 439(7075): 466–69.

Singleton, Royce A., Jr., and Jessica Vacca. 2007. "Interpersonal Competition in Friendships." *Sex Roles* 57(9–10): 617–27.

Smeeding, Timothy M. 2005. "Public Policy, Economic Inequality, and Poverty: The United States in Comparative Perspective." *Social Science Quarterly* 86(1): 955–83.

Smith, Eliot R., and Colin Ho. 2002. "Prejudice as Intergroup Emotion: Integrating Relative Deprivation and Social Comparison Explanations of Prejudice." In *Relative Deprivation: Specification, Development, and Integration,* edited by Iain Walker and Heather J. Smith. New York: Cambridge University Press.

Smith, Eliot R., Charles R. Seger, and Diane M. Mackie. 2007. "Can Emotions Be Truly Group Level? Evidence Regarding Four Conceptual Criteria." *Journal of Personality and Social Psychology* 93(3): 431–46.

Smith, Heather J., Thomas F. Pettigrew, Gina M. Pippin, and Silvana Bialosiewicz. 2010. "Does Relative Deprivation Predict? A Meta-Analytic Critique." Unpublished paper, Sonoma State University.

Smith, Kirsten P., and Nicholas A. Christakis. 2008. "Social Networks and Health." *Annual Review of Sociology* 34: 405–29.

Smith, Pamela K., Nils B. Jostmann, Adam D. Galinsky, and Wilco W. van Dijk. 2008. "Lacking Power Impairs Executive Functions." *Psychological Science* 19(5): 441–47.

Smith, Richard H. 1991. "Envy and the Sense of Injustice." In *The Psychology of Jealousy and Envy,* edited by Peter Salovey. New York: Guilford Press.

Smith, Richard H., David J. Y. Combs, and Stephen M. Thielke. 2008. "Envy and the Challenges to Good Health." In *Envy: Theory and Research,* edited by Richard H. Smith. New York: Oxford University Press.

Smith, Richard H., Heidi L. Eyre, Caitlin A. J. Powell, and Sung Hee Kim. 2006. "Relativistic Origins of Emotional Reactions to Events Happening to Others and to Ourselves." *British Journal of Social Psychology* 45(2): 357–71.

Smith, Richard H., and Sung Hee Kim. 2007. "Comprehending Envy." *Psychological Bulletin* 133(1): 46–64.

———. 2008. "Introduction." In *Envy: Theory and Research*, edited by Richard H. Smith. New York: Oxford University Press.

Smith, Richard H., W. Gerrod Parrott, Edward F. Diener, Rick H. Hoyle, and Sung Hee Kim. 1999. "Dispositional Envy." *Personality and Social Psychology Bulletin* 25(8): 1007–20.

Smith, Richard H., Terrence J. Turner, Ron Garonzik, Colin W. Leach, Vanessa Urch-Druskat, and Christine M. Weston. 1996. "Envy and Schadenfreude." *Personality and Social Psychology Bulletin* 22(2): 158–68.

Smith, Timothy W., Kelly Glazer, John M. Ruiz, and Linda C. Gallo. 2004. "Hostility, Anger, Aggressiveness, and Coronary Heart Disease: An Interpersonal Perspective on Personality, Emotion, and Health." *Journal of Personality* 72(6): 1217–70.

Spencer, Steven J., Steven Fein, Connie T. Wolfe, Christina Fong, and Meghan A. Dunn. 1998. "Automatic Activation of Stereotypes: The Role of Self-Image Threat." *Personality and Social Psychology Bulletin* 24(11): 1139–52.

Stapel, Diederik A., and Hart Blanton. 2004. "From Seeing to Being: Subliminal Social Comparisons Affect Implicit and Explicit Self-Evaluations." *Journal of Personality and Social Psychology* 87(4): 468–81.

Stapel, Diederik A., and Camille S. Johnson. 2007. "When Nothing Compares to Me: How Defensive Motivations and Similarity Shape Social Comparison Effects." *European Journal of Social Psychology* 37(5): 824–38.

Stapel, Diederik A., and Willem Koomen. 2001. "I, We, and the Effects of Others on Me: How Self-Construal Level Moderates Social Comparison Effects." *Journal of Personality and Social Psychology* 80(5): 766–81.

Stapel, Diederik A., and Abraham Tesser. 2001. "Self-Activation Increases Social Comparison." *Journal of Personality and Social Psychology* 81(4): 742–50.

Staub, Ervin. 1989. *The Roots of Evil: The Origins of Genocide and Other Group Violence.* New York: Cambridge University Press.

Steele, Claude M. 1997. "A Threat in the Air: How Stereotypes Shape Intellectual Identity and Performance." *American Psychologist* 52(6): 613–29.

Stephan, Walter G., and Krystina Finlay. 1999. "The Role of Empathy in Improving Intergroup Relations." *Journal of Social Issues* 55(4): 729–43.

Stephan, Walter G., and Cookie W. Stephan. 1985. "Intergroup Anxiety." *Journal of Social Issues* 41(3): 157–75.

Stephens, Nicole M., Hazel Rose Markus, and Sarah S. M. Townsend. 2007. "Choice as an Act of Meaning: The Case of Social Class." *Journal of Personality and Social Psychology* 93(5): 814–30.

Stouffer, Samuel A., Edward A. Suchman, Leland C. Devinney, Shirley A. Star, and Robin M. Williams, Jr. 1949. *The American Soldier: Adjustment During Army Life.* Studies in Social Psychology in World War II, vol. 1. Princeton, N.J.: Princeton University Press.

Suls, Jerry, René Martin, and Ladd Wheeler. 2000. "Three Kinds of Opinion Comparison: The Triadic Model." *Personality and Social Psychology Review* 4(3): 219–37.

————. 2002. "Social Comparison: Why, with Whom, and with What Effect?" *Current Directions in Psychological Science* 11(5): 159–63.

Suls, Jerry, and Ladd Wheeler, ed. 2000. *Handbook of Social Comparison: Theory and Research*. Dordrecht, Netherlands: Kluwer Academic/Plenum Publishers.

Swap, Walter C., and Jeffrey Z. Rubin. 1983. "Measurement of Interpersonal Orientation." *Journal of Personality and Social Psychology* 44(1): 208–19.

Tabibnia, Golnaz, Ajay B. Satpute, and Matthew D. Lieberman. 2008. "The Sunny Side of Fairness: Preference for Fairness Activates Reward Circuitry (and Disregarding Unfairness Activates Self-Control Circuitry)." *Psychological Science* 19(4): 339–47.

Tackett, Timothy. 2003. *When the King Took Flight*. Cambridge, Mass.: Harvard University Press.

Tajfel, Henri. 1974. "Social Identity and Intergroup Behavior." *Social Science Information/Sur les Sciences Sociales* 13(2): 65–93.

————. 1982. "Social Psychology of Intergroup Relations." *Annual Review of Psychology* 33: 1–39.

Takahashi, Hidehiko, Motoichiro Kato, Masato Matsuura, Dean Mobbs, Tetsuya Suhara, and Yoshiro Okubo. 2009. "When Your Gain Is My Pain and Your Pain Is My Gain: Neural Correlates of Envy and Schadenfreude." *Science* 323(February 13): 937–39.

Tassinary, Louis G., John T. Cacioppo, and Thomas R. Geen. 1989. "A Psychometric Study of Surface Electrode Placements for Facial Electromyographic Recording: I. The Brow and Cheek Muscle Regions." *Psychophysiology* 26(1): 1–16.

Tausch, Nicole, Jared B. Kenworthy, and Miles Hewstone. 2007. "The Confirmability and Disconfirmability of Trait Concepts Revisited: Does Content Matter?" *Journal of Personality and Social Psychology* 92(3): 542–56.

Taylor, Shelley E. 1989. *Positive Illusions: Creative Self-Deception and the Healthy Mind*. New York: Basic Books.

————. 1991. "Asymmetrical Effects of Positive and Negative Events: The Mobilization-Minimization Hypothesis." *Psychological Bulletin* 110(1): 67–85.

Taylor, Shelley E., and Jonathon D. Brown. 1988. "Illusion and Well-Being: A Social Psychological Perspective on Mental Health." *Psychological Bulletin* 103(2): 193–210.

Taylor, Shelley E., Vicki S. Helgeson, Geoffrey M. Reed, and Laurie A. Skokan. 1991. "Self-Generated Feelings of Control and Adjustment to Physical Illness." *Journal of Social Issues* 47(4): 91–109.

Taylor, Shelley E., Margaret E. Kemeny, Geoffrey M. Reed, Julienne E. Bower, and Tara L. Gruenewald. 2000. "Psychological Resources, Positive Illusions, and Health." *American Psychologist* 55(1): 99–109.

Taylor, Shelley E., Rosemary R. Lichtman, and Joanne V. Wood. 1984. "Attributions, Beliefs About Control, and Adjustment to Breast Cancer." *Journal of Personality and Social Psychology* 46(3): 489–502.

Taylor, Shelley E., and Marci Lobel. 1989. "Social Comparison Activity Under Threat: Downward Evaluation and Upward Contacts." *Psychological Review* 96(4): 569–75.

Tennen, Howard, and Glenn Affleck. 1990. "Blaming Others for Threatening Events." *Psychological Bulletin* 108(2): 209–32.

Tennen, Howard, Tara Eberhardt McKee, and Glenn Affleck. 2000. "Social Comparison Processes in Health and Illness." *Handbook of Social Comparison: Theory and Research,* edited by Jerry Suls and Ladd Wheeler. Dordrecht, Netherlands: Kluwer Academic/Plenum Publishers.

Tesser, Abraham. 1988. "Toward a Self-Evaluation Maintenance Model of Social Behavior." In *Advances in Experimental Social Psychology,* vol. 21, edited by Leonard Berkowitz. San Diego: Academic Press.

Tesser, Abraham, Jennifer Campbell, and Monte Smith. 1984. "Friendship Choice and Performance: Self-Evaluation Maintenance in Children." *Journal of Personality and Social Psychology* 46(3): 561–74.

Tesser, Abraham, Nicole Crepaz, Steven R. H. Beach, David Cornell, and Jon C. Collins. 2000. "Confluence of Self-Esteem Regulation Mechanisms: On Integrating the Self-Zoo." *Personality and Social Psychology Bulletin* 26(12): 1476–89.

Tesser, Abraham, Murray Millar, and Janet Moore. 1988. "Some Affective Consequences of Social Comparison and Reflection Processes: The Pain and Pleasure of Being Close." *Journal of Personality and Social Psychology* 54(1): 49–61.

Tesser, Abraham, and Del Paulhus. 1983. "The Definition of Self: Private and Public Self-Evaluation Management Strategies." *Journal of Personality and Social Psychology* 44(4): 672–82.

Tesser, Abraham, Constance J. Pilkington, and William D. McIntosh. 1989. "Self-Evaluation Maintenance and the Mediational Role of Emotion: The Perception of Friends and Strangers." *Journal of Personality and Social Psychology* 57(3): 442–56.

Tesser, Abraham, and Jonathan Smith. 1980. "Some Effects of Task Relevance and Friendship on Helping: You Don't Always Help the One You Like." *Journal of Experimental Social Psychology* 16(6): 582–90.

Testa, Maria, and Brenda Major. 1990. "The Impact of Social Comparisons After Failure: The Moderating Effects of Perceived Control." *Basic and Applied Social Psychology* 11(2): 205–18.

Thackeray, William M. 1879. *The Book of Snobs.* Philadelphia: Lippincott.

Thorndike, Edward L. 1920. "A Constant Error in Psychological Ratings." *Journal of Applied Psychology* 4(1): 25–29.

Thornhill, Randy, and Corey L. Fincher. 2007. "What Is the Relevance of Attachment and Life History to Political Values?" *Evolution and Human Behavior* 28(4): 215–22.

Tiedens, Larissa Z. 2001. "Anger and Advancement Versus Sadness and Subjugation: The Effect of Negative Emotion Expressions on Social Status Conferral." *Journal of Personality and Social Psychology* 80(1): 86–94.

Tiedens, Larissa Z., and Alison R. Fragale. 2003. "Power Moves: Complementarity in Dominant and Submissive Nonverbal Behavior." *Journal of Personality and Social Psychology* 84(3): 558–68.

Tocqueville, Alexis de. 1840. *De la démocratie en Amerique* [*Democracy in America*], vol. 2. London: Saunders and Otley.

Todorov, Alexander, Sean G. Baron, and Nikolaas N. Oosterhof. 2008. "Evaluating Face Trustworthiness: A Model-Based Approach." *Social Cognitive and Affective Neuroscience* 3(2): 119–27.

Todorov, Alexander, Chris P. Said, Andrew D. Engel, and Nikolaas N. Oosterhof. 2008. "Understanding Evaluation of Faces on Social Dimensions." *Trends in Cognitive Sciences* 12(12): 455–60.

Trampe, Debra, Diederik A. Stapel, and Frans W. Siero. 2007. "On Models and Vases: Body Dissatisfaction and Proneness to Social Comparison Effects." *Journal of Personality and Social Psychology* 92(1): 106–18.

Trapnell, Paul D., and Jerry S. Wiggins. 1990. "Extension of the Interpersonal Adjective Scales to Include the Big Five Dimensions of Personality." *Journal of Personality and Social Psychology* 59(4): 781–90.

Trautwein, Ulrich, Oliver Lüdtke, Herbert W. Marsh, and Gabriel Nagy. 2009. "Within-School Social Comparison: How Students Perceive the Standing of Their Class Predicts Academic Self-Concept." *Journal of Educational Psychology* 101(4): 853–66.

Tresemer, David. 1977. *Fear of Success*. New York: Plenum.

Triandis, Harry C. 1995. *Individualism and Collectivism*. Boulder, Colo.: Westview Press.

Tropp, Linda R., and Thomas F. Pettigrew. 2005. "Differential Relationships Between Intergroup Contact and Affective and Cognitive Dimensions of Prejudice." *Personality and Social Psychology Bulletin* 31(8): 1145–58.

Turner, Rhiannon N., Miles Hewstone, Alberto Voci, and Christiana Vonofakou. 2008. "A Test of the Extended Intergroup Contact Hypothesis: The Mediating Role of Intergroup Anxiety, Perceived Ingroup and Outgroup Norms, and Inclusion of the Outgroup in the Self." *Journal of Personality and Social Psychology* 95(4): 843–60.

Turner, John C., Michael A. Hogg, Penelope J. Oakes, Stephen D. Reicher, and Margaret S. Wetherell. 1987. *Rediscovering the Social Group: A Self-Categorization Theory*. Cambridge, Mass.: Blackwell.

Uchida, Yukiko, Sara S. M. Townsend, Hazel Rose Markus, and Hilary B. Bergsieker. 2009. "Emotions as Within or Between People? Cultural Variations in Lay Theories of Emotion Expression and Inference." *Personality and Social Psychology Bulletin* 35(11): 1427–39.

Updike, John. 1985. "Personal History: At War with My Skin." *New Yorker*, September 2, p. 61, 39–57.

U.S. Department of Labor. Bureau of Labor Statistics. 2009. *Highlights of Women's Earnings in 2008*. Report 1017. Washington: U.S. Government Printing Office (July).

Uslaner, Eric M., and Mitchell Brown. 2005. "Inequality, Trust, and Civic Engagement." *American Politics Research* 33(6): 868–94.

van den Berg, Patricia, Susan J. Paxton, Helene Keery, Melanie Wall, Jia Guo, and Dianne Neumark-Sztainer. 2007. "Body Dissatisfaction and Body Comparison with Media Images in Males and Females." *Body Image* 4(3): 257–68.

van den Berg, Patricia, and J. Kevin Thompson. 2007. "Self-Schema and Social Comparison Explanations of Body Dissatisfaction: A Laboratory Investigation." *Body Image* 4(1): 29–38.

van den Bos, Wouter, Samuel M. McClure, Lasana T. Harris, Susan T. Fiske, and Jonathan D. Cohen. 2007. "Dissociating Affective Evaluation and Social Cognitive Processes in Ventral Medial Prefrontal Cortex." *Cognitive and Behavioral Neuroscience* 7(4): 337–46.

van de Ven, Niels, Marcel Zeelenberg, and Rik Pieters. 2009. "Leveling Up and Down: The Experiences of Benign and Malicious Envy." *Emotion* 9(3): 419–29.

———. 2010. "Warding Off the Evil Eye: When the Fear of Being Envied Increases Prosocial Behavior." *Psychological Science* 21(11): 1671–77.

van Dijk, Wilco W., Jaap W. Ouwerkerk, Sjoerd Goslinga, and Myrke Nieweg. 2005. "Deservingness and Schadenfreude." *Cognition and Emotion* 19(6): 933–39.

van Dijk, Wilco W., Jaap W. Ouwerkerk, Sjoerd Goslinga, Myrke Nieweg, and Marcello Gallucci. 2006. "When People Fall from Grace: Reconsidering the Role of Envy in Schadenfreude." *Emotion* 6(1): 156–60.

van Yperen, Nico W., Veerle Brenninkmeijer, and Abraham P. Buunk. 2006. "People's Responses to Upward and Downward Social Comparisons: The Role of the Individual's Effort-Performance Expectancy." *British Journal of Social Psychology* 45(3): 519–33.

Vandello, Joseph A., and Dov Cohen. 1999. "Patterns of Individualism and Collectivism Across the United States." *Journal of Personality and Social Psychology* 77(2): 279–92.

Vandello, Joseph A., Nadav P. Goldschmied, and David A. R. Richards. 2007. "The Appeal of the Underdog." *Personality and Social Psychology Bulletin* 33(12): 1603–16.

Vanneman, Reeve, and Lynn Weber Cannon. 1987. *The American Perception of Class*. Philadelphia: Temple University Press.

Vecchio, Robert P. 1997. "Categorizing Coping Responses for Envy: A Multidimensional Analysis of Workplace Perceptions." *Psychological Reports* 81(1): 137–38.

———. 2000. "Negative Emotion in the Workplace: Employee Jealousy and Envy." *International Journal of Stress Management* 7(3): 161–79.

———. 2005. "Explorations in Employee Envy: Feeling Envious and Feeling Envied." *Cognition and Emotion* 19(1): 69–81.

Verkuyten, Maykal, and Arjan Reijerse. 2008. "Intergroup Structure and Identity Management Among Ethnic Minority and Majority Groups: The Interactive Effects of Perceived Stability, Legitimacy, and Permeability." *European Journal of Social Psychology* 38(1): 106–27.

Want, Stephen C. 2009. "Meta-Analytic Moderators of Experimental Exposure to Media Portrayals of Women on Female Appearance Satisfaction: Social Comparisons as Automatic Processes." *Body Image* 6(4): 257–69.

Wayment, Heidi A., and Shelley E. Taylor. 1995. "Self-Evaluation Processes: Motives, Information Use, and Self-Esteem." *Journal of Personality* 63(4): 729–57.

Webster, J. Matthew, Jamieson Duval, Leslie M. Gaines, and Richard H. Smith. 2003. "The Roles of Praise and Social Comparison Information in the Experience of Pride." *Journal of Social Psychology* 143(2): 209–32.

Weiner, Bernard. 1980. "A Cognitive (Attribution)-Emotion-Action Model of Motivated Behavior: An Analysis of Judgments of Help-Giving." *Journal of Personality and Social Psychology* 39(2): 186–200.

———. 2006. *Social Motivation, Justice, and the Moral Emotions: An Attributional Approach*. Mahwah, N.J.: Erlbaum.

Weinstein, Neil D. 1980. "Unrealistic Optimism About Future Life Events." *Journal of Personality and Social Psychology* 39(5): 806–20.

Wert, Sarah R., and Peter Salovey. 2004. "A Social Comparison Account of Gossip." *Review of General Psychology* 8(2): 122–37.

Whalen, Paul. 2007. "The Uncertainty of It All." *Trends in Cognitive Sciences* 11(12): 499–500.

Wheeler, Ladd, and Kunitate Miyake. 1992. "Social Comparison in Everyday Life." *Journal of Personality and Social Psychology* 62(5): 760–73.

Wilkinson, Richard G., and Kate E. Pickett. 2009. "Income Inequality and Social Dysfunction." *Annual Review of Sociology* 35: 493–511.

———. 2010. *The Spirit Level: Why Greater Equality Makes Societies Stronger.* New York: Bloomsbury Press.

Williams, Angie, and Howard Giles. 1998. "Communication of Ageism." In *Communicating Prejudice,* edited by Michael L. Hecht. Thousand Oaks, Calif.: Sage Publications.

Williams, Kipling D. 2007. "Ostracism." *Annual Review of Psychology* 58(2007): 425–52.

Williams, Kipling D., Christopher K. T. Cheung, and Wilma Choi. 2000. "Cyberostracism: Effects of Being Ignored over the Internet." *Journal of Personality and Social Psychology* 79(5): 748–62.

Williams, Lawrence E., and John A. Bargh. 2008. "Keeping One's Distance: The Influence of Spatial Distance Cues on Affect and Evaluation." *Psychological Science* 19(3): 302–8.

Wills, Thomas A. 1981. "Downward Comparison Principles in Social Psychology." *Psychological Bulletin* 90(2): 245–71.

Wilson, Anne E., and Michael Ross. 2001. "From Chump to Champ: People's Appraisals of Their Earlier and Present Selves." *Journal of Personality and Social Psychology* 80(4): 572–84.

Wilson, Timothy D., and Daniel T. Gilbert. 2005. "Affective Forecasting: Knowing What to Want." *Current Directions in Psychological Science* 14(3): 131–34.

———. 2008. "Explaining Away: A Model of Affective Adaptation." *Perspectives on Psychological Science* 3(5): 370–86.

Wojciszke, Bogdan, Roza Bazinska, and Marcin Jaworski. 1998. "On the Dominance of Moral Categories in Impression Formation." *Personality and Social Psychology Bulletin* 24(12): 1251–63.

Wojciszke, Bogdan, and Anna Struzynska-Kujalowicz. 2007. "Power Influences Self-Esteem." *Social Cognition* 25(4): 472–94.

Wong, Carol A., Jacquelynne S. Eccles, and Arnold Sameroff. 2003. "The Influence of Ethnic Discrimination and Ethnic Identification on African American Adolescents' School and Socioemotional Adjustment." *Journal of Personality* 71(6): 1197–1232.

Wood, Joanne V. 1989. "Theory and Research Concerning Social Comparisons of Personal Attributes." *Psychological Bulletin* 106(2): 231–48.

———. 1996. "What Is Social Comparison and How Should We Study It?" *Personality and Social Psychology Bulletin* 22(5): 520–37.

Wood, Joanne V., Shelley E. Taylor, and Rosemary R. Lichtman. 1985. "Social Comparison in Adjustment to Breast Cancer." *Journal of Personality and Social Psychology* 49(5): 1169–83.

Wright, Stephen C., and Linda R. Tropp. 2002. "Collective Action in Response to Disadvantage: Intergroup Perceptions, Social Identification, and Social Change." In *Relative Deprivation: Specification, Development, and Integration,* edited by Iain Walker and Heather J. Smith. New York: Cambridge University Press.

Yamagishi, Toshio, Karen S. Cook, and Motoki Watabe. 1998. "Uncertainty, Trust, and Commitment Formation in the United States and Japan." *American Journal of Sociology* 104(1): 165–94.

Yzerbyt, Vincent, Olivier Corneille, and Claudia Estrada. 2001. "The Interplay of Subjective Essentialism and Entitativity in the Formation of Stereotypes." *Personality and Social Psychology Review* 5(2): 141–55.

Yzerbyt, Vincent, and Stéphanie Demoulin. 2010. "Intergroup Relations." In *Handbook of Social Psychology*, vol. 2, edited by Susan T. Fiske, Daniel T. Gilbert, and Gardner Lindzey. New York: Wiley.

Yzerbyt, Vincent, Muriel Dumont, Bernard Mathieu, Ernestine Gordijn, and Daniel Wigboldus. 2006. "Social Comparison and Group-Based Emotions." In *Social Comparison and Social Psychology: Understanding Cognition, Intergroup Relations, and Culture*, edited by Serge Guimond. New York: Cambridge University Press.

Yzerbyt, Vincent Y., Nicolas Kervyn, and Charles M. Judd. 2008. "Compensation Versus Halo: The Unique Relations Between the Fundamental Dimensions of Social Judgment." *Personality and Social Psychology Bulletin* 34(8): 1110–23.

Yzerbyt, Vincent Y., Georges Schadron, Jacques-Philippe Leyens, and Stephan Rocher. 1994. "Social Judgeability: The Impact of Meta-Informational Cues on the Use of Stereotypes." *Journal of Personality and Social Psychology* 66(1): 48–55.

Zadro, Lisa, Kipling D. Williams, and Rick Richardson. 2004. "How Low Can You Go? Ostracism by a Computer Is Sufficient to Lower Self-Reported Levels of Belonging, Control, Self-Esteem, and Meaningful Existence." *Journal of Experimental Social Psychology* 40(4): 560–67.

Zagefka, Hanna, and Rupert Brown. 2005. "Comparisons and Perceived Deprivation in Ethnic Minority Settings." *Personality and Social Psychology Bulletin* 31(4): 467–82.

Zebrowitz, Leslie A., and Joann M. Montepare. 2005. "Appearance *Does* Matter." *Science* 308(5728): 1565–66.

Zell, Ethan, and Mark D. Alicke. 2009. "Self-Evaluative Effects of Temporal and Social Comparison." *Journal of Experimental Social Psychology* 45(1): 223–27.

Zucker, Gail S., and Bernard Weiner. 1993. "Conservatism and Perceptions of Poverty: An Attributional Analysis." *Journal of Applied Social Psychology* 23(12): 925–43.

Index

Boldface numbers refer to figures and tables.

Simon, Herbert, 38
small-business owners, 4
smiling, 36
Smith, Eliot, 8, 40–41, 43
Smith, Heather, 89
Smith, Richard, 13–14, 24, 58–59
snobbery, 59–60
social capital, 119
social class: behavioral cues, 52–53;
    beliefs about, 4; prevalence and
    persistence of distinctions, 2, 26;
    racial-ethnic issues, 49; self-
    identification, 4–6; social compari-
    son tendency, 65–66. *See also*
    social status
social cognition, 2–3, 30
social comparison: brain processes,
    19–20, 29–36, 142–45; cultural differ-
    ences, 71–76; at gym, 104–5; of hos-
    pital patients, 105–7; individuals,
    56–63, 80–88, 117–18; information
    seeking goal, 79–93; insecurity and,
    147–49; introduction, 1–4; manage-
    ment of, 76–78; protection of self
    goal, 94–113; reasons for, 79–82,
    148–49; in schools, 90–91; strategies
    for, 93, 110–13; tools, 82–88; univer-
    sal nature of, 26; at work, 91–92. *See
    also* downward comparison; group
    comparison; upward comparison
social comparison orientation (SCO),
    57–58
social conservatives, 68–71
social cues, 51
social dominance orientation (SDO),
    66–67
social identity theory, 123–24
social mobility, 127–28, 153
social selection, 136
social status: advantages of, 156;
    behavioral cues, 50–55; cognitive
    processes, 45–50; costs of, 156;
    emotions as signal for, 36–45;
    impression formations, 2–3;
    prevalence and persistence of
    distinctions, 2; relative nature of,
    46–47; and social comparison
    tendency, 65–66

social ties, 75–76
societies: BIAS Map, 3, 19, 21, 30,
    129–36; control of envy and scorn
    in, 162–63; social comparison
    impact, 149–55; status scripts,
    53–55; status stereotypes, 49–50
sororities, 115
South Korea, out-groups in, 131
Spears, Russell, 125
Spencer, Steven, 116
sports, 119–20, 126
Stapel, Diederik, 46, 86, 104, 123
status. *See* social status
status anxiety, 56, 153, 154–55
status quo policies, 53, 67, 69–70,
    128–29, 148
stay-at-home mothers, 49
Stephan, Cookie, 163
Stephan, Walter, 163
Stereotype Content Model, 165n1
stereotypes, **3,** 49–50, 131, 145–47,
    162–63
Sternberg, Emily, 44
stigma, 9
stigma by association, 37
Stouffer, Samuel, 88
strangers: impressions of, 2–3; social
    comparison standard, 84–85
stress, 22, 25
STTUC (Sensitivity to being the Target
    of a Threatening Upward
    Comparison), 99–100
subjective comparisons, 94
Suls, Jerry, 83–84
supplication, 113
Sweden, income inequality in, 7
Switzerland, social groups of, 153, **154**
sympathy, 159–60

Tajfel, Henri, 123–24
Taylor, Shelley, 105
teachers, 4
teamwork, 33
Tea Party movement, 149, 150
TED, 82
teens, 97
Tennen, Howard, 106
Tesser, Abraham, 107, 108